Thailand in the Cold War

Although Thailand formally allied itself to the United States from the start of the Cold War, Thai political leaders initially remained keen to present themselves as independent political actors. Nevertheless, throughout the 1950s Thailand became increasingly subservient to the United States. Politically, foreign policy was tied explicitly to a Cold War logic that presented communism as the principal threat to the country. Economically, Thailand became integrated into the US sphere of influence and Thai policy makers adopted much of the development agenda that firmly positioned Thailand as a third world economy. However, as this book argues, while state actors were responsible for seeing through this shift, it was Thailand's cosmopolitan urban communities that ultimately championed it. Committed for over a generation to developing a modern, consumerist lifestyle, it was this class that was instrumental in securing US hegemony in the country. Considering popular culture, including film, literature, fashion, tourism and attitudes towards Buddhism, this book shows how an ideology of consumerism and integration into a "free world" culture centred in the United States gradually took hold and became firmly established. This ideology, which emphasised popular ideas about what should be considered Thai culture, was fundamental in determining Thailand's international political alignment during the period.

Matthew Phillips is a Lecturer in the Department of History and Welsh History at Aberystwyth University, UK.

Routledge Studies in the Modern History of Asia

1. The Police in Occupation Japan
Control, corruption and resistance
to reform
Christopher Aldous

2. Chinese Workers
A new history
Jackie Sheehan

3. The Aftermath of Partition in South Asia
*Tai Yong Tan and
Gyanesh Kudaisya*

4. The Australia–Japan Political Alignment
1952 to the present
Alan Rix

5. Japan and Singapore in the World Economy
Japan's economic advance into
Singapore, 1870–1965
*Shimizu Hiroshi and
Hirakawa Hitoshi*

6. The Triads as Business
Yiu Kong Chu

7. Contemporary Taiwanese Cultural Nationalism
A-chin Hsiau

8. Religion and Nationalism in India
The case of the Punjab
Harnik Deol

9. Japanese Industrialisation
Historical and cultural perspectives
Ian Inkster

10. War and Nationalism in China
1925–1945
Hans J. van de Ven

11. Hong Kong in Transition
One country, two systems
*Edited by Robert Ash, Peter
Ferdinand, Brian Hook and
Robin Porter*

12. Japan's Postwar Economic Recovery and Anglo-Japanese Relations, 1948–1962
Noriko Yokoi

13. Japanese Army Stragglers and Memories of the War in Japan, 1950–1975
Beatrice Trefalt

14. Ending the Vietnam War
The Vietnamese
communists' perspective
Ang Cheng Guan

**15. The Development of the
Japanese Nursing Profession**
Adopting and adapting
Western influences
Aya Takahashi

16. Women's Suffrage in Asia
Gender nationalism
and democracy
*Louise Edwards and
Mina Roces*

**17. The Anglo-Japanese Alliance,
1902–1922**
Phillips Payson O'Brien

**18. The United States and
Cambodia, 1870–1969**
From curiosity to confrontation
Kenton Clymer

**19. Capitalist Restructuring and the
Pacific Rim**
Ravi Arvind Palat

**20. The United States and
Cambodia, 1969–2000**
A troubled relationship
Kenton Clymer

**21. British Business in
Post-Colonial Malaysia,
1957–70**
'Neo-colonialism' or
'disengagement'?
Nicholas J. White

**22. The Rise and Decline of
Thai Absolutism**
Kullada Kesboonchoo Mead

**23. Russian Views of Japan,
1792–1913**
An anthology of travel writing
David N. Wells

**24. The Internment of Western
Civilians under the Japanese,
1941–1945**
A patchwork of internment
Bernice Archer

**25. The British Empire
and Tibet**
1900–1922
Wendy Palace

**26. Nationalism in
Southeast Asia**
If the people are with us
Nicholas Tarling

**27. Women, Work and the Japanese
Economic Miracle**
The case of the cotton textile
industry, 1945–1975
Helen Macnaughtan

28. A Colonial Economy in Crisis
Burma's rice cultivators and the
world depression of the 1930s
Ian Brown

**29. A Vietnamese Royal Exile
in Japan**
Prince Cuong De (1882–1951)
Tran My-Van

**30. Corruption and Good
Governance in Asia**
Nicholas Tarling

**31. US–China Cold War
Collaboration, 1971–1989**
S. Mahmud Ali

32. Rural Economic Development in Japan
From the nineteenth century to the Pacific War
Penelope Francks

33. Colonial Armies in Southeast Asia
Edited by Karl Hack and Tobias Rettig

34. Intra Asian Trade and the World Market
A. J. H. Latham and Heita Kawakatsu

35. Japanese–German Relations, 1895–1945
War, diplomacy and public opinion
Edited by Christian W. Spang and Rolf-Harald Wippich

36. Britain's Imperial Cornerstone in China
The Chinese maritime customs service, 1854–1949
Donna Brunero

37. Colonial Cambodia's 'Bad Frenchmen'
The rise of French rule and the life of Thomas Caraman, 1840–1887
Gregor Muller

38. Japanese–American Civilian Prisoner Exchanges and Detention Camps, 1941–45
Bruce Elleman

39. Regionalism in Southeast Asia
Nicholas Tarling

40. Changing Visions of East Asia, 1943–93
Transformations and continuities
R. B. Smith, edited by Chad J. Mitcham

41. Christian Heretics in Late Imperial China
Christian inculturation and state control, 1720–1850
Lars P. Laamann

42. Beijing – A Concise History
Stephen G. Haw

43. The Impact of the Russo-Japanese War
Edited by Rotem Kowner

44. Business–Government Relations in Prewar Japan
Peter von Staden

45. India's Princely States
People, princes and colonialism
Edited by Waltraud Ernst and Biswamoy Pati

46. Rethinking Gandhi and Nonviolent Relationality
Global perspectives
Edited by Debjani Ganguly and John Docker

47. The Quest for Gentility in China
Negotiations beyond gender and class
Edited by Daria Berg and Chloë Starr

48. Forgotten Captives in Japanese Occupied Asia
Edited by Kevin Blackburn and Karl Hack

49. Japanese Diplomacy in the 1950s
From isolation to integration
Edited by Iokibe Makoto, Caroline Rose, Tomaru Junko and John Weste

50. The Limits of British Colonial Control in South Asia
Spaces of disorder in the Indian Ocean region
Edited by Ashwini Tambe and Harald Fischer-Tiné

51. On The Borders of State Power
Frontiers in the greater Mekong sub-region
Edited by Martin Gainsborough

52. Pre-Communist Indochina
R. B. Smith, edited by Beryl Williams

53. Communist Indochina
R. B. Smith, edited by Beryl Williams

54. Port Cities in Asia and Europe
Edited by Arndt Graf and Chua Beng Huat

55. Moscow and the Emergence of Communist Power in China, 1925–30
The Nanchang Rising and the birth of the Red Army
Bruce A. Elleman

56. Colonialism, Violence and Muslims in Southeast Asia
The Maria Hertogh controversy and its aftermath
Syed Muhd Khairudin Aljunied

57. Japanese and Hong Kong Film Industries
Understanding the origins of East Asian film networks
Kinnia Shuk-ting

58. Provincial Life and the Military in Imperial Japan
The phantom samurai
Stewart Lone

59. Southeast Asia and the Vietnam War
Ang Cheng Guan

60. Southeast Asia and the Great Powers
Nicholas Tarling

61. The Cold War and National Assertion in Southeast Asia
Britain, the United States and Burma, 1948–1962
Matthew Foley

62. The International History of East Asia, 1900–1968
Trade, ideology and the quest for order
Edited by Antony Best

63. Journalism and Politics in Indonesia
A critical biography of Mochtar Lubis (1922–2004) as editor and author
David T. Hill

64. Atrocity and American Military Justice in Southeast Asia
Trial by army
Louise Barnett

65. The Japanese Occupation of Borneo, 1941–1945
Ooi Keat Gin

66. National Pasts in Europe and East Asia
P. W. Preston

67. Modern China's Ethnic Frontiers
A journey to the West
Hsiao-ting Lin

68. New Perspectives on the History and Historiography of Southeast Asia
Continuing explorations
Michael Aung-Thwin and Kenneth R. Hall

69. Food Culture in Colonial Asia
A taste of empire
Cecilia Leong-Salobir

70. China's Political Economy in Modern Times
Changes and economic consequences, 1800–2000
Kent Deng

71. Science, Public Health and the State in Modern Asia
Edited by Liping Bu, Darwin Stapleton and Ka-che Yip

72. Russo-Japanese Relations, 1905–1917
From enemies to allies
Peter Berton

73. Reforming Public Health in Occupied Japan, 1945–52
Alien prescriptions?
Christopher Aldous and Akihito Suzuki

74. Trans-Colonial Modernities in South Asia
Edited by Michael S. Dodson and Brian A. Hatcher

75. The Evolution of the Japanese Developmental State
Institutions locked in by ideas
Hironori Sasada

76. Status and Security in Southeast Asian States
Nicholas Tarling

77. Lee Kuan Yew's Strategic Thought
Ang Cheng Guan

78. Government, Imperialism and Nationalism in China
The Maritime Customs Service and its Chinese staff
Chihyun Chang

79. China and Japan in the Russian Imagination, 1685–1922
To the ends of the Orient
Susanna Soojung Lim

80. Chinese Complaint Systems
Natural resistance
Qiang Fang

81. Martial Arts and the Body Politic in Meiji Japan
Denis Gainty

82. Gambling, the State and Society in Thailand, c. 1800–1945
James A. Warren

83. Post-War Borneo, 1945–1950
Nationalism, Empire and state-building
Ooi Keat Gin

84. China and the First Vietnam War, 1947–54
Laura M. Calkins

85. The Jesuit Missions to China and Peru, 1570–1610
Ana Carolina Hosne

86. Macao – Cultural Interaction and Literary Representations
Edited by Katrine K. Wong and C. X. George Wei

87. Macao – The Formation of a Global City
Edited by C. X. George Wei

88. Women in Modern Burma
Tharaphi Than

89. Museums in China
Materialized power and objectified identities
Tracey L-D Lu

90. Transcultural Encounters between Germany and India
Kindred spirits in the 19th and 20th centuries
Edited by Joanne Miyang Cho, Eric Kurlander and Douglas T. McGetchin

91. The Philosophy of Japanese Wartime Resistance
A reading, with commentary, of the complete texts of the Kyoto School discussions of "The Standpoint of World History and Japan"
David Williams

92. A History of Alcohol and Drugs in Modern South Asia
Intoxicating affairs
Edited by Harald Fischer- Tiné and Jana Tschurenev

93. Military Force and Elite Power in the Formation of Modern China
Edward A. McCord

94. Japan's Household Registration System and Citizenship
Koseki, identification and documentation
Edited by David Chapman and Karl Jakob Krogness

95. Itō Hirobumi – Japan's First Prime Minister and Father of the Meiji Constitution
Kazuhiro Takii

96. The Non-Aligned Movement and the Cold War
Delhi – Bandung – Belgrade
Edited by Nataša Mišković, Harald Fischer-Tiné, and Nada Boškovska

97. The Transformation of the International Order of Asia
Decolonization, the Cold War, and the Colombo Plan
Edited by Shigeru Akita, Shoichi Watanabe and Gerold Krozewski

98. Xinjiang and the Expansion of Chinese Communist Power
Kashghar in the early twentieth century
Michael Dillon

99. Colonial Counterinsurgency and Mass Violence
The Dutch Empire in Indonesia
Edited by Bart Luttikhuis and A. Dirk Moses

100. Public Health and National Reconstruction in Post-War Asia
International influences, local transformations
Edited by Liping Bu and Ka-che Yip

101. The Pacific War
Aftermaths, remembrance and culture
Edited by Christina Twomey and Ernest Koh

102. Malaysia's Defeat of Armed Communism
The Second Emergency, 1968–1989
Ong Weichong

103. Cultural Encounters and Homoeroticism in Sri Lanka
Sex and serendipity
Robert Aldrich

104. Mobilizing Shanghai Youth
CCP internationalism, GMD nationalism and Japanese collaboration
Kristin Mulready-Stone

105. Voices from the Shifting Russo-Japanese Border
Karafuto / Sakhalin
Edited by Svetlana Paichadze and Philip A. Seaton

106. International Competition in China, 1899–1991
The rise, fall, and eventual success of the Open Door Policy
Bruce A. Elleman

107. The Post-war Roots of Japanese Political Malaise
Dagfinn Gatu

108. Britain and China, 1840–1970
Empire, finance and war
Edited by Robert Bickers and Jonathan Howlett

109. Local History and War Memories in Hokkaido
Edited by Philip A. Seaton

110. Thailand in the Cold War
Matthew Phillips

Thailand in the Cold War

Matthew Phillips

LONDON AND NEW YORK

First published 2016
by Routledge
2 Park Square, Milton Park, Abingdon, Oxon OX14 4RN

and by Routledge
711 Third Avenue, New York, NY 10017

Routledge is an imprint of the Taylor & Francis Group, an informa business

© 2016 Matthew Phillips

The right of Matthew Phillips to be identified as author of this work has
been asserted by him in accordance with sections 77 and 78 of the
Copyright, Designs and Patents Act 1988.

All rights reserved. No part of this book may be reprinted or reproduced or
utilised in any form or by any electronic, mechanical, or other means, now
known or hereafter invented, including photocopying and recording, or in
any information storage or retrieval system, without permission in writing
from the publishers.

Trademark notice: Product or corporate names may be trademarks or
registered trademarks, and are used only for identification and explanation
without intent to infringe.

Every effort has been made to contact copyright holders for their permission
to reprint material in this book. The publishers would be grateful to hear
from any copyright holder who is not here acknowledged and will undertake
to rectify any errors or omissions in future editions of this book.

British Library Cataloguing in Publication Data
A catalogue record for this book is available from the British Library

Library of Congress Cataloging in Publication Data
Phillips, Matthew (Historian), author.
  Thailand in the Cold War / Matthew Phillips.
    pages cm. -- (Routledge studies in the modern history of Asia; 110)
    Includes bibliographical references and index.
  1. Thailand--Foreign relations--United States. 2. United States--Foreign
relations--Thailand. 3. Thailand--Foreign relations--1945-1988. 4. Popular
culture--Thailand--History--20th century. 5. Cold War. I. Title.
  DS575.5.U6P47 2015
  327.593009'045--dc23
            2015010101

ISBN: 978-1-138-01416-9 (hbk)
ISBN: 978-1-315-78096-2 (ebk)

Typeset in Times New Roman
by Taylor & Francis Books

Contents

List of figures		xii
Acknowledgement		xiii
Explanatory notes		xv
	Introduction	1
1	'A theatre with two stages': Jim Thompson's Thailand	21
2	In and out of *Vogue*: dressing for progress before and after 1945	54
3	If not 'Great', then what? Rethinking Thainess in post-war Bangkok	82
4	Cultural spectacle, political authority and the subversion of Thai modernity	117
5	The Tourist Organisation of Thailand and Cold War propaganda	145
6	*It's a small world after all*: Thailand's integration into free world culture	179
	Conclusion	199
	Bibliography	204
	Index	214

List of figures

1.1 Advert for Thaibok fabrics	43
1.2 Jim Thompson (far right) at his house with friends	44
1.3 Jim Thompson (far left), on balcony with friends	46
2.1 *Thongtiao Sapda* (Bangkok, 13 March 1941)	67
2.2 Front cover, *Suphap Satri*, 22 August 1943	70
2.3 'Fashion Show', *'Daily Mail' Pictorial News*, November 1953	74
3.1 Front cover of *Khon Muang*, July 1954	108
3.2 Front cover, *Phap Khao Sayam Nikon*, December 1953	110
4.1 Cartoon from *Phim Thai*, *'Honyai'* [The Prophet], 15 May 1954	126
4.2 Cartoon published in *San Seri*, 11 May 1957	134
4.3 The crowd at the opening ceremony, *Ta Khlong Thai Mai*, August 1957	137
4.4 Crowds watching the royal barges, *Ta Khlong Thai Mai*, August 1957	138
4.5 Crowds at Sanam Luang 'wait for the king', *Ta Khlong Thai Mai*, August 1957	139
5.1 Front page, *Anusan Osotho*, 2, 4 (1961)	166
5.2 Front Page, *Anusan Osotho*, 3.12, July 1963	169
6.1 King Bhumibol and Queen Sirikit with President Eisenhower and First Lady Mamie Eisenhower, The White House, June 1960	183
6.2 Queen Sirikit viewing Thai silk at Jim Thompson's shop in Bangkok	194

Acknowledgement

This book began life as my PhD dissertation, 'Oasis on a Troubled Continent: Culture and Ideology in Cold War Thailand'. It was completed at the School of Oriental and African Studies (SOAS), under the supervision of Ian Brown. I will be forever indebted for the support and encouragement I have received from him. I must also thank my examiners, Odd Arne Westad and Jonathan Rigg, for their insights into the current work. Completing the PhD would not have been possible without funding from the Arts and Humanities Research Council (AHRC).

Others who have helped include Angus Lockyer, Andrea Janku, Michael Charney, Shabnum Tejani, Teresa Bernheimer, Lifeng Han, Angela Chiu, Mark Clayden, Chris Chekuri, Naomi Wood and Sabrina Huettner. I must also thank Rachel Harrison, Janit Feangfu, Kullada Kesboonchoo-Mead, Naoko Shimazu, Thanes Wongyanawa, Thanet Apronsuvan, and everybody at the History Department at Chulalongkorn University for their generous support throughout the process of completing both the thesis and the current work. Special gratitude must be reserved for Arwut Teerak and Martyn Smith, both of whom were endlessly tolerant and supportive. I must also mention early conversations with Eugene Ford that were extremely helpful, and William Klausner who showed great kindness in the first few months of the research. I would like to reserve a special mention for Bianca Son whose friendship I miss.

Further thanks must be paid to the staff at the Library of Congress who made my stay in Washington both rewarding and enjoyable. In particular, Mary-Lou Recker and Carolyn Brown at the Kluge Center gave me the warmest welcome. The same sentiment is reserved for staff at Wheaton College Archives, the National Archives of Thailand and the Public Relations Department Archive, Bangkok. Thanks also to the Jim Thompson Foundation and Ton Chabab Publishing House for help in finding materials and further supporting the work. I must also thank the Project of Empowering Network for International Thai Studies (ENITS) for awarding me the 2011 ENITS scholarship. Thanks also to everybody at the Department of History and Welsh History, Aberystwyth University, and in particular Peter Lambert for looking through a portion of text.

xiv *Acknowledgement*

Finally, I must thank my family, all of whom have been forced to read and comment throughout the past few years, as well as my wife Mim for her support – emotional and practical. I would like to dedicate this book to the memory of my Grandfather, who would have enjoyed the conversations it spawned and would have no doubt put the whole messy story down to the 'herd instinct'.

Explanatory notes

Transcription

Where Thai has been transcribed into English this has been done using the 'General System of Phonetic Transcription' as set out in the Royal Institute, *Romanization Guide for Thai Script*, Bangkok, 1982. Proper names have been spelt according the preference of the person when known and the official spelling has been used for place names.

Dates and periods

During the period covered, two different dating systems were in use. Most Thai documents referred to the Buddhist Era (BE), which runs 543 years later than the Christian Era (CE). This means that the year 1957 CE, for example, will be referred to as the year 2500 BE in most Thai documents. Generally speaking, dates are converted to the Christian Era except when inappropriate.

Introduction

In just over two decades, from the late 1930s, ideas about what it meant to be Thai were overhauled. In particular, the widely held belief that Thai culture must adhere to international standards in matters such as dress or art was, by the 1960s, largely defunct. By then the country's cultural life revolved around endless assertions of a Thai character and Thai way of life that was unique and distinct from the modern centres of mass consumption. At the centre of this cultural universe, a young monarch, King Bhumibol, and his glamorous wife, Queen Sirikit, participated in grand re-enactments of ancient ceremonies resurrected from a near-forgotten past. In the imagined celestial periphery, rural communities engaged in a simple life on the land, unaware of the world outside. To prove the fact, trips were organised to transport urban residents of Bangkok, along with a stream of fascinated foreign visitors, into the provinces of the north and northeast. There, further re-enactments portrayed these 'pristine' communities as secure in their spiritual beliefs, living in harmony with nature. It was a vision of the country that was rooted in the internal prejudices and racisms of the past.[1] Yet it was also a symptom of Thailand's emergence as an unambiguous client to US power in the Cold War.

Since the end of the Second World War, Thailand had been repeatedly portrayed in the US media as a unique location in Asia or, as a 1953 Time Inc. documentary labelled it, an 'Oasis on a Troubled Continent'. With Thailand recognised as an American ally in the emerging Cold War, this depiction rested on the idea that Thailand sat in the centre of a region 'seething with intrigue and violence', which was 'usually communist inspired'.[2] By emphasising a continued commitment to traditional ways of life and a general satisfaction with the status quo, the Thai population were routinely depicted as uninterested in Communism. Rather, they were shown as open, not only to a political alliance with the US government, but also to establishing personal relationships with private American citizens. Be it the American tourist who wished to experience a fleeting glance of an unspoiled land, or the American businessman who sought to work with locals to bring new products to market, the Thai population were invariably presented as both hospitable and untroubled by an active American engagement with the country.[3]

2   *Introduction*

Underlying this creation of Thailand as a place where Americans could feel uniquely at ease was the country's historical independence. As *Life* magazine declared in 1951, Thailand was 'unlike other parts of Asia' because, 'an independent monarchy for six centuries', it had 'never been anybody's colony'.[4] This meant that, in contrast to most of Asia, where European colonialism had uprooted the population from local cultures and traditions, Thailand remained a place where 'the age old dreams of romantic Asia still come alive'.[5] Moreover, it was claimed that because in Thailand there was not the same desire to remove the presence of the 'white man' from the country's political and economic future, as was often the case elsewhere in the region, it was an ideal place for Americans to convert the lack of resentment of 'foreign imperialists' into a promise of the 'good life'.[6]

That American popular culture portrayed Thailand in such a way was the consequence of a number of political and economic realities.[7] At the end of the Second World War, American officials confidently adhered to the idea that their country was uniquely powerful in the world and that they must now work to establish a solid and lasting international presence. However, particularly in Southeast Asia, the period also saw America's position limited significantly by the returning European colonial powers.[8] In Indochina, the French refusal to recognise the Viet Minh as a legitimate political force had quickly escalated into a military confrontation.[9] In Indonesia, Dutch intransigence resulted in a prolonged conflict with a fragmented nationalist movement, and in Malaya the British return was marked by a rapid descent into civil war after the British confronted the Malayan Communist Party.[10] In Burma, British officials soon realised that hopes of a gradual transfer of power were unrealistic, while in the Philippines the American government maintained its pre-war promise to recognise Filipino sovereignty. Yet, throughout Southeast Asia, regardless of when independence was granted, the recent past made it difficult for new arrivals from the west to build relationships without first recognising the complex priorities of local populations.

To complicate matters further, toward the end of the 1940s communist insurgencies in Indochina, Burma, Indonesia, Malaya and the Philippines competed for the right to define independence in this new era, and invariably did so by attaching their message to an anti-imperialist rhetoric. Combined with the fear of increased Soviet Union propaganda in the region, and the seemingly inevitable coming to power of a Communist party in China, Asia as a whole now emerged as a front line in the US battle to contain Communism.[11] It also put the winning of Asian hearts and minds, which were deemed to be concerned principally with the issue of imperialism, at the centre of that battle. As the US Ambassador to Beijing wrote to Washington in February 1949, nine months before the final collapse of the US-supported Nationalist government, 'events in Asia confirms [*sic*] my conviction that communists cannot be stopped in this vast semi-colonial area by military force or economic aid alone'.[12] Rather, he went on to explain, 'the effective containment of Soviet expansion through communism requires in Asia a new

Introduction 3

approach with appropriate implementation ... of convincingly dramatized ideas'. The projection of these ideas 'principally to mind and heart', he made clear, would benefit from the UK, France and the Netherlands being invited to join the USA in a federation to assist in the restoration of 'complete independence to peoples of eastern and southeastern Asia'. Once established, this foundation should then work to protect Asian populations from more subtle forms of 'imperialism through highly organized minorities of their own people linked to international communism'.[13]

While such a federation was never established, the sentiment behind the idea was now commonplace among US policy makers. The desire to convince the European colonial powers to relinquish control of their Asian colonies and work with the United States to rebuild western credibility now dominated American concerns in Asia. By 1953, with full attention on French military operations in Indochina, the US Psychological Strategy Board (PSB) outlined plans for 'more active U.S. leadership in Southeast Asia' in order to 'mitigate the taint of imperialism, which surrounds the struggle against Communism in the minds of Asian nationalists everywhere'.[14] However, given the USA's inability to influence the French sufficiently, the strategy was to focus propaganda activity on Thailand. The principal reason for this, as outlined in the PSB documents, was that 'during the period of colonial expansion Thailand never fell under European domination as it succeeded in balancing the various Western powers which encroached on it'.[15] Moreover, while the Thai maintained suspicions of the British and the French, 'Thai feelings toward the United States have been friendly and at present Thai–US relations are more intimate than at any time previously'. This, combined with the country's geographical position at the centre of Southeast Asia, and its political climate that had become distinctly anti-communist since the end of the Second World War, meant that Thailand was now 'the most suitable base to initiate and develop a substantial US counter effort as long as Indochina remains a French responsibility'.[16]

Free from a colonial occupier, and largely sympathetic to the United States, Thailand was therefore cast in the early Cold War as an important field within which American hegemony could be achieved *psychologically*. Propaganda campaigns that focused on winning Thai hearts and minds increased, and the representation of Thailand in the American media continually reinforced the idea that the country was home to a friendly and hospitable population immune to the appeal of Communism. Documentaries, films and news articles endlessly reproduced the image of Thailand as a new Shangri-La on a continent at war or, as travel writer James Michener described it, 'the padded cell in the insane asylum'.[17] Free from the concerns that plagued American interests elsewhere on the continent, Thailand was a place where a new breed of forward-thinking Americans could counter the Communist claim that they were imperialists by working with an Asian population for the mutual betterment of their respective societies. To be sure, establishing Thailand as a bulwark against Communism always meant integrating it into a US-centred world order, but from an American perspective this was possible only because

4 Introduction

the Thai people were cast as a community who welcomed the US intervention as a sentimental embrace rather than an act of aggressive expansion.[18]

However, while US policy toward Thailand often placed it at the centre of Southeast Asia for propaganda purposes, this should not be confused with understanding Thailand as anything other than peripheral to the overall picture of the global Cold War. As a sphere of peace, rather than conflict, Thailand rarely featured in US discussions about the military confrontations they were engaged in. Particularly from the settlement of the First Indochina War with the Geneva Accords in 1954, Thailand quickly slipped from the most pressing US agendas, even when they concerned Southeast Asia.[19] Thailand was, as Jim Glassman has expressed it, a country 'at the margins' of a US imperial encounter with Asia, and while attention was at times paid to ensuring it would not be lost to American interests, the country very rarely featured as a primary concern.[20]

The fact, therefore, that Thai society was by the 1960s operating in ways that accorded to many of the assumptions of American visitors, can be understood only when viewed from a Thai perspective. Humiliated by the events that followed the Second World War, Thai communities struggled throughout the 1950s to make sense of the changing nature of the world, and how to orientate themselves within it. As a result, it was Thai communities that preoccupied themselves with the search for a version of Thai identity that made sense to international systems of governance and thought. Moreover, only those who could successfully do so were able to claim political legitimacy. Ideas about what it meant to be Thai during the Cold War thus evolved as a means through which small but important elite Thai groups were able to self-identify with American power.

National assertion and the Cold War in Southeast Asia: Thailand's case

The view of Thailand during the Cold War as an *Oasis on a Troubled Continent* sits neatly with the grand narrative of world history as it developed in the aftermath of the Second World War. As a result, it has remained largely unchallenged. An ally of America in the Cold War, Thailand was cast as a member of the 'Free World'; a partner, even if a small one, in the global fight between Capitalism and Communism. Yet, as recent studies have shown, such a binary view of the Cold War has invariably failed to acknowledge the complexity of the international situation.[21] Far from a period of stable boundaries, from 1945 onward the non-western world was defined largely by conflict. The majority of the world's nations were only just coming into being and sovereignty was in many places up for constant negotiation, in terms both of the meaning of sovereignty and of who should benefit. As a result, new nationalist elites, fixated on bolstering their own respective positions, sought to exploit the Cold War for their own ends.[22]

Just as an understanding of the colonial encounter has evolved to acknowledge exchange as well as imposition, cooperation as well as

Introduction 5

exploitation, local actors in countries on the periphery of the Cold War are increasingly being viewed as active in exploiting the rivalry between Communism and Capitalism for their own benefit. As Matthew Foley has explained, 'far from passive bystanders or unwitting pawns, robbed of agency by the exigencies of superpower confrontation, political leaders in capitals far removed from Washington and Moscow were in fact active and surprisingly independent authors of their own futures'.[23] Moreover, constrained by local political realities connected to decolonisation, legitimacy in the newly independent nations of Asia was often rooted in the need to assert distance from the centres of world power. This, in turn, made it vital in the early years of the Cold War to develop new and often ambiguous positions, framed largely under the banner of neutrality, and later non-alignment, in relation to global events. When alliances were formed with major world powers (and it is worth noting that by the middle of 1960s Southeast Asia *did* emerge as a region largely split along Cold War lines), they often involved an open manipulation of the conflict to serve the political ambitions of local elites. Alliance with the United States, while often lucrative, also had to be managed carefully when presented to the local population so that it might be seen to support the national interest.

In this complex political environment, Thailand's relatively rapid emergence as a staunch ally to the United States set the country apart from its Asian neighbours, and was arguably a consequence of the fact that Thailand did not have to contend with the challenges of decolonisation. Indeed, while the immediate aftermath of the Second World War had been a period of political uncertainty, the return to power of wartime Prime Minister Phibun Songkhram meant that by the late 1940s the country was once again ruled by a relatively stable administration. With Phibun keen to bolster his personal position in the country, there were clear advantages to asserting a firm personal commitment to US interests and to an anti-Communist position. Yet the decision was also to have significant implications for the ability of the country's leaders to shape an independent foreign policy. Despite his early commitment to the policy objectives of the United States, Phibun had initially shown a clear desire to maintain a degree of independence in shaping his country's foreign relations, only to be forced further into the American camp within a few short years.[24]

Daniel Fineman has established that from December 1949 to the middle of 1950, the Thai government shifted its stance considerably. Since his push for power in 1947, Phibun had already presented himself as instinctively anti-communist, and had shown a clear intent to utilise this stance to harness American support for his leadership of the country. Yet he was also keen to recognise the complexity of regional politics. In Vietnam, attempts to bolster French legitimacy and dampen support for the communist insurgency had led the French to install the final Emperor of the Nguyen dynasty, Bao Dai, as head of state. While even US officials were initially worried that the move would be interpreted as the imposition of a French puppet, the fall of China to Communism propelled the State Department to recognise the move as the only possible 'solution'. In turn, they were keen to win regional acknowledgement

6 Introduction

for Bao Dai. This included Thai support for the move. For Phibun, the choice as to whether his government should recognise Bao Dai was the first test of his commitment to US policy.

Ultimately, his interest in securing US aid convinced Phibun to accept the US request, in effect ending his government's ability to maintain neutrality in Indonchina. In the months that followed, the decision to send Thai troops to support the US defence of Korea from the communist North would further solidify this position, securing US military aid for the Thai government. For Fineman, it was a move that set Thailand on a path that the country's leaders had sought to avoid throughout the nineteenth and early twentieth centuries. During the period of high imperialism, Thai foreign policy had projected ambiguity and adaptability in order to protect the country from competing European interests in the country. Now, however, the 'mere prospect of military aid had sparked a revolution in post war Thai foreign policy amenable to American interests, and, once actually begun, the weapons flow secured Thai diplomatic support on nearly every issue of importance to the United States'.[25] In the following years, US support would also embed authoritarian politics into the Thai political system, as the two opposing forces of General Phao Sriyanond, director of the Thai police from 1951, and Field Marshal Sarit Thanarat, commander of the Royal Thai Army from 1954, sought to dominate the political system, each through his personal access to US financial resources.[26]

However, while Thailand's pro-American stance was largely set in political terms at the start of the Cold War, full cultural integration into the American sphere would be a much more challenging and drawn-out process. It would also be shaped dramatically by the country's historically ambiguous position on the world stage.[27] For over a century, the Thai elite had developed a sense of pride in their country's being Southeast Asia's only politically independent nation. As a result, cultural narratives were already well established as a means of projecting national strength. Promoting the view that Thais were a uniquely civilised race, they tended to assume racial superiority to the country's immediate neighbours, and commonality with the 'great' nations of the world. At the same time, the integration of Siam into the world economy had, particularly since the turn of the century, seen the widening of a small but important middle social stratum. Based primarily in the urban centre of Bangkok, these commoner Thais had become preoccupied by ideas of progress driven from a Western centre, and were fully committed to a consumer culture dependent on imports from the colonial powers. During the Cold War, it was this urban-based community that would ultimately decide the extent to which Thailand would become an ally of the United States.

The emergence of a self-aware 'national' community

In 1932, a revolution in what was then called Siam had removed the country's absolute monarchy and replaced it with a system of government that sought to redefine Thai notions of citizenship. For the generation who lived through

Introduction 7

the period that followed, it was unlike anything their parents could have imagined. New priorities and new opportunities combined with increased demands on the psychological development of the population. As larger numbers became involved in the activities of a growing bureaucratic state, now led principally by commoners, so individual Thais were encouraged to understand themselves in relation to that state. Government-owned media proliferated, and new technologies were mobilised in order to saturate daily life with information about what it meant to be a member of the Thai nation.[28] Invariably, the public relations campaigns of the new government focused on the country's international status. The struggle to establish and defend Thai economic as well as political sovereignty was repeatedly connected to the country's position within global systems of knowledge and representation.[29]

For the new leaders, resituating the country within a system of competing nation states was central to securing their own political legitimacy. The renegotiation of the unequal treaties, which were seen as humiliating reminders of the country's subservience to the European colonial powers, was a priority. At the same time, the Thai economy would have to be decoupled from its dependence on imports, the importance of agricultural production reduced, and new internal industries established to restrict the flow of capital out of the country. In turn, it was hoped, an expanding nation state would be able to bring ever-increasing numbers into the system of governance, providing new avenues for taxation, and bolstering claims that the Thai nation should be treated with respect on the international stage.[30]

However, by the end of the 1930s the global descent into war, and the collapse of the League of Nations as a forum within which to negotiate a fairer deal for the country, pushed Thailand once again onto the very periphery of world politics.[31] As actors of 'great' nations played out what in many ways seemed the end game of international competition, fear struck Thai leaders that the country would be permanently reduced to the role of a minor player. Government propaganda became fixated upon the idea that there was an international conspiracy to cast the Thai as a barbarian race, unsuitable for self-government, and claiming that building a successful nation state was now implicitly connected with a fight for survival.[32] In a climate where imperial ambitions seemed to be dictating the course of world politics, the threat that Thailand could be swallowed up altogether was presented as a very real concern.

Particularly under the military regime of Phibun Songkhram, who came to power in 1938, the need to transform the condition of the nation was viewed in direct relation to the conditions created by the international system. Changing the name of the country from Siam to Thailand, Phibun repeatedly located the emergent nation state within a global hierarchy: Thailand must prove its 'great' status, and be permanently removed from the curse of 'barbarism' that had been used for over a century to reduce its status.[33] Committed to exploiting the full range of socio-political weapons that were driving statecraft in the rest of the world, the post-1932 regime had seen public relations as vital to the new state. However, only under Phibun did government propaganda seek to

8 *Introduction*

marry the need to protect the country from foreigners with a wide range of messages that intended to transform the day-to-day behaviour of the population. Between 1938 and 1944, conformity to certain 'universal' standards in diet, dress and overall behaviour was promoted as essential to securing a Thai ascendency in a world turned upside down.

The period from 1932 onward, and particularly following 1938, thus saw a rapid escalation in the production of state-led media that sought to reference state ideology in practices that were, for many urban Thai, already part of daily life. Dressing well, eating well and behaving well were not alien to city dwellers. For decades, status in urban Thailand had been dependent upon maintaining a high standard in such practices. Yet it was only through state propaganda that these practices became attached to an all-encompassing message that sought to transform the individual into a representative of a developing nation state. As Thailand itself mobilised for war, first in its campaign against the French in Indochina in early 1941, and then as an ally of the Japanese from early 1942, individual behaviour continued to be viewed as an essential tenet in the defence of the nation, which, according to propaganda, remained under a perilous threat.

Following the end of the Second World War, a weakened Thai state, and the collapse in legitimacy of those who had taken Thailand into war against Britain and America, were combined with an expansion of the public sphere as state censorship was lifted. As different personalities battled for popular support, the proliferation of new media products saturated the Bangkok market, competing for new constituencies. This diffusion of power from a highly centralised arena to new sets of politically distinct groups transformed the portrayal of daily life into a series of contested representations about what it meant to be Thai. Meaning was regularly imposed onto social situations which both undermined existing forms of power and supported new ones in a climate where ideology was 'sustained and reproduced, contested and transformed, through actors and interactions which include(ed) the ongoing exchange of symbolic forms'.[34] Assertions about what it meant to be Thai, therefore, were not only narratives that secured the interests of particular individuals or groups, they were also subtly woven into discussions that sought effectively to represent the experience of urban life in relation to the nation. Once disseminated, such representations would often be reproduced, with new meanings imposed and further contested.

In this climate, the idea of what it meant to be Thai changed, and over time a surprising coalition of Sino-Thai, leftists, royalists, military elites and urban consumers settled on the image of the rural Thai village and other proposed vestiges of pre-modern culture as the key site of the nation's identity. In doing so, they relieved urban populations, where nationalist ideology continued to be produced, from the burden of associating modernity and civilisation with the universal desire for participation. They offered in its place a type of nationalism that emphasised, above all, the unity of urban society as distinct from a rural 'other'. They also, however, located this exploration of Thainess

Introduction 9

within the context of the principal political and economic transformation of the time, namely, the integration of the Thai state into an American imperial order.

Under these conditions, cultural production during the early Cold War was to establish many of the narratives that would be exploited from 1958, when Field Marshal Sarit Thanarat took full control of the Thai state in a coup that he labelled a 'revolution'. Describing the transition of power over which he presided as a move from a 'Westernised' political community to a more indigenous form of leadership, Sarit was able to build his legitimacy by embedding his rule in assumed Thai cultural norms. He was also able to replace the rhetoric of Thai state building, which had previously asserted a struggle for real economic and political freedom within the international system, with assertions of cultural independence alone. This in turn allowed him to embed the Thai political system into the US orbit without drawing attention internally to the consequences for Thai sovereignty.

Thai distinctiveness and US imperialism

According to Benedict Anderson, in his 1978 essay on studies of the Thai state and the state of Thai studies, the study of Thailand had, since the end of the Second World War, been vulnerable to scholarly assumptions that the country was unique when compared with its Asian neighbours.[35] As Anderson explained, area specialists who worked on Asia during the Cold War were invariably imbued with the 'pro-indigenous sympathies' that were vital in dealing with the realities of decolonisation. Thai specialists, who 'were not confronted by a formidable body of colonial scholarship', tended to approach the 'Thai, Thai government and Thai history with the same tender spirit' as their academic colleagues. Unlike elsewhere in Asia, where there was a need to confront the stark realities of the past, the same forces in the Thai case tended to 'reinforce a timid – if not conformist – outlook'. The search for an autonomous Asian history, which in other cases provided the intellectual means of establishing a rich and complex scholarly engagement with the region, in the Thai case 'meant that scholars could – and did – proudly assume uniqueness'. As a result, 'ambiguous rubrics' such as 'uniquely Thai values' or assertions such as 'the monarchy is essential to the Thai national identity' had, according to Anderson, encouraged scholars 'to base our thinking on a wholly imaginary eternal Thai essence'.[36]

The essay offered a profound intervention into the study of Thailand, and has inspired a proliferation of studies that have tried to better understand Thai society and the Thai state. In particular, the charge that scholars of Thailand, both inside and outside the country, had been prone to promote a form of Thai exceptionalism is now viewed as a significant complication in understanding the country's modern history.[37] Since Benedict Anderson's article was published, there has been considerable discussion concerning the extent to which Thai nation building should be understood as a process determined by global forces.[38] Most of these have sought to understand how Siam's integration into

10 *Introduction*

the world political economy during the late nineteenth and early twentieth centuries had a considerable impact on the country's early development as a nation state, while others have sought to understand the impact of those processes on more recent cultural phenomena. However, despite the proliferation of such studies, there remains a lack of literature that seeks to understand the early Cold War through the same analytical lens, or to recognise that foreign involvement, generally by the United States, was to play an equally important role in shaping the Thai state during the period as those European countries that had preceded it as the leading power in the country. This has tended to mean that while international pressures are considered vital to understanding early state formation in Siam, Thailand's political development since the Second World War has continued to be viewed within a framework that pays greater attention to the distinctive nature of Thai state formation.

This is particularly true of the military dictatorship of Sarit Thanarat, which has invariably been viewed as a regime embedded in specifically Thai characteristics or, as Thak Chaloemtiarana argues, was the product of specific 'historical and cultural constraints' on the development of modern Thai politics. Rooting his argument in Sarit's popular appeal during his period in office (1958–63), Thak claims that despite his 'harsh, repressive, despotic, and inflexible rule, it nevertheless resonated strongly with much of the population'.[39] This, he argues, was due to his commitment to indigenous forms of governance; the rejection of 'foreign theories of representation' to be replaced by ones conceived as being in a 'Thai mold'. Sarit, Thak claims, 'was a realist in that he thought that objective social facts had to be considered in developing a political ideology'; but he was also 'a romantic in his emphasis upon the stability of a traditional style social system, however administered'.[40] Recognising how Sarit based much of his political thought on ancient markers of Thai leadership, and in particular on the image of the father figure portrayed on the Ramkhamhaeng inscription, Thak postulated that 'perhaps if Sarit had lived in ancient times, he would have founded a new dynasty', or in other words, would have made himself a King.[41]

Ultimately, Thak's analysis recognises that Sarit exploited cultural narratives to bolster his own authority. Yet, by committing himself to the idea that there is a specifically 'Thai mold' from within which such narratives emerged, his study downplays the extent to which the assertion of such 'Thai' characteristics were historically contingent upon forces far beyond the control of the Thai state. Moreover, by asserting Sarit's political philosophy as one rooted in a form of 'despotic paternalism', Thak understates the possibility that, despite his rhetoric, Sarit was largely responding to challenges that were distinctly modern. As a result, Thak's study has minimised the role of international pressure in asserting what could be understood as local culture, and the way in which the Sarit regime's popularity was determined by its ability to project those ideas of Thainess during the Cold War.

Nevertheless, what Thak successfully identified, in what is the foundational study of the period, is both the distinctive nature of the Sarit regime, and the importance of the Cold War in re-defining notions of Thai citizenship from 1958. More recently, in considering the impact of the Cold War on Thai statecraft, David Strekfuss has argued that, 'as "abnormal times" became increasingly normal, "culture" moved toward the centre of official ideology'.[42] Loose in its definition of the term, culture was, by the late 1960s, formally included in Thai law, when undefined violations against the cultural life of the nation could lead to up to 10 years in prison. Drawing from the work of Giorgio Agamben, Strekfuss argues that cultural narratives were instrumental in clearing constitutional space for a 'state of exception', where power was given free rein to assert itself. This, he claims, helped to consolidate a 'vision of the relationship between insiders and outsiders' and 'between those who love the nation and those who work for its destruction'. As a result, a positive identification of what it meant to be 'Thai' was used to enforce the power of the state to exclude anybody who could be said to be 'un-Thai', not through the right of birth but through commitment to a cultural identity in support of the state.

Elsewhere, studies that have recognised the fluidity of cultural narratives during the period have helped to undermine the view that Thainess holds any particular 'essence'. In particular, the work of Saichon Sattayanurak has provided valuable insight into the individual prejudices and historical contexts that gave rise to different versions of what it meant to be Thai.[43] By focusing on key figures in the formation of these ideas, she shows how a discourse of what it meant to be Thai was highly contingent upon the relationship of the individual in question to the regime of the time, their understanding of the international situation, and their relationship to the body politic. In particular, her deconstruction of the work of Kukrit Pramoj sheds important light on how a loose definition about 'Thainess' allowed him to shift his political philosophies and allegiances depending on the climate in which he wrote.[44] More recently, her work on Phya Anuman Rajadhon has placed further emphasis on how personal connections and priorities helped shape his particular view of what encompassed *being* Thai.[45]

In another study, this time from the perspective of Leftist intellectuals during the early years of the Cold War, Sopha Chanamool asserts how ideas of Thainess evolved as a response to the internal condition of the country and in order to fit within the ideological assertions of the international Left.[46] Focusing particularly on the middle of the 1950s, Sopha has identified how left-wing intellectuals explored alternative forms of Thainess that reversed received wisdom by locating Thai culture in rural areas rather than in elite urban centres. Seeing the 1950s as a vital time for debate about Thainess, and recognising the impact of change internationally on such ideas, Sopha further emphasises the way in which cultural narratives about Thailand were adapted to suit particular ideologies.

Building upon these insights, this work seeks to further problematise the search for a Thai essence, but does so by placing greater emphasis on the relationship between Thailand and the United States during the Cold War. Once again, this cue is taken from Benedict Anderson who, by labelling the period of Thai

12   Introduction

history following the Second World War as the 'American era', has sought to draw attention to the powerful impact of American intervention, economically, militarily and politically, in determining Thai cultural priorities during the Cold War.[47] More recently, there has been an increased focus on how US influence on the development of the Thai political system was far more pervasive than previously thought. In particular, Nattupoll Chaiching has cast invaluable light on the role of the United States in shaping Thai government policy during the 1950s.[48] Elsewhere, new studies have shown that, from the mid-1960s, the escalation of the Vietnam War had a significant impact on Thai identities. Exploring Thai cinema, Rachel Harrison has demonstrated that Cold War themes proliferated during the period, reflecting the way in which a discourse set within an international context had an extraordinary impact on Thai mass culture.[49] Janit Feangfu, on the other hand, has shown how Thai–US relations throughout the Cold War had a direct impact on how Thai writers viewed themselves and their society.[50]

Overall, the impact of these studies has been to raise questions about how Americans influenced the emergence of new ideas about what it meant to be Thai during the Cold War. By viewing cultural transfer as a key process in the development of Thai nationalism, this study seeks to look at how new political and economic realities at the end of the Second World War combined with ideological factors to make Thailand particularly susceptible to a version of the Thai nation that made sense within a trans-pacific arrangement of power. Recognising the role of the American media, the study also seeks to locate other key actors who helped, from the American side, to mediate new ideas about the Thai nation. As well as authors, publishers, filmmakers and translators, tourists, businessmen, spies, diplomats, musicians and academics all contributed to re-orienting Thai views of their own country.

At the same time, local Thai actors worked closely with American visitors and permanent residents to re-define their understanding of the nation and present their new understandings to the various constituencies from which they sought appeal.[51] They did so by engaging in a process of appropriation and rejection that, over time, made them transmitters of information about both the outside world, and what should be considered Thai. In doing this, they came to adopt a culturist vision of the nation that was gradually to re-impose orientalist notions of distance between Thais and Americans, and in turn bolster US hegemony over the country. Similarly to how the US relationship developed with other close allies during the period, this study thus argues that, in Thailand, the United States was able to dominate by endowing the Thai people with a sense of Thai tradition as the grounds for their nationalism. By fostering ideas of Thai uniqueness, American actors were to promote a sentimental nationalism that fundamentally re-drew what it meant to be Thai and subsequently pulled them into a US orbit.

Thailand's alliance with America during the Cold War was therefore much more than a merely political or military relationship. It was overtly imperial, built upon a complex cultural mode that sat at the apex of America's imperial

Introduction 13

engagement in the world.[52] As Christina Klein has shown, American cultural producers during the Cold War established a 'sentimental dream' in which cultural difference was used to determine the status of one country in relation to the other. In an international context, where misunderstandings were seen to be the root cause of arrested development and the principal obstacle to world peace, this process of relationship building as identity formation was fuelled by the idea that the 'human connection' was the 'highest ideal'. It also placed acknowledgement of society's emotional response to international exchanges as on a par with the more cerebral conception of national citizenship or international order under a US-oriented world system. As Klein explains, texts such as *the King and I*'s (1951) 'Getting to Know You' were testaments to how 'cultural producers imaginatively mapped a network of sentimental pathways between the United States and Asia that paralleled and reinforced the more material pathways along which America's economic, political and military power flowed'.[53]

It is therefore important to recognise that, despite the often banal-sounding narratives that underpinned American–Thai cultural exchanges, such interactions in fact reflected very real economic and political transformations happening at the level of both individual and state. As Jim Glassman has demonstrated, the evolution of the Thai state has been marked by a growing process of 'internationalisation', which has served to secure Thailand's status within a system of uneven capitalist development, confirming its status as a third world entity in the mid- to late-twentieth century. Recognising the long roots of this process, Glassman nonetheless sees US Cold War involvement as a watershed in the creation of a national system of development that has secured Thailand's subservient status globally to the detriment of its rural population, but to the advantage of the urban-centred elite. As he explains:

> Under U.S. hegemony, the Thai peasantry was more fully incorporated into the international market economy, and the project of export manufacturing was initiated, with former peasants supplying much of the industrial labour. The Thai state, acting in coordination with U.S. advisors, developed a wide range of state institutions and projects to further this transformation ... All these endeavours facilitated high rates of economic growth throughout the decades after World War II, and set the stage for the even higher growth rates that were to follow. They also encouraged the Bangkok-centric and regionally imbalanced growth that has become such a hallmark of development in Thailand.[54]

The proliferation of debates about Thainess that featured in cultural and ideological production throughout the 1950s can thus be said to have occurred at the early stages of a process in which the country's development became determined by institutions that were external from the Thai state itself. As a result, such debates can be explored to illuminate that process. In doing so, it is important to recognise not only complicity with US demands, but also

14 *Introduction*

resistance to them, in order to trace how the ideological foundations of the relationship developed and were then sustained. Indeed, throughout the early part of the 1950s, despite political closeness with the USA, state cultural policy continued to emphasise Thai parity with the 'great' nations of the world, and increasingly attempts were made to associate the country more explicitly with non-alignment rather than with a foreign policy that unflinchingly supported US interests. This changed only following the 1958 'revolution', when the public relations messages of the Thai government became explicitly tailored to the demands of US diplomats, in all their guises, and located Thai citizenship under a system of US-centred governance.

However, the institutionalisation of unbalanced development that followed the 1958 political transformation was not to reject the emotional concerns of Bangkok's urban elite and the anxieties that had underwritten Thai identity formation since 1932. Concerns about how to represent the nation, about how to frame rural life, and about what independence should really look and feel like remained central to governmental ideological production in the attempt to capture the imagination of disparate urban communities. Rejecting existing assertions of a world ordered by race, it replaced them with new culturist versions of distinction that opened up being Thai to a wider catchment. Now, as Thainess became associated with the sentimental engagement with a way of life disconnected from urban lifestyles, they lent themselves to commodification and fetishisation more than ever. Trips to the floating market, or to distant rural communities to appreciate Thai culture, unthinkable during the era of nation building that preceded the Sarit revolution, now became principal sites of self-exploration for urban Thais. Yet, accompanied by representatives from the United States, these experiences of Thailand were 'authenticated' through their relevance to a global consumer culture that urban communities could now feel a clear part of. While these experiences seemed to re-define what it meant to be Thai, re-locating and broadening cultural narratives to incorporate more of the population and their shared history, in fact participation was more exclusive and restricted than ever.

Structure of this book

Although the book takes a broadly chronological approach, it is also organised so as to identify the complex way in which American and Thai narratives about Thainess emerged. Recognising the vital role of US cultural and ideological production during the period, the first chapter focuses on how Thailand was presented in the US media, and how that vision of the country fitted with the broader themes of US expansion during the early part of the Cold War. Focusing on the figure of Jim Thompson, the American ex-Office of Strategic Services officer who established the Thai silk industry, this chapter explores how Thai silk became a brand that made Thailand 'known' to America. As a result, there is a specific focus on New York, where Thaibok fabrics sold Jim Thompson's silk to wealthy Americans. Acknowledging the city as a key

Introduction 15

centre for cultural production during the Cold War, the chapter pays particular attention to the publication houses that helped create the myths that surrounded Thompson and his product. In particular, it shows how the creation of the Thai silk brand was intertwined with the theme of abundance and a sense of a common American mission, all of which sat neatly within the logic of the Cold War from an American perspective.

From here, the next five chapters scrutinise how ideas of culture were transformed from the 1930s through to the height of the Thai–US relationship during the 1960s. Chapter 2 identifies the historical trends and developments that set the scene for the post-war era. Taking its cue from the first chapter, it looks at how ways to dress had long been connected in the minds of Thai consumers with ideas of economic sovereignty and political independence. Through a study of Thai state propaganda and post-war lifestyle magazines, the chapter seeks to determine why, in the aftermath of the Second World War, ideas about how to dress permeated Thai understanding of the country's status internationally. Finally, the chapter asks why early interactions with American cultural producers were often characterised by misunderstanding and misappropriation on the part of Thai writers, who would often view American interest in Thailand through the prism of the country's wartime experience.

The third chapter takes a more detailed look at the post-war period, and how wartime declarations of Thai cultural parity were undermined. Once again, it looks at post-war Thai interactions with American culture, but shows how, from early on, there was a desire to question the kind of relationship Thailand should forge with the new 'great' power. Using problem pages from one of the most influential Thai newspapers of the time, as well as lifestyle magazines, it shows how the proliferation of private media encouraged an active engagement with changes occurring globally, and sought to make sense of the apparent decline in Thailand's international status. In a region where Thailand had once been the only independent nation, decolonisation raised new questions about how the country should engage in diplomacy, forcing an acknowledgement of new centres of power outside the 'West'. At the same time, US interest in Thailand began to increase as the Cold War in Asia became hotter. Offering one of the few safe havens for American academics who wished to study an Asian nation, Thailand became a human laboratory for investigating how 'traditional' culture was being transformed by modernity. Overall, the chapter shows how these ideas began to seep into Thai public debate and consciousness, and how they gradually helped to secure new narratives about an alternative political system.

With Chapter 3 focused on popular, and more framings of Thainess, the fourth chapter once again places the spotlight on the Thai state. In particular, it looks at how state actors, and particularly Phibun Songkhram, sought to re-invigorate state power and re-ignite confidence in the constitutional system. Largely in response to increased hostility to American political intervention among urban Thai communities, but also to the growing confidence as a capital of the non-aligned movement, the Thai state sought to re-orient Bangkok as

16 *Introduction*

capital city defined not by a relationship to the West, but rather to the rest of Asia. Looking in particular at the months leading up to the coup that would finally remove Phibun from power, specific attention is paid to the celebrations of the twenty-fifth centenary of the Buddhist calendar. The chapter illustrates how the state increasingly struggled to employ the symbolic capital of the nation. It also shows how commentaries in the country's media added credence to the idea that there might be an alternative vision of the nation that was yet to be realised.

Following the Sarit revolution, cultural production again shifted, and was used by the new regime to secure the hegemony of American power inside the Thai political system. With a particular focus on the Tourist Organisation of Thailand, the fifth chapter explores how this new institution was created in order to service state propaganda in the context of the Cold War. The chapter looks at how the organisation of state-led spectacle projected coherent representations of Thainess outside 'modern life', and in doing so provided new opportunities for urban Thai communities to form a new conception of 'high society' dominated by interaction with American visitors. The grandstand, for example, became a prized international space, within which Thai culture could be viewed from a distance and appreciated as part of a cosmopolitan experience of the country, and the Erawan Hotel became a site for the production of exclusive insights into the value of Thai culture. Encouraging urban Thais to rethink their place in the world, such spaces also promised the prospect of parity and relevance, even if just for a fleeting moment, to US imperial culture.

Finally, the sixth chapter reflects on the significance attached to two events that in many ways marked the height of the Thai–US relationship, when a Thai 'victory' on the world stage was most explicitly defined in terms of acceptance into an American imperial order. First, the King and Queen's visit to the United States at the start of the 1960s was celebrated in newspapers as a moment of pride for all Thais. The ability of the Queen in particular to represent the Thai nation effectively to the world was highlighted. Second, in 1965, the crowning of a Thai woman as Miss Universe at Miami Beach was heralded as a watershed in Thailand's national history. Both of these moments were also fleeting. They were tied to the supremacy of the USA on the world stage and to the ongoing logic of the Cold War. Thai unity, just like the global relevance of international beauty pageants, remained vulnerable in a world where the only constant was an ongoing change in the priorities and fashions that continued to shape and re-shape global culture.

Notes

1 Thongchai Winichakul has written extensively on the 'other within', meaning the rural classes who live outside the urban centres (principally Bangkok). For Thongchai, the emergence of such 'othering' practices began during the era of European imperialism, as a result of orientalist identity markers of ethnic differentiation based on European models of civility and racial hierarchy. See Thongchai Winichakul, 'The others within: travel and ethno-spatial differentiation of Siamese

Introduction   17

subjects 1885–1910', in Andrew Turton (ed.) *Civility and Savagery, Social Identity in Tai States,* Richmond: Curzon, 2000.

2 *March of Time: Oasis on a Troubled Continent,* Time Inc., 1953.
3 These examples are taken from the Time Inc. film, but are widely replicated elsewhere.
4 'For Westerners the good life', *Life,* 31 December 1951, p. 37.
5 Ibid.
6 Ibid.
7 There is a large and growing scholarship that recognises the way in which decolonisation frustrated and, indeed, shaped the early Cold War in Asia. One of the most important is Odd Arne Westad, *The Global Cold War,* Cambridge: Cambridge University Press, 2007.
8 There is a range of literature that deals with the rapid breakdown of American optimism in the aftermath of the Second World War. For details on the how American officials recognised the problems posed by decolonisation, see Frank Ninkovich, *Modernity and Power: A History of the Domino Theory in the Twentieth Century,* Chicago, IL: University of Chicago Press, 1994. Also, for a discussion on how America's position globally was 'frustrated' by events happening globally, and in particular by the successful Russian test of an A-bomb in 1949, see Stephen J. Whitfield, *The Culture of the Cold War,* Baltimore, MD: Johns Hopkins University Press, 1996.
9 For a synopsis of the initial stages of the conflict see John Springhall, '"Kicking out the Vietminh": how Britain allowed France to re-occupy South Indochina 1945–46', *Journal of Contemporary History,* 40(1) (2005): 115–130.
10 On the return of the Dutch to Southeast Asia, see Anne L. Foster, 'Avoiding the "Rank of Denmark": Dutch fears about loss of empire in Southeast Asia', in Christopher Goscha and Christian Ostermann (eds) *Connecting Histories: Decolonization and the Cold War in Southeast Asia,* Stanford, CA: Stanford University Press, 2009.
11 National Security Council Staff Paper NSC48/2, produced toward the end of 1949, stated that the USA was not willing to accept further Soviet encroachment into Southeast Asia, and outlined plans to defend the Asia region through a range of policies.
12 US Ambassador in China (Stuart) to the Secretary of State, 15 February 1949. 'Foreign relations of the United States (FRUS). The Far East and Australasia' in two parts, 1949, p. 1117.
13 Ibid.
14 White House Office, National Security Council Staff Paper 1948–1961 / NSC Registry Series, 1947–62, Box 15 A82-18. Psychological Strategy Board (PSB), Washington, 'US Psychological Strategy with Respect to the Thai Peoples of Southeast Asia', July 2 1953, p. 16.
15 Ibid.
16 Ibid.
17 James A. Michener, *The Voice of Asia,* New York: Random House, 1951, p. 138.
18 The idea of the 'sentimental embrace' is explored more later; see Christina Klein, *Cold War Orientalism, Asia in the Middlebrow Imagination, 1945–1961,* Berkeley, CA: University of California Press, 2003.
19 This can be seen best in the uncertainty expressed by John Foster Dulles in 1955 about the need to welcome Phibun Songkhram to Washington, and the subsequent discussions with the Ambassador in Thailand about why the country should be considered important. See chapter 4 for more details.
20 Jim Glassman, 'On the borders of Southeast Asia: Cold War geography and the construction of the other', *Political Geography,* 24(2005): 784–807.
21 A particularly good example of this in relation to Southeast Asia is Christopher E. Goscha and Christian Ostermann, *Connecting Histories: Decolonization and the*

18   *Introduction*

Cold War in Southeast Asia 1945–1962, Stanford, CA: Stanford University Press, 2009.

22 For a specific exploration of the Cold War in Asia, and of the way local leaders used the Cold War to support their own needs, see Immanuel Wallerstein, 'What Cold War in Asia, an interpretative essay', in Yangwen Zheng, Hong Liu and Michael Szonyi (eds) *The Cold War in Asia: The Battle for Hearts and Minds*, Leiden: Brill, 2010, pp. 15–24.

23 Matthew Foley, *The Cold War and National Assertion in Southeast Asia: Britain, the United States and Burma, 1948–1962*, Abingdon: Routledge, 2010, p. 2.

24 Daniel Fineman, *The Special Relationship: The United States and Military Government in Thailand, 1947–1958*, Honolulu, HI: University of Hawaii Press, 1997.

25 Daniel Fineman, 'Phibun, the Cold War, and Thailand's Foreign Policy Revolution of 1950', in Christopher E. Goscha and Christian Ostermann, *Connecting Histories.*

26 The political relationship between these two figures and Phibun Songkhram is known in Thai political history as the Triumvirate. See Thak Chaloemtiarana, *Thailand: The Politics of Despotic Paternalism*, Ithaca, NY: Cornell Southeast Asia Program, 2007.

27 The term 'ambiguous' is a reference to a recent collection of essays that deal with Thailand's 'semi-colonial' status during the period of European imperialism and the ongoing impact of that historical experience. See Rachel Harrison and Peter Jackson (eds) *The Ambiguous Allure of the West: Traces of the Colonial in Thailand*, Hong Kong: Hong Kong University Press, 2010, p. 174.

28 Kenneth Osgood has noted how it is 'often overlooked that the Cold War coincided with a moment in world history when technologies and information resources were everywhere exploding'. Particularly from the First World War onwards, states became increasingly skilled at monopolising such channels to distribute ideological material for the sake of capturing hearts and minds. People such as Edward Bernays, who straddled the world of advertising and public relations, increasingly incorporated psycho-analysis as a tool, for selling either products or, indeed, ideologies. See Kenneth Osgood, *Total Cold War: Eisenhower's Secret Propaganda Battle at Home and Abroad*, Lawrence, KS: Kansas University Press, 2006, pp. 3–9. Also see Edward Bernays, *Propaganda*, Brooklyn, NY: Ig Publishing, 1928.

29 Prasenjit Duara has argued that sovereignty became recognisable during the period before the Second World War through the integration of states in international systems of knowledge and representation. This meant that countries such as Thailand became particularly vulnerable to changes in the distribution of power globally. See Prasenjit Duara, *Sovereignty and Authenticity: Manchuko and the East Asian Modern*, Lanham, MD: Rowman & Littlefield, 2004.

30 For supporting material see Benjamin Batson, Siam's *Political Future: Documents from the End of Absolute Monarchy*, Southeast Asia Program, Department of Asian Studies, Ithaca, NY: Cornell University, 1974.

31 For an account of the importance of the League of Nations in Siam's development as a nation state, see Stefen Hell, *Siam and the League of Nations, Modernization, Sovereignty and Multilateral Diplomacy 1920–1940*, Bangkok: Riverbooks, 2010, p. 4.

32 Particularly during the Phibun Songkhram's first term as Prime Minister (1938–1944), frequent reference was made to 'foreigners' as enemies of the Thai state, and government propaganda emphasised that the categorisation of the Thai people as 'barbarian' by outsiders represented an existential threat to the nation.

33 Bangkok was transformed into a stage for this purpose, with new modern buildings erected to encourage Thais to take pride in their surroundings. See Pinai Sirikiatkul, '*Na thi ni mai mi "Khwamsueam" thanon ratchadamnoen pho so*

Introduction 19

2484–2488' [A place without "cultural slackness": Rajadamnern Boulevard, 1941–1945], *Warasan nachua, Wa duai prawattisat sathapattayakam lae sathapattayakam thai* (NAJUA) Vol. 6, Bangkok: 2010, pp. 9–50.

34 John B. Thompson, *Ideology and Modern Culture: Critical Social Theory in the Era of Mass Communication*, Cambridge: Polity Press, 1990.

35 Benedict Anderson, 'Studies of the Thai State: the state of Thai studies', in Eliezer B. Ayal (ed.) *The Study of Thailand: Analyses of Knowledge, Approaches, and prospects in Anthropology, Art History, Economic, History and Political Science*, Athens, OH: Centre for International Studies, Ohio University, 1978, pp. 193–247.

36 Ibid.

37 Thongchai Winichakul has been particularly scathing about the conservative nature of Thai scholarship that has failed to undermine state-led calls for Thailand to be viewed as distinct. See Thongchai Winichakul, 'Nationalism and the radical intelligentsia in Thailand', *Third World Quarterly*, 29(3) (2008): 575–591.

38 There is a vast range of material on this. For work that traces the impact of Siam's integration into a world determined by European imperialism, see Thongchai Winichakul, *Siam Mapped: A History of the Geo-body of a Nation*, Chiangmai: Silkworm Books, 1994; Tamara Loos, *Subject Siam: Family, Law and Colonial Modernity in Siam*, Ithaca, NY: Cornell University Press, 2006; Maurizio Pellegi, *Lord of Things: The Fashioning of the Siamese Monarchy's Modern Image*, Honolulu, HI: University of Haiwai'i Press, 2002. For a discussion on Thai nation building that has influenced this work, see Craig J. Reynolds, *Seditious Histories, Contesting Thai and Southeast Asian Pasts*, Singapore and Seattle, WA: University of Washington Press, 2006. Also see Michael Herzfeld, 'The conceptual allure of the West: dilemmas and ambiguities of crypto-colonialism in Thailand', in Rachel Harrison and Peter Jackson (eds) *The Ambiguous Allure of the West: Traces of the Colonial in Thailand*, Hong Kong: Hong Kong University Press, 2010.

39 Thak Chaloemtiarana, *Thailand: The Politics of Despotic Paternalism*, Ithaca, NY: Cornell Southeast Asia Program, 2007, p. 10.

40 Ibid., 109.

41 Ibid., 119.

42 David Strekfuss, *Truth on Trial in Thailand: Defamation, Treason, and Lese-majeste*, Abingdon: Routledge, 2011, p. 237.

43 Saichon has written about HRH Prince Damrong Rajanubhab, Luang Wichitwathakhan, Kukrit Pramoj and Phya Anuman Rajadhon. A similar approach to the construction of Thainess can be found in Scott Barme, *Luang Wichit and the Creation of a Thai Identity*, Singapore: Institute of Southeast Asian Studies, 1993.

44 Saichon Sattayanurak, *Kukrit kap praditthakam 'Khwam pen Thai' lem 1 yuk chomphon Po Phibun Songkhram* [Kukrit and the construction of Thainess during the era of Phibun Songkhram], Bangkok: Samnak phim matichon, 2007; and *Kukrit kap praditthakam 'Khwam pen Thai' lem 2 yuk chomphon Sarit thueng thotsawat*, 2530, [Kukrit and the construction of Thainess from the Sarit era to the 1980s], Bangkok: Samnak phim matichon, 2007.

45 Saichon Sattayanurak, *Phraya Anuman Rajadhon: Prat saman chon phu niramit 'khwam pen Thai'*, Bangkok: Samnak phim matichon, 2013.

46 Sopha Chanamool, *Chat thai nai thatsana panyachon hua kao na* [The Thai Nation from the perspective of progressive intellectuals], Bangkok: Samnak phim matichon, 2007.

47 Benedict Anderson (ed.), *In the Mirror: Literature and Politics in Siam in the American Era*, Bangkok: Duang Kamol, 1985. In particular see the Introduction.

48 Nattupoll Chaiching, '*Kanmueang thai samai rattaban Chomphon Po Phibun Songkhram phai tai rabiap lok khong Saharat America phoso 2491–2500*', Bangkok: Witthayaniphon ratthasat dutsadi bandit sakha wicha ratthasat Chulalongkorn Mahawitthayalai, p. 2552.

20 Introduction

49 Rachel Harrison, 'The Man with the golden gauntlets: Mit Chaibancha's *Insi Thong* and the hybridization of red and yellow perils in Thai Cold War action cinema', in Tony Day (ed.) *Cultures at War: The Cold War and Cultural Expression in Southeast Asia*, Ithaca, NY: Cornell University, 2010.

50 Janit Feangfu, '(Ir)resistably modern: the construction of modern Thai identities in Thai literature during the Cold War era, 1958–1976', PhD thesis, University of London, 2011.

51 An interesting essay that deals with a similar process in Japan during the same period is Naoki Sakai, '"You Asians": on the historical role of the West and Asia binary', in Tomiko Yoda and Harry Harootunian (eds) *Japan after Japan: Social and Cultural Life from Recessionary 1990s to the Present*, Durham, NC: Duke University Press, 2006.

52 Notable studies that look at the role of US Imperialism in constructing various locales that have strongly influenced this study include Christine Skwiot, *The Purposes of Paradise, U.S. Tourism and Empire in Cuba and Hawai'i*, Philadelphia, PA: University of Pennsylvania Press, 2010; Christina Klein, *Cold War Orientalism, Asia in the Middlebrow Imagination, 1945–1961*, Berkeley and Los Angeles, CA: University of California Press, 2003; Christopher Endy, *Cold War Holidays: American Tourism in France*, Chapel Hill, NC: University of North Carolina Press, 2004. Also, particularly on the role of culture in forming conceptions of world order during the Cold War, Akira Iriye, *Cultural Internationalism and World Order*, Baltimore, MD: Johns Hopkins University Press, 1997.

53 Christina Klein, *Cold War Orientalism*, p. 17.

54 Jim Glassman, *Thailand at the Margins: Internationalization of the State, and Transformation of Labour*, Oxford: Oxford University Press, 2004, p. 5.

1 'A theatre with two stages'

Jim Thompson's Thailand

In the latter half of March 1967, just a few days before Easter Sunday, three men were spending an evening together in Bangkok. It was an uneventful evening, spent between men who knew each other well. Jim Thompson was one of Southeast Asia's best known American residents, famous for making Thai silk known to the world. Charles Sheffield was acting manager of the Thai Silk Company, which Thompson had founded two decades earlier. William Warren was a writer and journalist who, based in the city for many years, had long made Thompson one of his most prized contacts. This time, the book he was writing was about Thompson's house, a hotchpotch of old wooden buildings and palaces from around the country that combined to create one of the city's most spectacular and opulent residences. The book was near completion, and all that was now needed was to catalogue the collection of historic artefacts accumulated by Thompson during two decades in Southeast Asia. As the three proceeded to walk through the different levels of the dwelling, measuring Buddha statues and commenting on the origins of various Burmese tapestries, the only thing of note about Thompson's demeanour was that he seemed tired.[1] Yet this was to be the last time that William Warren would spend time with the man who had been one of his most important subjects. It was the height of summer, and Jim Thompson was about to make a trip he knew well, into the cool Malaysian highlands. After a couple of days relaxing with his long-standing friend Connie Mangskau and the owners of the cottage, Dr Ling and his wife Helen, the small group marked Easter Sunday with a picnic. That afternoon, he was supposed to be taking a nap in his room. Yet at some point, Dr Ling later reported, he had left, leaving his suit jacket and his cigarettes back at the house. Little else is known about what happened to Jim Thompson that afternoon, except that he was never seen again.[2]

For the American public, headlines about the disappearance of Jim Thompson made little impact. In January of the same year, Martin Luther King had written an article linking the civil rights movement with the Vietnam War. In doing so, he had made a powerful connection between American military involvement in Southeast Asia and the calls for racial equality at home.[3] A generation of black Americans were beginning to join forces with a

22 *A theatre with two stages*

bourgeoning anti-war movement based largely in US universities, and central to the movement was the charge of hypocrisy made against US policy in Southeast Asia. A day before Thompson's disappearance, 5000 had marched against the war in Chicago, and two weeks later 400,000 marched on the United Nations in New York. Fuelled by the draft, and driven by a rising uncertainty over the purpose of the US fight in Southeast Asia, the transformation in US public opinion was rapid. In a short few months, the idealism that had shaped American attitudes to the Cold War from the end of the Second World War were to come under a scrutiny from which it would never quite recover.[4]

However, while Jim Thompson's disappearance might have quickly slipped from the American public's attention, his legacy within the minds of the international community was already secured. Since his arrival in Asia in 1945, Thai silk had become integral to the branding of the Thai nation, and his house, nestled on the banks of a Bangkok canal, had become an unmissable attraction for tourists to the country. As a result, Jim Thompson's disappearance immortalised his status as a 'good' American, and his story was quickly re-located from the difficult years of the mid-1960s to the memory of a now fading post-war American moment.[5] During those early years of the Cold War, a 'climate of victory' had intoxicated writers, editors and film producers with regard to their thinking about America's status in the world.[6] Tied to the ideological logic promoted through the idea of an 'American Century', figures such as Jim Thompson, who left America to live in places like Thailand, were revered as central to the country's future as a global leader.

Jim Thompson's story was particularly compelling. He had originally been sent to Thailand as part of an Office of Strategic Services (OSS) mission to liberate the country at the end of the Second World War. After a trip back to New York, made only a few months into the occupation, Thompson returned to Thailand intending to stay. After a short period spent working on the refurbishment of the Oriental Hotel, he soon refocused his attention on a different project, selling the silk that he had found being produced in some of Bangkok's poorest communities.[7] He worked hard to support the development of this small cottage industry into a set of commercial processes and social relations that made it possible to produce a product tailored specifically for the post-war American market. Over a few short years he developed dyes, patterns and techniques that resulted in the production of a high-quality fabric available in quantities sufficient for both export to the metropolitan centre of New York, but also for an increasing number of American visitors to the country.[8]

With his silk production already a successful business by the late 1950s, Thompson refocused once again, putting considerable effort and resources into building a new house. Put together to create a building that Thompson regarded as distinctly Thai, the house was from the start of the project designed to be a space made specifically for entertaining guests from America.[9] Already a celebrity among the engaged American public, Thompson was clear about the fact that the house was to be a theatre, in which guests, including diplomats, film stars, academics, journalists and spies, could sit and view the comings and goings of Thai communities living below on the canal.[10] Soon after finishing construction of the house, Thompson increased his constituency, opening it up to tourists for a number of days a week. By the start of the 1960s, with American policy makers continuing to receive the broad support of US media outlets, Jim Thompson remained one of Thailand's best known American residents. More than that, however, the vision of Thailand that he had invested so much in asserting was now providing the predominant framework through which US visitors experienced the country. As a result, while the man's physical disappearance in the latter half of the decade remained little more than an intriguing mystery to the American public, the cultural narratives that Jim Thompson had both exploited and constructed continued to shape American, and increasingly global, visions of the country.

Imagining an age of abundance

Unlike the time he spent in Thailand, Jim Thompson lived the first half of his life in relative mediocrity. Born into an upper-middle-class family on the east coast of America, in 1928 he graduated from Princeton University. He then went on to study at the University of Pennsylvania's School of Architecture, but his failure to complete the post-graduate course there left his career as an architect frustrated. While he found employment with Holden, McLaughin and Associates in New York, the fact that he had not graduated meant he was unable to sign off on his designs. Yet, while his diminishing prospects in the city were, before the Second World War, becoming ever more apparent, his experiences there would nevertheless prove invaluable. Coming from a good white family, and already financially secure, his work with a leading architect firm in the city would have brought him frequently into contact with the New York financial and political elite.[11] Over his years in Bangkok, his knowledge of New York-based culture, and his understanding of how that culture was disseminated to the American nation at large, would prove vital to his success.

In the first half of the twentieth century, New York stood out as culturally, socially and economically distinct when compared with other American cities.[12] Throughout the country, lifestyles had at the turn of the century been clearly split. The first was an elite cultural life, confined to opera houses, museums, clubs and concert halls. The other was the world of working men and women, where cultural institutions such as neighbourhood associations, the union hall, and the mutual aid societies were the basis of community identification. While this same split existed in New York, there began to develop from the end of the nineteenth century, first around Broadway, and increasingly throughout the city, a new form of cultural production.[13] William R. Taylor has described this environment as a 'cultural marketplace', in which appeals to a broader market went some way to breaking down the earlier class distinctions.[14] Beginning with 'itinerants and storefront theatricals', he explains how there emerged 'new cultural institutions that collected and displayed entertainment, just as

24 *A theatre with two stages*

the new department stores displayed goods'.[15] While this commercialisation of cultural life may have held within it the disavowal of class distinction, or the oppressive reality of city life, Taylor points out how 'the new newspapers, the popular songs, and the graphic and photographic art had an open, and non-prescriptive function for consumption' that helped 'consumers from across the social spectrum to decode the city'.[16] As someone who traversed the space between a New York-based ruling elite and what Barbara and John Ehrenreich have described as the 'professional–managerial class', Jim Thompson would have been immersed in such a cultural life.[17] Moreover, by moving to New York in 1928, he would also have been privy to a decade in which that kind of cultural production was scaled up to provide ideological narratives for the nation at large.

With many of the country's major publishing houses already located in the city, the 1920s also saw New York become the centre of the burgeoning advertising industry.[18] With the economy booming, fuelled to a great extent by speculation on Wall Street, New York was cemented as the location of a set of industries focused on the production of modern American life. However, during October 1929, the decade of growth came to an abrupt end when prices on the New York Stock Exchange fell dramatically. Whether cause or symptom, the stock market crash was nevertheless followed by a decade in which a vast number of Americans suffered from unemployment, the rapid decline in personal incomes and poverty inducing malnourishment and illness.[19] It also resulted in an ideological shift in American politics. When Franklin D. Roosevelt was elected President in 1932, free market capitalism began to be challenged with strong and popular state-led policies that sought to protect working Americans from the excesses of unfettered capitalist growth. Unionisation was promoted, taxes were imposed that sought to redistribute wealth, and social welfare programmes were implemented in order to offer relief to the most destitute families.[20] Also included in the ideological framework of the 'New Dealers' was the view that during the preceding decade, Americans had been taken advantage of by the capitalist system and, as a result, credit had been extended while people were encouraged to purchase substandard or unnecessary products. As a result, it became increasingly popular in Washington to see normal Americans as what Lizabeth Cohen has described as 'citizen consumers' who needed to be represented, and therefore protected, from those advertising agencies and salespeople who over the preceding decade had invested so much time and energy in seeking out their valuable incomes.[21] Throughout the decade this consumer movement picked up pace, receiving strong support from the academic community, and resonating strongly with ethnic minority groups, women's groups and workers in both the industrial and the professional sectors.[22]

However, while the consumer movement grew in popularity, the large corporations and the financial business elite fought against its ideological logic. For them, American consumers remained central, but rather than seeing them as citizens who needed to be protected from big business, these groups sought

A theatre with two stages   25

to promote the idea that the citizen was a purchaser who, if allowed unfettered access to the market, could stimulate the economic growth that would lead to higher employment and, in turn, create greater levels of consumption. In quoting directly from a film made by Chevrolet in 1937, entitled *From Dawn to Sunset*, Lizabeth Cohen notes how this vision worked in direct opposition to the consumer movement that had gained momentum under the stewardship of the Roosevelt government. In it, the film suggested that consumers should be given the 'pleasure of buying, while trapping "the purchasing power of pay packets" to fuel "a prosperity greater than history has ever known".'[23]

What is particularly noticeable about this group's message was the way that, in the immediate aftermath of the crash, it sought to view the crisis as a momentary failure of systems that would eventually return the economy to growth. Rather than making strong commentaries on the economic climate of the day, instead it sought to draw from a memory of the 1920s combined with the emotional appeal to a brighter future for all. Moreover, exploiting New York's unrivalled position as a 'cultural market place' during the 1920s, it was the financiers who resided in the city who emerged as central to the production of an American future undeterred by the temporary failings of the system. The Rockefeller Center, for example, was built at the height of the depression as a physical reminder on the New York skyline of what had been achieved during the 1920s, and what might come next. It was also intended to act as a site for 'cultural diffusion and transmission', which, by exploiting the latest in public relations practices, quickly became a physical centre for a New York media industry that was increasingly focused on a national market. As William Buxton has noted, the Rockefeller Center, by integrating 'philanthropy, knowledge and commerce, as well as family connections and personal networks', was to become a powerful mediator of culture and ideology.[24] When Henry Luce moved his Time Life publishing corporation into the top six floors of the main building in April 1937, the formidable power of the site was confirmed.

Toward the end of the decade, as war loomed in Europe, the New York World Fair continued to reinforce the message of its main financial backers. Opening under the motto 'Building the World of Tomorrow', the Fair, and in particular the 'Consumers Pavilion', sought to locate at its centre the consumer as purchaser rather than citizen, as one exhibit, described by Lizabeth Cohen, explained:

> 'As mass production depends upon mass purchasing power, we cannot hope to build lasting prosperity under such conditions of inadequate purchasing power.' But, it continued, with 'the techniques and the power to produce abundance' within our grasp, soon all Americans should be able to live 'the good life'.[25]

The New York Fair was a financial disaster, and yet ideologically it was to set a strong agenda for the future. While the American economy was yet to exit

26 *A theatre with two stages*

from its decade-long difficulties, the New York World Fair was nevertheless to set the scene for a wartime narrative about American culture and identity that would allude to the potential for 'prosperity and abundance' once peace arrived.

These were also themes that Henry Luce exploited strongly in his influential editorial, 'The American century', which was written to urge the country to see itself as a global leader, clear and confident about its role in the Second World War. Published on 17 February 1941, the editorial argued that while the government languished in indecision, American society was already in the conflict, and that normal people knew exactly which side they were on. He therefore wanted Americans to recognise the fact that if the country was to enter the war, there would be 'no shadow of a doubt that we Americans will be determined to win it – cost what it may in treasure or life'.[26] This assertion first that there was no question about sides, and second that America would be victorious, was crucial to the article's argument. It also emphasised the idea that the choice to enter into war existed within a broader ideological narrative about the role of America in the world. Indeed, his assertion was that America was a powerhouse from which the best ideals of the world emerged, and that American society not only should mobilise for war, but also should act to achieve the swift spread of those ideals across the world. Reprinted in *The New York Times*, *The Washington Post* and *The Readers Digest*, all paid for by Luce himself, the article was to prove crucial in convincing American society that it should enter the war.[27]

While *Life* magazine provided political direction to American readers, other publications that normally concerned themselves with lifestyle alone began to exploit their position within the cultural world of New York to further support an ideology of consumption as the primary marker of American identity, and increasingly coupled this to a new kind of internationalism that located America at the apex of Western civilisation. Condé Nast's *Vogue*, for example, had since its birth in 1892 sought to inform American society about European fashion and taste. Yet on the eve of the Second World War, the publication began to challenge the assumption that the old world was still the global centre of cultural production, with the publication of the very first *Americana* edition. A decade on, in the editorial for the tenth annual *Americana* edition, the original issue was described as a 'new direction not only for *Vogue*, but for the fashion publishing world', a moment when the magazine 'turned its usually international eye, singly on the ideas, the women, the life, the fashion of its own country'. 'In those days', it went on to explain, 'when France was the fashion heart of the world, it was dramatic, unique, and even newsworthy for a fashion magazine to produce an issue with no touch of Europe in it.'[28]

When America did enter the war, the idea that America had 'arrived' was employed by the magazine to support the war effort. It also, in line with the stance taken by the New York World Fair and with Henry Luce's notion of the American Century, sought to encourage Americans to think about the future. Now more explicitly linked to the current conflict, particular emphasis

A theatre with two stages 27

was placed on the role readers might play in the reconstruction of the world in its aftermath. During the years of conflict, the *Americana* edition was to offer a powerful narrative about how its readership might conceive of the global conflict as a basis upon which to build the ideological foundations of a post-war American engagement in the world. Only years after *Vogue* had established American fashion and design as a world leader, the war gave it an opportunity to re-internationalise the newly confident nation in relation to the 'old' world of Europe.

Writing in the 1943 edition, the 'humanitarian anthropologist' Margaret Mead made the case for a new emphasis on the exceptional status of American society.[29] She did so by asserting a base difference between the people of America and the rest of the world: 'We know it from inside,' she exclaimed. Drawing from her theoretical commitment to understanding culture through family structures and learned psychologies, Mead argued that American confidence would prove difficult to manage in the post-war years. She explained how diplomatic brains are already 'grappling with how to handle the inevitable "We won the war" which will come from millions of American throats at the end of this war'. The Russians, the Chinese, the British, 'working hard with stolid, unyielding courage in a bombed and narrow land', none of them, she continued, will be impressed with an American society that already perceives itself to be the reason the war will be won. However, for Mead it was important that this should not weaken American resolve; neither did it mean that Americans should shy away from what was, nevertheless, their innate character. In times of war, she went on to explain, Americans must conclude that fighting was 100 per cent the right thing to do, and that this would be proven following the end of hostilities. 'If there is to be a better world after the war' she concluded, 'a world with widening horizons for work and effort and visible rewards; if, as we draw the whole world closer together, we turn it also into a world of opportunity'.[30]

Mead's impassioned declaration therefore, asked American society not to think simply about the war as a moment in time, but to embrace the sense of unity achieved during the conflict as the potential dawn of a new historical epoch. The war, she argued, provided a point at which unease or anxiety about how America might relate to the rest of the world could be resolved inside the black-and-white morality of the conflict. Confident that they were on the 'right side', Americans should be encouraged to think of themselves as the somewhat reluctant centre of expanding opportunities for all the world's citizens. By promoting action and intervention as the underlying themes of American identity, Mead also alluded to a post-war world in which whole countries would have to be rebuilt, and where the furtherance of human progress would have to be driven from an American centre. Capturing the spirit of Henry Luce's American Century, Mead gave it extra meaning, and indeed academic legitimacy, by imposing upon it the science of cultural difference. The barren lands of past 'old' civilizations, as well as the contested regions of the world for which Americans ultimately fought, were being constructed into

28 *A theatre with two stages*

a new stage, onto which the expansion of the American frontier might once again rest at the heart of American identity.

In the early months of the war, Jim Thompson, who was newly married, remained in America, now living in Washington. However, he was soon to be recruited into an elite and clandestine military organisation, the OSS, which would later become the CIA. As a result, his work involved much more than simple fighting. Rather, as William Warren has suggested, he was more than likely to have been involved in 'raids behind German lines, liaison with local resistance groups, and probably a good deal of personal risk'. While the exact details of his movements remain little known, Jim Thompson's role in the war certainly moved beyond the narrow confines of conflict, for it is clear that the State Department, and the elite core of the OSS, kept one eye firmly on the post-war world. Making good on the promises made by Henry Luce and Margaret Mead, Jim Thompson, it can be assumed, would have been privy to conversations which sought to foresee America's role in the world once the war had come to an end.

American national character in a climate of victory

Jim Thompson arrived in Thailand in August 1945, days after the Japanese surrender in Asia. He therefore came to a country that had officially been at war with the United States. However, due to the clandestine operations of the OSS and the organisation of a group made up of the Thai economic and political elite known as the *Seri Thai*, or the Free Thai movement, Thompson was welcomed to the country as part of a liberating force. For a few months, he spent his time mixing with the Thai establishment, supporting the American presence in the country. However, in the middle of November he got news from home that his wife wanted a divorce, and a few days later he returned to the United States.[31] When he got there, he would have found a place that, according to Howard Zinn, was 'overcome with the Grandeur of its mission'.[32] The predictions of Luce and Mead had been correct, and American editors and journalists now spent their time thinking about how the successes won during the war could be translated into a similarly successful post-war period. Mixing a strong belief in the power of American consumer culture with a determination to remain central to a global future, he would also have found an American society eager to learn about a distant country that was now working closely with the United States.

While the Second World War had temporarily solved the immediate problems facing American families during the Great Depression, it was only in its aftermath that the ideology of consumer-driven capitalism took firm root in American society. During the war, while much of the population, both male and female, had been employed either in the military services or on the home front, the rationing of goods had meant that there were few avenues for Americans to spend their wages. When the war came to an end, and when the rationing of goods was lifted, there was an enormous demand for consumer goods. American homes, now flush with capital, were eager to spend their new-found wealth. Moreover, because the American mainland had not been attacked during the war, the infrastructure, built to produce armaments and industrial equipment, was quickly and cheaply converted into factories that produced civilian consumables.[33] As Randall Bennett Woods has explained, 'depression followed by war had rendered the material dimensions of the American dream elusive for most', but 'now that peace was at hand, many sought to transform their postponed hopes – for new housing, automobiles, electrical appliances and so forth into practical shopping lists'.[34]

This post-war interest in commodity, coupled with the technological and industrial advances made during the conflict, made for a smooth transition from the heavily state-subsidised war economy to one fuelled largely by the private sector. However, echoing Margaret Mead's prediction, the new confidence that America was entering an era of unprecedented abundance was coupled with an interest in the nation's status in the world. On one hand, American writers remained confident. They made no apology for their view that America was the most developed society on Earth. Yet there remained an anxiety that the war had thrust the country into the spotlight with such speed that it would struggle with its new-found power. In the 1947 Americana edition of *Vogue*, in an article entitled 'We are responsible to the world', Eric Sevareid, a correspondent for CBS during the war, claimed that now the war was over, 'it will be hard for America to be a country in the world: harder than ever because America is so big and so much in the world's eye'. Speaking with authority to his American audience, he claimed that 'The big searchlight of Time is burning directly down on us, and if we aren't dazzled, it's only because we haven't yet quite opened our eyes. God's finger is resting on our heads, and if we don't feel it, it must be because we have heads of stone.'[35]

Sevareid's argument was that America had received the accolade of world leader not because it had intended to, but because it had 'come of age' at a time when the rest of the world faced calamity. Moreover, in this vision of a unipolar world, how America managed its arrival as the principal world power needed to be managed with care. Clearly alluding to, among other things, the development of nuclear armaments, he emphasised the idea that America had been granted 'the leading responsibility of an era at the precise moment when the driving forces of science have made it inevitable that if this era is mishandled, there will be no more forthcoming, not in terms of Western civilisation, at any rate'.[36]

By identifying American society as the unwitting inheritors, and now protectors, of Western civilisation, Sevareid also imagined the nation as one that must act wisely if it was not to fall into the same traps as the old European powers. Of all those that had inherited global leadership, he claimed that 'the British had made the best job of it', but even they had 'carried it off without much dignity or mercy'.[37] To succeed where others had failed, he sought to encourage Americans to recognise that 'henceforth the relationship of any American with the other peoples of the world is going to be different ...

30 *A theatre with two stages*

Make no mistake about it – vast, historic changes in world power positions are sensed and responded to by the lowliest Sardinian fisherman or Shanghai coolie'.[38]

Elsewhere, the importance placed upon how Americans behaved when they met the peoples of the world was emphasised. Here, however, Americans need not worry too much about cultivating a good attitude. Instead, they should simply draw from what came naturally. Writing in the same edition, Henry Steele Commager presented his thesis on 'the American character'.[39] Like Mead, Commager drew from the idea that cultural identities were the product of past experiences, mixed with environmental conditions. The American character, he argued, had come about from the unique nature of the American past. While Americans had inherited much from the 'old' world, their character had been shaped by the 'environment of the New World, and the experiences of the American people', creating 'one of the most distinctive of national characters'. The war, in bringing so many Americans into full contact with the rest of the world for the first time, had proven the point. No more, he argued, could anybody doubt that Americans were unique. More importantly, the American character was one that held an emotional hope for the future, combined with a keen and pragmatic interest in material prosperity. The American, he concluded, had an optimism that 'led to a cheerfulness and carelessness: as the present and the future were both reasonably sure'. At the same time however, he 'was never unconscious of the power and might and wealth of his country'. He was a materialist, finding deep satisfaction in statistics of wealth and growth, and concerned with material comforts which could be translated in "standard of living" generalizations.[40]

Later in the year, in the July edition of *Glamour*, sister publication to *Vogue*, similar themes to those of the Americana edition were explored. In an editorial, it was explained that in celebration of 'our greatest national holiday, Independence Day, GLAMOUR, as a public duty, departs a little from its predominating fashion formula to devote some space to what it conceives to be a current national problem that is a great concern to all Americans'.[41] It went on to explain that 'today, we think it is important to lay before our readers, some of the reasons why we must think deeply and act wisely, in the matter of the whole world's interdependence under our inescapable leadership'. What followed was an essay, published in French and Russian as well as English, and written by the Russian-American political scientist Vera Micheles Dean. In it she claimed that, as a result of the war, America now possessed the 'most highly developed industrial system known to history'.[42] Moreover, she explained, because America's industrial areas remained intact, unlike Russia's, America alone was in a position to convert that system into one channelled toward peacetime production; an 'arsenal of democracy, which successfully filled the manifold necessities of global war, could contribute with equal success to the creation of global peace'.[43] A year later, and the 1948 *Americana* edition of *Vogue* would put it more simply, stating that 'in the twenties, the U.S.A. ducked both responsibility and spotlight', but that now, 'we cannot modestly fade out of the light ... We have the food, the money, the machinery, and the arms. We plan to use them wisely. It will take both our brains and our hearts'.[44]

Thus, in the early years of the post-war period, these nationalist editions of *Vogue* and *Glamour* promoted the rise of America to world leadership as an undeniable fact, and argued that it was up to Americans to use the opportunity for good. This, it was made clear, needed to be achieved through a commitment to two fundamental beliefs. The first was that the industrial processes developed in America were now the best in the world, and should be employed to bring 'peace and prosperity' to the world. The second was that American cultural identity, or 'character', was unique from the old colonial powers, and indeed, from any other nation on Earth. By understanding this identity (in its weaknesses as well as its strengths), Americans would be able to convince the world that their intentions were genuine.

However, this notion of a unique cultural character, promoted through such elitist publications, was ultimately rooted in the ideological shift that had been promoted in New York since the stock market crash of 1929. It incorporated the key tenets of an emotional commitment to an American ideal, and an internal concern for material comfort for all. Published in *Vogue* in 1949, an excerpt from Margaret Mead's most recent book epitomised the theory. For Mead, the American character was sustained through an insistence in a 'future dream' and a 'refusal to rest content with the present'. This, she explained, meant that 'Americans depend more upon the eye than upon the sense of touch ... more upon the living room as a stage set than a living room into which one sinks deeply into remembered warmth.' While this meant that being American came with a price attached to it, the reward was that Americans 'feel that no one in the world can be disinherited simply by being born in some other kind of house as long as there is a possibility that someday, later in life, he can live in the ideal house'.[45]

During the immediate aftermath of the Second World War, a commitment to such ideas was responsible for the widespread belief in American society that it had a responsibility to bring prosperity, or abundance, to the world. Seeing itself as the most modern nation on Earth, this American idealism drove academic theories about both cultural identity and development. The rise of modernisation theory, in particular, combined the presumed supremacy of American modernity in the world with an analysis of localised cultural norms.[46] While these norms were not deemed scientifically inherent in racial identity, they *were* located within the new science of a humanitarian anthropology, pioneered by Ruth Benedict and Margaret Mead. Their belief was that it was possible to understand 'patterns of culture' that, like the American example, were determined by engrained historical narratives and the national landscape.[47] For those who employed the anthropological conclusions of Mead to understand the supremacy of American culture, the emphasis was invariably upon the country's status as an abundant society. Importantly, while these notions were rooted in a mythology about the American frontier, they were also caught up

32   A theatre with two stages

in the current situation, with the desire for a different kind of abundance, provided by the post-war American industrial model.

By the time Thompson had permanently settled in Thailand, and had committed to working with Thai silk, the ideological value of such arguments had heightened as the result of rising uncertainty about the uniqueness of American progress. Indeed, by the end of the decade it was becoming increasingly obvious that Russia, too, had emerged from the war with its own sense of victory, and more importantly that it was also capable of the technological advances that had transformed the status of the United States in the world, made evident by the successful test of a Soviet atom bomb in September 1949. As a result, the inevitable progress of American interests and values became 'frustrated' by the haunting presence of a strong Soviet Union and the spectre of communist ideology.[48] US media outlets were to instinctively support the broad political and social drive that sought to promote American society as ideologically superior to Russia. At the same time, with Europe established as a place where the ideological battle was already being fought, the attention of newspaper and magazine editors increasingly fell upon Asia as a second front in that battle. When China fell to a Communist regime in October of the same year, the fear that Asia would come under Communist influence started to seem a strong possibility.[49]

A second 'frustration' to the American 'climate of victory' was the fear that the fuel driving the economy, the consumption of goods bought with wartime savings, would dry up once those savings had been spent. In 1948, the rapid growth of the post-war period started to slow and the project to expand American economic interests globally became ever more important. While policy makers first sought to integrate Europe into an American-centred model of development, many in both New York and Washington had already identified Asia as the place where that expansion would be most important for the country's future. As Robert Herzstein has identified, for Henry Luce, Asia was the real prize for post-war American expansion: 'a veritable garden of souls, and, being underdeveloped, it was also subject to American influence'.[50]

Significantly, however, Asian nations were not to be treated equally. While policy toward Japan would seek to establish it as a secondary economy to the United States, it also sought to promote the reintegration of the less developed economies of Southeast Asia as 'tertiary' economies. Drawing from National Security Document NSC 48, Christina Klein has noted how the American system of production, consumption and resource management sought to 'maximise the availability, through mutually advantageous relationships, of the material resources of the Asia area to the United States and the free world generally, and thereby correspondingly deny those resources to the communist world'.[51] This 'pattern of trade', as Jim Glassman has put it, 'would involve the export from the United States to Japan of such commodities as cotton, wheat, coal, and possibly specialized industrial machinery; the export from Japan of such items as low-cost agricultural and transportation equipment, textiles and shipping services to Southeast Asia; and the export from the latter area of tin, manganese, rubber, hard fibres and possibly lead and zinc to the United States'.[52] Throughout the 1950s, the American expansion into Asia would conform to these policy requirements. Ideologically, policy remained tied to the beliefs that the United States had come to represent: abundance, prosperity, peace and freedom.

Thailand: *Oasis on a Troubled Continent*

By the end of the 1940s, therefore, the confidence that had been such a characteristic of post-war America had evolved into anxiety over its political and economic supremacy in the face of a communist presence that, it was feared, might de-rail the central role of America globally. The invasion of Communist forces from North Korea into the South in June 1950 heightened that anxiety. For policy makers in Washington, the expansion of Communism was likened to the Nazi expansion into Europe that had led to the Second World War.[53] Located within the walls of the Kremlin, Communism was conceived of as a monolithic goliath that would, if given the chance, swallow up the smaller, weaker nations of the world, a view emphasised by the National Security Council in April of that year. In document NSC 68, the National Security Council had advised President Truman to engage in a massive re-armament programme in order to halt the spread of Communism and prevent a Third World War. While the plan was initially rejected, the June invasion of South Korea and the subsequent escalation of an American-led ground war during the latter half of the year once again established open warfare as an integral part of the US political, economic and cultural landscape. It did so, however, in the context of a growing sense of crisis that Asia might be lost altogether.

Writing in *Life* in June 1951, travel writer and journalist James A. Michener summed up the new importance of Asia for American readers.[54] 'For so many decades', he began, the continent had seemed 'mute, mysterious and almost impersonally remote to most Americans'. Now, however, with 'almost 70,000 Americans dead, wounded or missing' in Korea, and with questions raised in the 1950 elections for the House of Representatives about Truman's initial leadership, Asia had become 'terrifyingly alive and urgent'. The continent, he said, 'had exploded into the centre of American life', and 'it will stay there forever'. The problem, however, was that while the Asian nations would, according to Michener, 'make or crush us', it was nevertheless a place where 'the American is utterly unwelcome'. In China, Malaya and Indochina, he explained, the American runs the risk of being murdered, and throughout Asia 'wise Americans stay indoors'. 'Never in our National history have we been so feared and despised', and though Americans had often helped win national freedoms for the people of Asia, 'those very nations today condemn us as reactionary and imperialistic'.[55]

These might have been tough facts to face but, according to Michener, they were nevertheless crucial to an American future in the continent. The 'fact' of

34 A theatre with two stages

the local nationalist movements and the inevitability of self-rule from the European empires was, like it or not, something that had a direct bearing on how Americans were viewed. Following centuries in which the continent had been under colonial domination, Americans faced the ever-present reality that 'imperialism is absolutely finished' and 'any white men who try to re-establish it will be murdered ruthlessly'.[56] If Americans were going to integrate their world with the world of the Asian peoples, they would not only have to embrace decolonisation as a historical certainty, but would also have to convince Asian populations that America had no imperial intentions. Published in the same year, Michener's book, which recorded his trips through Asia and his encounters with various Asian people, advised Americans that to achieve this they should 'proclaim that we are a democracy and that we, like almost all Asiatic nations, won our independence through revolting against our alien masters'.[57] Entitled *The Voice of Asia* (1951), it asserted the idea that victory in Asia would be won only through the ability of the American people to see themselves not as superior, but rather as 'an intelligent and moral nation trying to find its way'.[58] The book, like the article, made no mention of the American colonisation of the Philippines.

The Cold War was used to emphasise urgency. With the dismantling of the colonial empires, Asia was presented by Michener as a land that sought 'progress and power' independently of any foreign coloniser. Yet, it was also a place that was home to a 'huge power vacuum'. As a result, Asia was presented as a place that, while heavily influenced by local nationalist movements, remained in search of a leader. Michener himself seemed to think that one of the 'big three', China, India or Japan, would rise to the position of regional leader. However, in the global context, these local powers would inevitably be split by the underlying conflicts that determined the Cold War. As the struggle between these three local powers continued, he explained, 'it will increasingly affect the war for the world between Communism and the West'.[59]

In his *Life* article, Michener spoke only indirectly about the potential benefits for America should the battle for Asia be won, yet he was also to allude strongly to the economic penalties that might emerge should they fail. If Americans could not convince Asian nations that they were different from the 'white men' of old, he argued, 'American capital will soon be thrown out of Indonesia just as peremptorily as British capital is being thrown out of Iran'.[60] What Americans therefore needed to do was to find a way of doing business on the continent that did not offend Asian sensibilities regarding sovereignty. By echoing themes developed both before and during the Second World War, Michener's narrative was deeply related to a belief in the American Century as the best outcome for the world. 'Throughout our history', he concluded, 'we have won futures, which in dark moments seemed worse than dubious. Here the cost of failure is too staggering to allow us to proceed with anything less than confidence.'[61]

The final edition of *Life* that year focused exclusively on Asia and, like Michener, presented it as a continent central to an American future. Also like

Michener, the special edition presented Asia as a place of potential difficulty as well as opportunity, arising from the twin problems of antipathy toward 'Westerners' and the ability of the Communists to gain legitimacy from the fight against imperialism. In an article entitled 'Decline of the Westerner', *Life* photographer–reporter David D. Duncan sought to report on a 'Free Asia', where the 'ghost of empire haunts his outposts in the East as Asians prepare to run Asia – even if badly – for themselves'.[62] However, the magazine also sought to emphasise that the American belief in the morality of its cause was already playing a strong role in 'Free Asia', and that rising interest in the continent was increasingly determining what it meant to be an American. Using the Korean War as its starting point, the magazine explained that Asia had for decades lain 'beyond the farthest horizon of any average American interest or comprehension', but that had changed, and now 'the US is inextricably involved in Asia, both as the chief force of the free world, defending itself against the new aggressive force of Communism and as a global good neighbour'.[63]

The various articles in the Asia edition, like Michener's text, presented the idea that Asia could be lost through a global misunderstanding about the real nature of American intentions in the region. Indeed, it is particularly noticeable that writers such as Michener and Duncan, when seeking to confront American society with such stark 'truths', accepted that the reader was quite certain of the inherent morality of the American role in the world. Behind the backdrop of Communist-inspired conflict or the violence directed toward the 'white man' was a different version of Asia that was yet to be achieved, but that required American engagement if it was to be achieved. The hope, therefore, was that if a dialogue between these different populations could be secured, then victory would finally be won. As Christina Klein has explained, Michener's appeal was that through re-telling his own stories of encounter with Asia, he was able to enter into 'an ideal state of multiracial, multinational collectivity'. In doing so, Klein continues, 'he reassures the reader that Asia is still accessible to an American, that exchange is still possible, and that the alienation of Asia from America is not inevitable'.[64]

In *Life's* Asia edition, however, it was not David Duncan who showed the potential for Asians and Americans to achieve harmony. Instead, the magazine's centre pages, just after a long piece covering the 'Rise of the Red Star' and a shorter article on 'Why we fight', both printed in black and white, the pages gave way to a glossy picture of Bangkok at dusk. Described as a 'peaceful city', the capital was presented as a place unaffected by the troubles elsewhere, and therefore as a place where Americans were able to feel at home. Here, unlike elsewhere, where Michener had demanded that Asian country names no longer be prefaced by 'inscrutable' or 'mysterious', Americans could continue to find a place where 'the age old dreams of romantic Asia still come alive today'. Bangkok, the article explained, home to a Buddhist people, 'still fulfils the most romantic fairytale dreams of the Orient'. After a pictorial trip through the city, the article returned to the primary narrative of the magazine, for Thailand

36   *A theatre with two stages*

was presented as the only place in Asia where a Westerner need not feel threatened. Using the example of a recent coup and change of government, the *Life* article explained that, 'unlike other parts of Asia, where Americans and other Westerners now have to step carefully, the changes in the Thai government have had absolutely no effect on the foreigners in Bangkok'. This, the author explained, was because 'Thailand, an independent monarchy for six centuries, was never anybody's colony' there was no resentment of 'foreign imperialists'.[65]

By presenting Bangkok as a 'peaceful city' for Americans, the article thus promoted the idea that it was possible to settle in the city. Moreover, the magazine explained, 'because Thailand is the only country in Asia which produces more rice than it can consume, the cost of living is low', meaning it was also a place where Americans could achieve the post-war dream of living 'the good life'. By establishing Thailand as a place that, because of its history, its religion and its environment, was already a peaceful and abundant society, it therefore imagined the country as a reflection of what Americans already recognised as 'good' in their own exceptional society. The difference was that the American version of abundance was rooted in their status as the most advanced society on Earth, while Thailand had achieved its own self-assured status as a free country in the world as a consequence of its intact traditional society. As James Michener had explained in the *Voice of Asia*, Thailand had 'prospered under its own haphazard guidance for some 2,000 years'.[66]

The idea that Thailand was a place not caught up in the violent business of establishing freedom from the West was further emphasised in a documentary film produced in 1953. Produced by *Life's* sister company, Time Incorporated, as part of the *March of Time* series, the documentary was entitled *Oasis on a Troubled Continent* (1953), and once again presented the country as a land at peace, nestled on a continent at war. At the start of the film, Thailand was introduced as exceptional, first and foremost because its people remained unaware of the troubles afflicting the world in which it was situated:

> In recent weeks, the March of Time has taken you to several Asian countries where the even tenure of daily life is constantly interrupted by open warfare, and guerrilla activity, usually communist inspired. Today we concern ourselves with a land whose people have in recent years lived peacefully, surrounded by countries seething with intrigue and violence. This is idyllic Siam, also called Thailand.[67]

From there, the film introduced Thailand as a place where the 'even tenure of life' continued unabated, as if in a historical bubble when compared with the rest of Asia. It looked at what it described as a traditional kite-flying contest, and showed images of Thai temples. It showed the King attending a sporting event, and noted the deep veneration that the Thai people have for the nation.

Like the *Life* article, Bangkok's Thai population and images of their daily life were used as a backdrop to tell the story of American involvement in the country. From the half-way point of the film, the narrator, who had been describing this daily life, introduced the American community who were said to be 'living comfortably in this easy-going country' and were 'taking an active part in Siamese life'.[68] Included in the list of people interviewed was Bill Davies, who had set up a soft drinks company with Thai partners and was distributing Coca-Cola throughout Bangkok, and Alexander MacDonald, a fellow OSS officer who had established the *Bangkok Post*. Speaking directly into the camera, MacDonald explained to the viewer back in America that he found his work at the *Post* 'very rewarding', and that 'other Americans are beginning to feel the way I do, and they're coming here to Bangkok'. He went on to explain that, once settled, such Americans invariably 'find the kingdom hospitable, and they find the Thai a friendly and good natured people'. Yet by far the most time in the documentary was spent looking at the character of Jim Thompson, who with his associates was reported to 'have made Thai silks world famous once again, and have given a new life to an important Siamese industry ... New York interior decorators, French fashion designers, and South American textile houses', it was reported, 'are among those asking for his silks'. Today, the documentary informed the viewer, 'Thompson inspects the looms on which are woven the materials for the costumes of the London production of *The King and I*, the hit musical whose locale is Siam'. The film's focus on Jim Thompson concluded by suggesting that 'Siam has proven a country of opportunity to Thompson as it has to other enterprising Americans.'[69]

Thus, just as with the article in *Life*, the *March of Time* documentary presented Thailand as a place where Americans were not the enemy. It also located Thailand in the context of a news agenda that sought to narrate the ongoing struggle in the region. Thailand, as a peripheral yet peaceful location in the day-to-day realities of the global conflict, gave credence to the idea that there remained parts of the world where the fight for freedom could exist alongside the expansion of American interests. However, Jim Thompson stood out by engaging in a business activity that spoke directly to the logic of the Cold War in America; not only was he making Thailand known to the West by single-handedly bringing the silks of Thailand to global attention, but he had done so by supporting weaving families less well off than himself.

Adorning progress with morality: Thai silk as a global commodity

Thai silk was first tested on the American market in 1948, when Jim Thompson launched to the American public not only the product, but also the New York end of his business, Thaibok fabrics. In the lobby of the Pierre Hotel, just off Central Park in Upper Manhattan, the Siamese silks were introduced as a product steeped in a history of which Americans were presumed to be ignorant. *The New York Times* described the silks as 'products of native weavers in remote Siamese provinces' that 'represent traditional designs and techniques that are said ... to have been almost unknown outside of the country'.[70] It was a powerful narrative that would quickly begin to shape the commercial

38 *A theatre with two stages*

identity of the product among elite American society. Moreover, by casting it not merely as a material entity with an aesthetic value, but also as a product with a rich background, Thai silk was to speak directly to the sensibilities of post-war American society, and was to support the construction of Thailand as an *Oasis on a Troubled Continent* (1953).

Nevertheless, it is unlikely that Thai silk would have received significant interest from American consumers had it not been for the Rogers and Hammerstein production of *The King and I*, which opened on Broadway in 1951. The timing was significant. Although the cultural influence of New York was being challenged by Hollywood in the first half of the decade, the theatre-going public of the city maintained an important role in governing the success of such a production. Since the turn of the century, theatre companies in New York had done much to attract a broad spectrum of society. Yet the social processes that governed whether or not a play was successful remained determined by a relatively small number of people.

On one hand, markers of social distinction within the theatre itself had been discarded. The removal of side boxes for elite guests, a range of ticket prices in the stalls, and the free movement of all visitors in the lobby provided an egalitarian feel to the theatre, and helped to establish theatre going as an activity that was marketable to the masses. However, by maintaining the prestige of the opening night, the theatre continued to assert a hierarchy over access to the cultural life it represented. As Bruce A. McConachie has noted, the opening night was an occasion when a ruling class of New Yorkers held the right to make or break a production's future. Together with the review writers in the popular press, McConachie sees this hit-or-flop system of Broadway productions as a tool through which 'the ruling class exercised a kind of veto over all shows', meaning that, despite the apparent equality, 'productions during the Cold War had to pass through the eye of a needle held by a conservative ruling elite before gaining success and widespread distribution'.[71]

The King and I opened on 29 March to a rapturous reception. The success of the play was never really in question. Throughout the previous decade, Rogers and Hammerstein had built a reputation for producing musicals with a strong mass-market appeal. The press response to the opening night confirmed that they had triumphed once again. As that week's edition of *Collier's* stated, '*The King and I* seems destined to be a success; another hit to harass Rogers and Hammerstein's already harried accounts.'[72] *The Saturday Review* also celebrated what it described as an 'enchanting evening in theatregoing'. The article then went on to comment on the fact that the production had been achieved with impeccably 'good taste, the kind of perfect taste which characterizes the staging, the dancing, the performances, the settings, the costumes, and the writing'.[73] Having received the broad support of the theatre-going elite, *The King and I* soon became a hit on Broadway, before it was taken on tour across the United States.

While the play's plot was a narrative about Siam in the mid-nineteenth century, it was also deeply imbued with the ideological logic of the Cold War.

As Christina Klein has explained, the production was to utilise a semi-factual story about an English governess employed by a Thai king in the 1860s to put forward ideas tied to US ideals about a post-war engagement in the world. In particular, Klein recognises that *The King and I* asserted a belief that through the exploration and acceptance of difference, great and little powers could learn to work together. However, in emphasising a strong opposition between tradition and modernity, as if located on two ends of a single continuum, the play also identified the terms upon which such mutually beneficial relationships must work. Because the play focused on the steps the Thai court needed to take if it was to deflect the interest of the imperial powers, it implicitly recognised the developmental superiority of the West. The story of *The King and I* thus resonated with American audiences because, as Klein explains, it 'made the transition to modernity seem painless, as long as native elites followed the West's instructions and knew when to step aside'. While the imperial powers were cast as outsiders, with little sensitivity, the hero of the play is Anna, who modernises not though force but through 'an intimate embrace'.[74]

The King and I was therefore to support the idea that, by acknowledging and appreciating difference, and by 'getting to know' other ways of life, Americans would be able to secure friendship with the peoples of Asia. Yet it is important to remember that *The King and I* remained a cultural product firmly rooted in the cultural world of New York. Attending the play, and having an opinion about it, was a marker of social identification rooted in the ideology of post-war American internationalism; and, as with other such products, identification with the play and its message soon became a mark of social distinction. Indeed, since the 1920s Broadway's success had been predicated upon its ability to combine the spectacle of the stage with fashion consumption. As Marlis Schweitzer has described, the 'fusion of spectatorship and consumption represented a crucial step in the formation of a mass market for consumer goods and the cult of celebrity, two intertwined cultural projects designed to fuel the American economy and overwrite anxieties about the exploitation of labour and the loss of individuality'.[75] In the case of *The King and I*, the interplay between the messages of the play and the products associated with it was to provide a similar function, but now in relation to an Asian nation.

By the end of the summer of 1951, *The King and I* had made Siam one of the most recognisable place-names associated with Asia. It had also made anything 'Siamese' highly sought after. Now, the iconography of ancient Siam could be employed by New York-based retailers as a way to familiarise their audience with a new product, new because Siam was newly famous within the local market. The department store Saks Fifth Avenue placed an advert in *The New York Times* that drew directly from the success of the play to launch a new line of products. 'From Broadway to your jewellery box,' the advert proclaimed, 'Siam is all the hue and cry this season.' The new season provided by the Siamese-inspired products also drew from the product best known from the play. Costumes designed by Irene Sharaff, which had used Jim Thompson's

40   *A theatre with two stages*

Thai silk, were reflected in the assertion that 'these imported, hand-turned glass beads mirror the fantastic colours of native cloths'.[76]

In October, another Condé Nast magazine, *House & Garden*, went further, to state that the play had made the silks an important fashion commodity and the latest marker of the new season. Siam, it explained, was a 'country, whose wealth of colour and design inspired the costumes of a Broadway hit "The King and I",' and now 'provides ideas for your home'.[77] The magazine devoted page after page to the country, giving meaning to images from Bangkok for an American audience by placing them next to scenes from the play. Then, in those pages devoted to new ideas for the home, the magazine encouraged readers to think about how they might use 'ideas from Siam to brighten your room'. Once again, the magazine combined materials imported to New York with ideas taken directly from the play. While on one side of the page it invited the reader to 'add colour to a black-and-white room' by covering a shade in 'Siamese plaid', on the other it said that 'if you admired the costume Yul Brynner wore in *The King and I*, try it out on a table cover by sewing on crocheted cotton balls'. The magazine also introduced Jim Thompson to the American audience. It did so in order to make it clear to its New York readers that if they wished to redecorate in a Siamese fashion, they did not need to visit Thailand. They could instead go to Jim Thompson's shop in New York. Interestingly, it did not introduce Thaibok fabrics as a business but as an organisation, which, run by Thompson, was actively supporting the silk industry and 'constitutes a heartening Four Point program'. The implication was that the silk-weaving industry was contributing to Thailand's post-war reconstruction and future development, in line with government plans to support less developed nations.

The Four Point plan was a policy developed by the Truman administration at the end of the 1940s to counter the Russian claim that America was not interested in sharing its wealth. Important for the magazine was that in Jim Thompson's case, he was doing so without direct aid. When Thompson had arrived in the country, it explained, he had been 'both impressed by the products of the local weavers and depressed by the fact that they were deprived of necessary materials by the extended fighting in the Far East'.[78] This was erroneous. It was not war that had deprived the weavers, but the lack of interest, local or international, in their products. However, by linking the product with Thailand's post-war reconstruction, and by casting Jim Thompson as an independent American using his resources as an American to better the lives of the Thai people, the article in *House & Garden* idealised him as an emblem of post-war US expansion. The story presented was that of a man who, by drawing from his own ingenuity, good intentions and love of the product, had pre-empted State Department policy in a project that was winning the hearts and minds of an Asian population. More importantly, the magazine made it clear that the American reader could play a part in that story. They, too, could support the organisation by purchasing the product.

A theatre with two stages 41

Lizabeth Cohen has explained how, during the Cold War, the idea that American consumer goods would be able to 'win the hearts and minds of the people in the so-called developing world' was combined with an understanding that the expansion of US consumables into those markets would 'fatten' the purses of American manufacturers.[79] In the story put forward by *Life*, and then the *March of Time* documentary, figures such as Bill Davies were fulfilling that dream by bringing a product such as Coca-Cola to a large Asian market, enriching not only himself but also his Thai partners. Thai silk, however, held a more subtle location in the ideological framework as a product that identified the extent to which a 'faith in a mass consumption postwar economy' was regarded as a tool with which American consumers could change the world. *House & Garden* affirmed the idea that wealth being created in America could be used to support the development of Asian economies. It also affirmed the importance of valuing the exotic distinctiveness of such a society in the context of the Cold War. Here, for example, Thailand was presented as a country that, despite its development lag, prospered in its inherent, cultural knowledge of colour; it was 'a country where colour is splashed by man and nature across the land with a lavish hand'.[80]

House & Garden, by using *The King and I* (1951) as its point of reference, took the opportunity to take the reader on a virtual trip to Bangkok. Through the purchase of silk and through the memory of the play, they were encouraged to imagine the country from afar. Yet it also made it clear that, for those who had the means, Bangkok was a place they could actually visit. The travel data section, which gave flight details and a brief description of the hotels available in the country, was one of the first occasions when the country was presented as a desirable place for American tourists. Over the next few years, a small number of Americans did take this advice, contributing on a small scale to the rising interest in and knowledge of the country. However, like the article in *House & Garden*, the play and the place were often used to inform the trip, and at times even to re-inform the experience of watching the play. For Eleanor Roosevelt, writing in *The Washington Daily News* in May 1952, a recent trip to Bangkok had inspired her to return and watch the production a second time. Seeing the city, she said, had 'really added to my enjoyment of the play'. It had convinced her of the authenticity that the play had been able to achieve: 'Dorothy Sarnoff as Lady Tiang is remarkably good. She looks and acts just like the little ladies who piloted me around on my sightseeing tour of Bangkok.'[81]

By the middle of the decade, the idea that a 'real' experience must involve an actual trip to the country was becoming more pronounced. In an article that appeared in *Vogue* in September 1957, the purchase of Thai silk was presented as a journey into the true heart of the country. This article told the story of a visit to a silk shop in central Bangkok where the author intended to buy material to take back home.[82] As she entered, however, she found a vast array of coloured silk which, she explained, 'dazzled' her eyes and forced her to back away. The young girl who, according to the author, misunderstood

42   *A theatre with two stages*

the movement as evidence that she was about to lose a sale, responded by asking her if she would like to see the factory where it was made. She then described the journey as she travelled first in a little car through increasingly narrow streets, and then in a boat into the heart of a Bangkok canal or *klong*. Finally, she arrived at the place, a unique location where she might be able to witness an authentic Thai family producing a traditional commodity. As she entered the house and commented on the different members, all involved in their own part of the assembly line, she also took pleasure in witnessing a traditional social and economic life that she was about to support through a consumption choice. In doing so, she confirmed to herself the underlying morality of the exchange, identifying that the true value of the product was not only its beauty, but also what it represented to her American readership. The five yards, she explained, were now a dress over which her friends would exclaim, 'Thai silk, how lovely'. 'Dyed in a gasoline can, washed in the turgid *klong* water, woven through long patient hours by a girl whose feet hardly reached the pedals of her loom', the dress was, according to the article, woven of much more than silk, it was 'woven of intimate moments in the life of a *klong* family', and was 'like no dress I shall ever own'.[83]

Written in 1957, the article emphasised a journey that took the author off the beaten track and into an encounter with the 'real' Thailand. In doing so, it reinforced the standard trope of modernisation theory, that the modern city was not the genuine home of an authentic Thai culture, which could be viewed only by a visit to an authentic cultural site. The fact that this cultural site was a family living in relative poverty was acceptable because the American consumer was able to sustain (and of course maintain) the family by finding value in a product produced in Thailand's own 'haphazard ways'. As a result, it reinforced the idea that the true abundance found in Thailand was rooted in a traditional cultural life.

It also incorporated such products into a New York-centred fashion culture that saw international travel, and the moral implications of US leadership in the world, as fundamental to the conformation of America's elite status. Mirrored in Thaibok's own advertising back in New York, Thai silk was thus sold as both a morally laudable investment in the future of Thai society, and as a luxury commodity that elevated American consumers into near royalty on the world stage. An American woman depicted wearing a lavish item of jewel-covered Thai headwear was transformed in an advertising image into a monarch of the East through her visit to a New York boutique selling silks from Thailand (see Figure 1.1). Promoting itself as a product that represented the complexities of Cold War relations, it also therefore, served to confirm the emergence of an American based global elite.

Thompson's Thailand: a theatre with two stages

Toward the end of the 1950s, Jim Thompson began construction of his house on the banks of a Bangkok *klong*, a structure that would become his most

A theatre with two stages 43

Figure 1.1 Advert for Thaibok fabrics
The New Yorker, 11 December 1955

profound material legacy upon the city's landscape. It was an ambitious project, the intention of which was to create a home both suitable for his personal needs, and at the same time explicitly 'Thai' in character. To achieve this, on one hand he would use existing structures, a collection of old wooden buildings taken from Bang Krua and from Ayutthaya; on the other he would assemble them to create a space suitable for his life in the city. Most noticeable of these 'adaptations' was the lobby and internal staircase, an important feature for a man who took such pleasure and meaning from entertaining guests. Once complete, this idea, that the house was an amalgamation of two distinct qualities, a fine balance between being 'as authentically Thai as possible' while at the same time home to 'certain Western comforts', was consistently repeated by journalists who wrote about it.[84] It was, just like *The King and I*, to act as an important addition to the cultural and ideological tools needed by American visitors to support their engagement in the country.

By the time Jim Thompson had finished his house, in April 1958, Southeast Asia as a distinctive region was rising in the American consciousness. With the Korean War settled, and with the majority of the nations in the region now independent from the European powers, the idea that Americans needed to win over these newly emerging national populations was becoming increasingly prevalent. Yet the sense of 'sentimental crisis' about possibly losing Asia, depicted by James Michener in 1951, continued to haunt American encounters with the region. The Bandung conference in April 1955 had been followed by a year in which an alternative to both Communism and American-led Capitalism had been openly discussed in capitals across the region, including Bangkok. News of widespread hostility toward America, present even in an 'oasis' like Thailand, trickled back to American readers, and in turn fed anxiety about America's position in the world. Despite this, American literature continued to depict Thailand as a generally 'safe' location, and remained committed to the idea that the Thai people had, for the time being at least, very little interest in Communism. In turn, this added fuel to the idea that the country was an ideal location for American visitors to engage with a Southeast Asian public.

Figure 1.2 Jim Thompson (far right) at his house with friends
By permission of the James H.W. Thompson Foundation, Bangkok.

A theatre with two stages   45

In the same year, the publication of *The Ugly American* (1958) reinforced the point. The book, written by William Lederer and Eugene Burdick, depicted a fictional Southeast Asian country named Sarakhan, and re-told a number of failed American encounters with the population there.[85] Like Michener's *The Voice of Asia* (1951), the book contained a number of opinions supposed to be from 'local' perspectives that castigated Americans for failing to engage with the people of Asia. In particular, it ridiculed the diplomatic corps, and those elite American visitors who kept themselves isolated in gated buildings. Instead, the book sought to emphasise the value of moving out of one's comfort zone to engage directly with the local population. *The Ugly American* was a best seller, and would soon be made into a major movie to be filmed in Thailand and starring Marlon Brando. The success of the book also ran alongside, and no doubt influenced, a rise in American interest in travel to the region. In this climate, the completion of the Thompson house could not have happened at a better time. Keen to feel like they were moving beyond indulging simple desires, Jim Thompson's house provided an alternative space from which to experience the Cold War in Asia, a space that was emphasised as uniquely 'Thai', and that was nestled within a distinctly 'Thai' community. In the following years, Jim Thompson would become increasingly defined by the US media as one of the 'good' Americans of Asia.[86]

It is unsurprising, therefore, that those who wrote about Jim Thompson's house placed a great deal of emphasis upon the man himself and his interest in maintaining as much of the 'traditional' Thai design and atmosphere as possible. It also, however, presented that commitment to a Thai authenticity as a difficult task, which involved a retreat from the modern city in which he had lived for over a decade. As William Warren would later write, 'Thompson's nostalgia for the unprogressive Bangkok of the past' had been a decisive factor in his choice of a location that, while 'now squarely in the middle of a modern city', was suitable only because it 'still retained a flavour of its country past, the city noises muted by trees and the pace perceptibly slower'.[87] It is also significant that this retreat from the modern city was framed in terms of Jim Thompson's own character, as a rather peculiar individual when compared with other expatriate inhabitants. In an almost direct replication of what had become the standard narratives around his silk, the house was in turn cast as a service to a Thai cultural world that had lost its value to Thais themselves. As an article from *Life International* emphasised in 1960, Jim Thompson's skill with both his silk and his home was his skill in valuing material culture previously ignored by their Thai owners. The silk industry had been built up, 'despite the head shaking of Thais who argued that their boldly patterned silks were only for "peasants"'.[88] Now Thompson had decided 'to build himself an authentic Thai home' by blending together six old teakwood houses 'which had been torn down by their owners to make way for more modern, westernized houses'.[89]

Writing in *House Beautiful* magazine, William Warren was in the same year to reassert the point, describing Thompson as an American who stood out in

Figure 1.3 Jim Thompson (far left), on balcony with friends
By permission of the James H.W. Thompson Foundation, Bangkok.

Bangkok because, rather than replicating 'a miniature America in the foreign place', had instead become 'happily and overwhelmingly involved in the culture of the place'.[90] Quoting Jim Thompson on the reasons why he was so committed to the project, the article explained that he had 'got reckless' and 'decided to go all the way'. Moreover, like the *Life* article, Warren repeated the point that the Jim Thompson house was an oddity in a city where locals were aspiring to more modern, by which was meant 'Westernised', homes.

However, despite the claim that Jim Thompson was unique in rejecting a modern American-style home for something more traditional, he was in reality not the only American who followed such a narrative. Throughout the 1960s, the *Bangkok World*'s Sunday Magazine, an English-language publication owned by another fellow ex-OSS officer, Darrell Berrigan, featured a number of Americans who had done a similar thing.[91] While the scale of the Jim Thompson project was unprecedented, and stood out in the fact that it had been rebuilt from scratch, others had also become well known for their commitment to finding a residence within one of Bangkok's poorer communities. Keith Lorenz, for example, was introduced as an American businessman who had bought a place that overlooked a canal, allowing him an unrivalled mid-morning spot to sit and watch what was going on.[92]

Wally Besecker was another, whose quest to find 'a simple little wooden construction' had come from 'nostalgia for the simple country life', and had taken him to the 'jungle suburbs' of Thonburi.[93] Once there, he described how he had hungered for a spot from which to observe the daily life of the local Thai, and so had built himself a small structure at the back for that very purpose. In this respect, Jim Thompson was no different. For him, the veranda that he had built looking out upon the *klong* below was a central aspect. Talking in the *House Beautiful* article, Thompson described it as a 'theatre with two stages', a spot from which he was able to sit and watch the daily lives going on around him. 'They watch me and I watch them,' he explained. 'They probably think I'm a little crazy to prefer this to one of those new, Western-style houses, but they've been very hospitable.'[94]

What is clear, therefore, is that Jim Thompson's house was not exceptional. It was merely the pre-eminent example of such a home in the city, both because of what he had done, and because of his high-profile position in the American media. Indeed, the idea that the *klong*, or the 'floating market', offered an important site of encounter with Thailand during the Cold War had been widely emphasised and, as with the article that had appeared in *Vogue*, its portrayal as home to an 'original' and therefore authentic Thai community was often presumed. Earlier films such as *Oasis on a Troubled Continent* (1953) and *Walt Disney's Siam* (1954) had reinforced this idea, casting the *klongs* as the Thai alternative to an American supermarket.[95] In another US film, *Golden Temple Paradise* (1954), those Thai who lived, worked and played in the dirty water were explicitly described as happy despite being poor.[96] What the Jim Thompson veranda provided, therefore, was a 'real' glimpse of this world already depicted in the US media, a place to observe the spectacle of a poor yet abundant Thai society. Moreover, the reference to the modern city as a place that had to be left in order to witness the 'real' Thailand reinforced the notion that these 'unprogressive' areas of Bangkok were also home to the true social and economic life of the country. By continually berating urban Bangkok for its lack of interest in protecting and learning about this cultural life, the story of the Thompson house inferred that modernity, if left to Thais alone, might threaten this harmony.

Jim Thompson's house thus sat squarely at the centre of a narrative in which Thai traditions needed to be protected, despite the incorporation of Western lifestyle needs and economic systems; a story that resonated with the idea that a successful, and indeed authentic, Thai modernity could be achieved only under US guidance. The house's portrayal in the US media as a 'harmonised' environment echoed the projected hopes and dreams of New York consumers who, in the 1951 edition of *House & Garden*, had been encouraged to do the same thing in their own Manhattan homes.

Over the following decade, the Jim Thompson abode was to become an important destination for Americans visiting the capital, and as tourist numbers

48 A theatre with two stages

increased, Jim Thompson took the decision to open up the house for tours twice a week. Serving to further cement his role as a cultural icon to the American visitor, the tours were important signs of the extent to which the building became a site of cultural production, a place for people to consume the house and the Cold War narratives that it espoused. What the tours also did, however, was to identify the fact that with the rise of mass tourism, Bangkok was increasingly mimicking the social scene of New York in the way it reinforced social hierarchies. While the construction of difference between the world of the American and the Thai provided for a sense of united social identification among American visitors, there was nevertheless a clear distinction made between those who came purely to consume the site, and those for whom the house was really established to serve.

According to William Klausner, Jim Thompson's house was the 'centre of the social and cultural universe, at least among the expatriate and foreign visitors who came to Thailand', with Jim Thompson entertaining 'almost every day'.[97] But this access was restricted, with Klausner likening it to the exclusive environment of an eighteenth-century French salon; a place where notable elites could refine their tastes and gain knowledge of each other's personal work under the guidance of an interesting and considerate host. If anyone who came to Thailand, 'from prince to pauper, to movie star to academic', wanted to gain entrance, they would have to do it by means of a letter of introduction from somebody back at home. When they got there, they were guaranteed a memorable evening where anybody, including celebrities, major leaders of business and diplomats, might be found. From the lobby through to the veranda, the house was a creation designed specifically to serve an international guest list.

Anne Tofield, recalling her time spent at the house, remembered it as a place of beauty, but also as a truly exclusive location, an extension of the cultural and political world of New York and Washington. On one evening, for example, she recalled meeting Ted and Joan Kennedy, as well as US World Fair Commissioner to the Brussels World Fair, and Philip Morris representative Howard Cullman with his wife. In this exclusive environment, she remembered how the men sat together, busily discussing the politics of the Cold War in Asia while the women took in their surroundings. Joan Kennedy, she remembered, had described it as 'the most beautiful house in Thailand', and it was clearly a sentiment with which Anne agreed. In her description of her first visit to the house, she drew heavily on the theatre analogy to describe the experience, presenting the arrival, the lighting, the sound track and the script as if it was a choreographed event.

> Going to dinner at Jim's house was wonderful … that first night when we arrived in Bangkok … we got in the car, and drove up, and we went into the parking lot, and down the stairs came this terribly elegant man, always dressed in Thai silk, coming out of the foyer … and the lights were always slightly dim, always on the person getting out of the car, behind Jim, and he came forward, with that wonderful warm smile on his

face saying, 'how wonderful that you could come', as if *we* were doing *him* a great favour. And he led us through the marble hallway, and up the stairs, past all those wonderful old Thai prints ... and we got to the top, and walked out onto the terrace, and it was dark and it was lovely. And we sat for a few minutes in that drawing room, and then we went down for dinner, down the steps onto the terrace, which was on the *klong*. There were lights in the trees, the air was soft ... and we sat down at the table, and felt just this, glow. It was the magic kingdom ... and all through dinner we kept time with the click clack of the weavers across the *klong*, it was one of life's magic moments. And I've never forgotten it.[98]

In recognising the theatrical nature of the event, Anne Tofield's account is both revealing and illustrative. She describes her experience as one in which Jim Thompson was the star, lit from behind as if by a spotlight. Thai life, or more explicitly a Thai community engaged in productive labour well into the night, provided the ambience and was to act as the backdrop for the night's entertainment. In this sense, the memory of a night at Jim Thompson's house reaffirmed the fact that Thompson was the central narrative, the man who brought all the strands together. By describing her entrance into this 'magic kingdom', what she unwittingly referenced was the idea that the economic and political relationship Jim Thompson had crafted with his Thai workers was a positive 'harmonised' engagement. The theatrical elements had transformed this relationship into a pleasant background noise that added to the overall production. While tourists might, the following day, have tried to imagine what that wonderland of a night at Jim Thompson's might be like, and while they might have very well understood the narrative, they were nevertheless only con-suming a potential entrance into that elite world. By restricting access, Jim Thompson's house was thus to become a perpetual opening night which, like a Broadway show, acted as a tightly controlled site of social negotiation in which elite ownership of the cultural and ideological Cold War was maintained.

In this sense, the analogy of the theatre referred to more than the spectacle to which it gave precedence. Rather, it referred to the fact that the house *was* a theatre, both in the way it reproduced American narratives about Thailand as a cultural location, and in the way it reinforced the social relations of Broadway. Like productions such as *The King and I*, this site of cultural explanation was focused on maintaining the prescribed relationship between the ruling class and those Americans who would later seek association with that world through their consumption choices, in this case achieved through purchasing silk or visiting his house as a tourist. Whether Jim Thompson could ever be considered a member of this elite community himself is debateable. What is clear, however, is that during the 1950s and early 1960s, he made himself highly relevant to US high society. By drawing from his experience of New York before the war, and his background as a member of the 'professional managerial' class, he owned the social tools needed to become a principal producer of Cold War culture and ideology. By reflecting strongly the prerogatives of magazines

50 *A theatre with two stages*

such as *Life* and *Vogue*, Jim Thompson committed himself to reproducing the narratives to which wealthy Americans were deeply committed. He did this by projecting himself as a benevolent lord, ruler over a small feudal kingdom at the back of his house, over which he held sway due to his kindly nature and his love for the Thai, but most importantly, because of his understanding of what constituted international commodity.

Notes

1 Interview with William Warren, Bangkok, 3 November 2006 (The Jim Thompson Oral History Project), available for viewing from the Jim Thompson Foundation Library, Bangkok.
2 This chain of events is as retold by William Warren, although there are others who question even this most basic recounting of what happened. See William Warren, *Jim Thompson: The Unsolved Mystery*, Singapore: Archipelago Press, 1998, pp. 8–10, 132–134. For more recent and well researched biography of Jim Thompson, see Joshua Kurlantzick, *The Ideal Man, The Tragedy of Jim Thompson and the American Way of War*, Hoboken, NJ: Wiley, 2011.
3 Max Elbaum, *Revolution in the Air: Sixties Radicals Turn to Lenin, Mao and Che*, New York: Verso, 2002, pp. 1–58.
4 Henry Kissinger, *Ending the Vietnam War: A History of America's Involvement in and Extrication from the Vietnam War*, New York: Simon & Schuster, 2003 pp. 7–12. Kissinger's own admission was that the war ended the unity felt by American society with regard to the country's foreign policy. At a conference held at the State Department in September 2010, Kissinger put it like this: 'To me, the tragedy of the Vietnam War was not that there were disagreements. That was inevitable given the complexity of the subject. But that the faith of Americans in each other became destroyed in the process. It was America's first experience with limits in foreign policy, and it was something painful to accept.' 'The American experience in Southeast Asia, 1946–1975', Address by Dr Henry Kissinger, 29 September 2010, http://history.state.gov/conferences/2010-southeast-asia/secretary-kissinger.
5 There is wealth of literature on post-war America and the powerful impact of the Second World War and its aftermath on American society. One account is Randall Bennett Woods, *The Quest for Identity, America since 1945*, Cambridge: Cambridge University Press, 2005.
6 The term 'climate of victory' is borrowed from US government documents that dealt specifically with Southeast Asia during the early Cold War. However, I also understand the term as related directly to the American sense of expectation that dominated US culture in the post-war era and that haunted American society throughout the Cold War.
7 The area is known as Bang Krua in downtown Bangkok, and the community who live there are generally Mon and Muslim.
8 Fellow OSS officer and founding editor of the *Bangkok Post*, Alexander MacDonald in 1948 explained the problems Thailand faced in producing the silk for Americans. He noted how 'very little of the silk weaving is of Siamese origin, although it has long provided the courts of the Kingdom with the beautiful costumes worn in other days'. He also explained how local weavers 'get bored after weaving enough silk on long length and want to change the colour and pattern', but that 'Jim's prospective buyers on the other hand want the silk on long lengths so it can be marketed'. Alexander MacDonald, 'The Postman Says', *Bangkok Post*, 13 January 1948, p. 1.
9 Interview with William Klausner, Bangkok, 6 November 2006 (The Jim Thompson Oral History Project, 2006). In the interview he described Jim Thompson's house as 'the centre of the social and cultural universe' in Bangkok.

A theatre with two stages 51

10 For details of Jim Thompson's connections to the intelligence community, and in particular his role as the local contact for the World Commerce Corporation (WCC), see Anthony Cave Brown, *The Last Hero, Wild Bill Donovan, Founder of the OSS and 'Father' of the CIA, from Personal and Secret Papers and the Diaries of Ruth Donovan*, New York: Times Books, 1982, p. 797. Also see Peter Dale Scott, 'Operation Paper, the United States and drugs in Thailand and Burma', *Asia Pacific Journal* (Online, November 2010), www.japanfocus.org/-Peter_Dale-Scott/3436.

11 Interview with Ann Donaldson, New York, 26 October 2006 (The Jim Thompson Oral History Project, 2006). According to her, Jim Thompson was already a millionaire due to an inheritance from an elderly friend earlier in his life.

12 Martin Shefter (ed.), *Capital of the American Century: The National and International Influence of New York City*, New York: Russell Sage Foundation, 1993. In particular see Chapters 5 and 6.

13 John Mollenkopf (ed.), *Power, Culture, and Place: Essays on New York City*, New York: Russell Sage Foundation, 1988. In particular see William R. Taylor, 'The launching of a commercial culture, New York City, 1860–1930'.

14 Ibid., p. 107.

15 Ibid.

16 Ibid., p. 129.

17 Barbara and John Ehrenreich, 'The professional–managerial class', in Pat Walker (ed.) *Between Labor and Capital*, Political Controversies Vol. 1, Boston, MA: South End Press, 1979, pp. 5–24. This category has been contested, but nevertheless seems to hold clear value in exploring Jim Thompson's relationship to New York society. He cannot be said to be a member of the New York elite, or at least not until the 1950s. Yet throughout the 1930s he was able to mix in elite circles through his role as an architect. In the aforementioned essay, it was people like Thompson who from the turn of the century became principal actors in society, not because they owned the means of production, but because they carved out a role for themselves through the reproduction of capitalist ideology and culture. Reference to this group is made in a number of works on the cultural world of the Great Depression. One of the most useful is Jeff Alfred, *American Modernism and Depression Documentary*, Oxford: Oxford University Press, 2010, pp. 1–27.

18 Roland Marchand, *Advertising the American Dream: Making Way for Modernity, 1920–1940*, Berkeley, CA: University of California Press, 1986.

19 Arthur G. Neal, *National Trauma and Collective Memory: Major Events in the American Century*, New York: M.E. Sharpe, 1998, pp. 41–59.

20 Jeff Manza, 'Political sociological models of the U.S. New Deal', *Annual Review of Sociology* 26(2000): 297–322. Also see Edwin Amenta, *Bold Relief: Institutional Politics and the Origins of Modern American Social Policy*, Princeton, NJ: Princeton University Press, 1998.

21 Lizabeth Cohen, *A Consumers' Republic: The Politics of Mass Consumption in Postwar America*, New York: First Vintage Books, 2004, p. 19.

22 Ibid.

23 Ibid., p. 60.

24 William J. Buxton, 'From the Rockefeller Center to the Lincoln Center: musings on the "Rockefeller half Century"', in William J. Buxton, *Patronizing the Public: American Philanthropy's Transformation of Culture, Communication and the Humanities*, Lanham, MD: Lexington Books, 2009, p. 25.

25 Lizabeth Cohen, *A Consumers' Republic*, p. 61.

26 Henry Luce, 'The American Century', *Life*, 17 February 1941, p. 62.

27 Robert E. Herzstein, *Henry R Luce: A Political Portrait of the Man who Created the American Century*, New York: Charles Scribner's Sons, 1994, pp. 181–183.

28 'Vogue's eye view of the 10th Americana Issue', *Vogue*, Americana Edition, 1 February 1947, p. 65.

52 *A theatre with two stages*

29 Margaret Mead, 'What makes Americans tick', *Vogue*, Americana edition, 1 February 1943.
30 Ibid., p. 67.
31 Margaret and Kenneth P. Landon Papers, 1824–2000; 1/6 38/10, Kenneth Landon's Diary, 27 October 1945–26 February 1946, Wheaton College Archives, Illinois, p. 28.
32 Howard Zinn, *Postwar America, 1945–1971*, Cambridge, MA: South End Press, 2002, p. 6.
33 Randall Bennett Woods, *The Quest for Identity*, p. 121.
34 Ibid.
35 Eric Sevareid, 'We are responsible to the World', *Vogue*, Americana edition, 1 February 1947, p. 180.
36 Ibid.
37 Ibid.
38 Ibid., p. 226.
39 Henry Steele Commanger, 'The permanent and the transient in the American character', *Vogue*, Americana Edition, 1 February 1943, p. 174.
40 Ibid., p. 226.
41 *Glamour*, Young American Edition, July 1947, p. 21.
42 Vera Micheles Dean, 'Wise American leadership is the hope of the world', *Glamour*, Young American Edition, July 1947, p. 21.
43 Ibid.
44 Editorial, *Vogue*, Americana Edition, 1 February 1948.
45 Margaret Mead, 'Reality and the American dream', *Vogue*, Americana Edition, 1 February 1949, p. 87.
46 Walt W. Rostow, *The Process of Economic Growth*, New York: WW Norton, 1952. See chapter 3 for further discussion on this point.
47 David Noble in his analysis of American notions of cultural exceptionalism is enlightening on this matter, see David W. Noble, *Death of a Nation: American Culture and the End of Exceptionalism*, Minneapolis, MN: University of Minnesota Press, 2002, pp. 250–286.
48 Stephen J. Whitfield, *The Culture of the Cold War*, p. 5.
49 Immanuel Wallenstein, in setting out the specific conditions that shaped the Cold War in Asia, has noted how while Europe was essentially distributed between two powers before the end of the Second World War, the situation in Asia was always less clear, making it a natural centre for tensions to spill over into proxy wars and contestations. Hong Liu and Michael Szonyi (eds), *The Cold War in Asia*, p. 15.
50 Robert Herzstein, *Henry R. Luce*, p. 2.
51 Cristina Klein, *Cold War Orientalism*, p. 127.
52 Economic Considerations, 1949 draft, 18–19, NCS 48 File, 7 October. As quoted in Jim Glassman, *Thailand at the Margins*, p. 43.
53 Gary Donaldson, *Abundance and Anxiety, America 1945–1960*, Westport, CT: Greenwood Publishing Group, 1997, p. 58.
54 James A. Michener, 'Blunt truths about Asia', *Life*, 4 June 1951, p. 96.
55 Ibid., p. 96.
56 Ibid., p. 110.
57 James A. Michener, *The Voice of Asia*, New York: Random House, 1951, p. 242.
58 Ibid.
59 *Life*, 4 June 1951, p. 115.
60 Ibid., p. 110.
61 Ibid., p. 121.
62 David D. Duncan, 'Decline of the Westerner', *Life*, 31 December 1951, p. 15.
63 Ibid., p. 13.
64 Christina Klein, *Cold War Orientalism*, p. 132.
65 'For Westerners the good life', *Life*, 31 December 1951, p. 37.

A theatre with two stages 53

66 James A. Michener, *The Voice of Asia*, p. 138.
67 *March of Time: Oasis on a Troubled Continent* (1953).
68 Ibid.
69 Ibid.
70 'Decorative silks from Siam shown', *The New York Times*, 4 November 1948.
71 Bruce A. McConachie, *American Theatre in the Culture of the Cold War: Producing and Contesting Containment 1947–1962*, Iowa City, IA: University of Iowa Press, 2003, p. 4.
72 James J. Poling, 'Gertie and the King and I', *Collier's*, 7 April 1951, p. 25.
73 'Seeing things', *Saturday Review*, 17 April 1951, p. 44.
74 Christina Klein, *Cold War Orientalism*, p. 222.
75 Marlis Schweitzer, *When Broadway was the Runway: Theatre, Fashion, and American Culture*, Philadelphia, PA: University of Pennsylvania Press, 2009, p. 4.
76 *The New York Times*, 16 September 1951, p. 101.
77 'Siam', *House & Garden*, October 1951, p. 160.
78 Ibid.
79 Lizabeth Cohen, *A Consumers' Republic*, p. 127.
80 *House & Garden*, October 1951, p. 189.
81 'Mrs Roosevelt', Eleanor Roosevelt, *The Washington Daily News*, 26 Monday 1952, p. 30.
82 'Five yards of Thai silk', *Vogue*, 15 September 1957, p. 124.
83 Ibid.
84 I am quoting directly from William Warren who, like other writers of the time, repeatedly emphasised this fact. William Warren, *Jim Thompson*, p. 105.
85 William J. Lederer and Eugene Burdick, *The Ugly American*, New York: Fawcet, 1958.
86 For an example: Keyes Beech, 'Good American gets Ugly Deal in Thailand', *Chicago Daily News*, Chicago, IL: 13 November 1962, p. 16.
87 William Warren, *Jim Thompson: The Unsolved Mystery,* Singapore: Archipelago Press, 1998, p. 103.
88 'House too lovely to be a home', *Life International*, April 11, 1960, p. 90.
89 Ibid.
90 William Warren, 'In fabled Siam, a truly fabulous house', *House Beautiful*, April 1960, p. 212.
91 For information on Derrell Berrigan, see Peter Jackson, 'An American death in Bangkok, the murder of Darrell Berrigan and the hybrid of origins of gay identity in 1960s Thailand', *Journal of Lesbian and Gay Studies*, 5(3) (1999): 361–411.
92 Keith Lorenz, 'The view from a klongside hammock, musings by a klong Bangkunthian chronicler', *Bangkok World*, Sunday Magazine, 9 September 1961, p. 2.
93 'The jungle suburbs, a Bangkokonian's retreat in the orchards of Bangkok Noi', *Bangkok World*, September 1962, p. 2.
94 *House Beautiful*, April 1960, p. 212.
95 *Walt Disney's Siam*, Walt Disney Production, Buena Vista Distributing Corp, 1954.
96 *Golden Temple Paradise*, Circle Film Enterprises, 1953.
97 Interview with William Klausner, Bangkok, 6 November 2005 (The Jim Thompson Oral History Project).
98 Interview with Anne Tofield, Tallahassee, 28 October 2006 (The Jim Thompson Oral History Project).

2   In and out of *Vogue*

Dressing for progress before and after 1945

> Of all the different kinds of white people (*farang*) who come to Thailand, they recognize that of the women in the East there isn't another nation whose women have the kind of skin, aura, or dress sense as this one.[1]
>
> Mom Kopkaeo, President of the Thai Women's Association, Bangkok, 1947

Speaking in 1947 to the Thai photo magazine *Phap Khao Sayam Nikon*, the statement by Mom Kopkaeo that Thai women were uniquely well dressed in Asia demonstrated an air of confidence and self-assurance about how Thais were viewed by foreigners from the West. The interview, published in the regular section entitled *Phuying*, or 'Women', told of a recent visit that the President of the Thai Women's Association had received from *Vogue* magazine in New York. In it, she revealed the importance of dress as a means for Thai people to present themselves to the world. In doing so, she evoked a long and complex past, during which time dress had been promoted as a key marker of relevance to, and participation with, the international community. Specifically, she sought to reassure readers that they could feel secure that Thai society continued to maintain high standards in dress, and as a result that they remained relevant to foreigners. As she went on to explain, the visitors from New York came 'to look at all the different kinds of Thai fabric we have; they took many, many photos and they admired the fact that Thai women dress beautifully'.[2]

However, the article also came with a caveat, for as Mom Kopkaeo concluded, while Thais might be uniquely able to dress well, this was an art that continued to need a level of individual self-awareness. As she explained, Thai women needed to think carefully about adapting their wardrobe, mastering the art of keeping with the fashions of the moment, while at the same time acknowledging their local environment, the climate in which they lived, and the colour of their skin. It was an admission that, speaking directly to the sensibilities of her audience, located the issue of dress within a set of underlying anxieties that dominated Thai society during the post-war period. After more than a generation for whom dress had become deeply attached to the projection of Thailand as a progressive nation of the world. Now, however, poor economic conditions inside the country combined with a changing international situation to raise serious questions about the ability of Thailand to maintain its status as an important nation to the outside world. With ways of dress intimately connected to ideas of progress, the article therefore revealed not only the interest of Thais in maintaining a modern look; it also identified how maintaining that look required an ongoing commitment to self-improvement. Perhaps most revealing, however, was that the article fundamentally misunderstood the purpose of the *Vogue* visit, missing the fact that of all the photos taken of Thai women, none would appear in the American magazine back at home.

Planning for the *Vogue* trip had begun earlier in the year, in June 1947, when the Thai government in Bangkok received a letter from the Office of the Commercial Attaché at the Royal Siamese Legation in Washington, DC. The Embassy wished to inform Bangkok that it had received a visit from two individuals: one representing the office of International Information and Cultural Affairs at the Department of State, New York; the other, Condé Nast Publications Incorporated.[3] The reason for the visit, the attaché explained, had been to inform him of a tour around Asia which the publication house intended to make the coming fall. Describing it as an 'editorial mission', the trip was outlined as an opportunity to gather material, including photographs and motion pictures, that could be used across the company's magazines, *Vogue, House & Garden* and *Glamour*, reaching a potential readership of 1,250,000 Americans.[4] Furthermore, the material would also be displayed in exhibitions at New York's Museum of Modern Art and used in the films of Paramount Pictures.[5] In the attached letter from the President of Condé Nast Publications, it was explained that the magazine had 'felt for some time that the readers of our magazine would be interested, and should be more informed about the cultural life in the countries which, on the whole, we have so far had very little contact, such as Siam, India and the Dutch East Indies'.[6] Crucially, he went on to explain, the point of the mission was not a concern with politics but rather with the 'cultural life' of the nation; 'the subjects to be covered will be in the realm of educational, arts and crafts, architecture, gardens, personalities etc'.[7]

Yet, while the trip clearly went ahead, the readers of all Condé Nast publications would, for the time being at least, remain ignorant of the stylish women of a civilised Siam, renamed Thailand for a second time in 1947.[8] Instead, the journey through Asia would be explored in a 10-page special of photographs entitled the 'Colour of India'. There, readers were introduced to a six-month trip made by two *Vogue* correspondents who witnessed 'village life and the richness of the princely states'.[9] India, they claimed, was a place where a 'knowledge and feeling for colour are born in the princes of India' and 'in the peasants who intuitively understand how to use colour without having to learn it'.[10] What followed was a journey across the Indian subcontinent. Colour photographs, reserved for those features that warranted it, lavishly took up whole pages and placed India into the definitive context, through their captions, of a vibrant and stable social harmony built upon an attachment to the Indian past. Film actresses and Maharajas were placed next to untouchables and even the dead, in a parade of golds and silvers, reds and blues, greens and almost

56   *In and out of Vogue*

fluorescent pinks. Keeping to its word, as expressed in the letter to the Siamese Embassy, the magazine avoided politics. Not only did it omit the fact that the country had only just become independent from British rule, it went further, juxtaposing in the text the instability of that new political world with the *actual* cultural life of its citizens; the correspondents, it was said, looked not only at the people, but also at 'the conflict when tradition was confronted with modern politics'. The latter was not depicted in the photos.[11]

We can only hypothesise as to why India was privileged over Thailand. Yet what can be noted is that, if the *Vogue* journalists who had travelled from New York were looking for images of women dressed in vibrant and colourful fabrics to splash on their centre pages, post-war Bangkok was not the place to go. The city was struggling to recover from the war, and the people of Bangkok had little money to spend on lavish wardrobes. At the same time, ideas about how to dress in the country were highly prescribed, and only if they had chosen to go to one of the many fancy dress parties that littered the Bangkok social calendar might they have found a wealthy group of socialites dressed up in the unusual costumes that would fit their editorial agenda.[12] Outside the walls of such garden parties, the *Vogue* journalists would have found a city where the dress code was set within very narrow parameters. For women, a blouse and skirt, and for men, a shirt and trousers were the essential clothes to wear for anyone who sought participation in public life.[13] Post-war Bangkok, now adorned with a new modernist architecture, was also populated with a conservative urban class who held very particular notions of what it meant to be Thai, and of how a Thai should dress.

That is not to say that the population of post-war Bangkok was particularly confident about what they should be wearing, especially in front of foreign visitors from the publishing houses of New York. What it does identify, however, is the extent to which Thai society had become conscious during the years preceding the Second World War about dress as a key marker of what it meant to be Thai. While this chapter focuses largely on the years before 1945, it does so to illustrate how issues concerning dress were, in the aftermath of the war, intimately connected to ideas about Thailand's status within the international community, and driven largely by the desire to be seen as modern and relevant to foreign centres of power. As Maurizio Peleggi has argued, since the late-nineteenth century Siam's rulers had seen dress as an important way to present themselves as civilised to the colonial powers. Then, in the early decades of the twentieth century, dress had become a powerful identifier of an emergent Thai middle class claiming to be part of a community who were 'up to date' or 'with the times'; the harbingers of a modernity viewed as emanating principally from the West.[14]

Importantly, however, throughout the 1930s, and then during the Second World War, state propaganda had sought to connect the issue of dress with more complex matters concerning the country's political and economic condition. To be sure, the state continued to assert the idea that the way Thai people dressed had a direct impact on the country's international standing.

In and out of Vogue 57

Yet by connecting the issue of dress with the need to build a new society and develop a functioning and independent internal economy, state propaganda had made the issue of dress significantly more complicated for urban consumers. In the post-war environment, magazines that sought to report on Bangkok's cultural re-engagement with the world often replicated the long-term emphasis on dress as an important marker of the country's international standing. Now, however, they did so in an era of unprecedented anxiety about what that standing actually was. While, by the start of the 1950s, dress remained a central talking point, such conversations would often reveal as much uncertainty about how to measure progress as any long-standing confidence that Thais could achieve the kind of civilised status they sought.

Consumed by progress: nation building following the 1932 revolution

On 24 June 1932, a small group of bureaucrats and military officers, members of a political group named the People's Party, staged a revolution that ended absolute monarchy in Siam. It was widely anticipated, coming after a decade in which the reputation of the ruling elite had been emphatically undermined. Emphasising their role as nationalists who sought economic development for the whole of Thai society, and who believed in the near sacred importance of a constitution, it was also well received. In the days that followed the coup, informed people across the country confirmed their support, and in Bangkok, business leaders, labour groups and members of the general public flocked to join the party. While still only a fraction of the country's total population, the support was nevertheless enough to buoy the new government. Over the next decade, those in control of the Thai state would seek to change the political, economic and cultural landscape of the country.[15]

For the next three years, the monarch and his supporters tried to maintain a role for themselves, both politically and financially, within the new state. Yet they were ultimately to find it impossible to reconcile their demands with enthusiasm for the new government. After a number of failed attempts to regain control for the royalists, King Rama VII travelled to Europe. While there, following a disagreement over government legislation, and with clear fears for his personal safety, he abdicated on 2 March 1935. Few mourned the loss, symptomatic of a society that hungered for change and that had grown tired of any romanticised conservatism. In this new era, the past was something to be memorialised and historicised, and that included the achievements of the Chakri monarchs.[16]

For decades, open debate about the country's future, and criticism of the absolute monarchy, had been widespread among what Scott Barme has described as an 'emergent middle stratum'.[17] Made up of networks and alliances of people with connections to the government bureaucracy, but from a commoner background, this group also included entrepreneurs who had developed a private publishing industry that became highly skilled at 'fusing both imported and local elements to create a new hybrid form of mass culture'.[18] In an

58 *In and out of Vogue*

international climate where the world's last absolute monarchies were all but dismantled, this group increasingly sought to identify itself as opposed to 'the social order fostered by absolutism' that it saw as 'moribund and profoundly corrupt'.[19] Convinced that Thailand had important ground to make up if it was to compete on the international stage, this group routinely promoted the idea that they were the 'bearers of modernity', involved in a struggle for 'human equality, individual freedom, and female emancipation'.[20]

As a result, when the new government came into power, it drew much of its support from those who were already engaged in the workings of the state and the associated economy. This in effect linked the revolution's success to legitimacy gained from Thai communities who resided in urban centres, in particular in Bangkok and the surrounding area. It also tied the revolution ideologically to the fulfilment of moral, political and economic progress, that would be traceable through the expansion of the state and its resources to ensure wider participation for this class of middle-stratum commoner Thais. By opening up new government departments, expanding professions such as teaching and nursing, and widening access to professional education, including the founding of Thammasat University, the bureaucratic state presented itself as a central guarantor to social advancement.[21]

Building its legitimacy upon advancing the interests of the nation, the new government also sought to promote the state as central to the country's improved economic conditions. One of the principal factors in securing support for the 1932 revolution was the economic calamity that followed the onset of the Great Depression. Between 1930 and 1932, the price of Thailand's main export, rice, collapsed by nearly two-thirds, leading to an equally catastrophic drop in land prices. Faced with having to implement cuts to spending, the government continued to take the advice of a British financial advisor who successfully convinced Thai leaders to stay on the gold standard. This left Siamese rice priced much higher than that of countries that had abandoned the standard. Falling living standards combined with shock at the apparent vulnerability of the Thai economy to the international economy. In the decade following 1932, the new government was thus able to build legitimacy upon taking credit for improving economic conditions.[22]

As a result, the 'victory' of the revolution was framed largely in terms specific to the urban hunger for a modern lifestyle, meaning improved access to consumer goods and increased protection from external economic forces. State ideology often merged with the messages of private advertisers, who themselves employed the new terminologies of statecraft in selling their products: those such as Asahi beer, which was promoted as a product loved by 'the majority of the masses',[23] or Cock Brand Worcestershire sauce, which could now be enjoyed by a 'commoner or a King'.[24] At the same time, state-sanctioned media would seek to harness urban aspirations by asserting the idea that modernity was a global process of change, and that the government was working hard to improve the conditions of the people by increasing access to a society governed by consumption.

State media also focused on projecting a message that sought to promote the widening of access to consumerism as a major task of the government. Magazines and newspapers under the People's Party were tightly controlled, and would therefore adhere strictly to the ideological premise of the revolutionary government. Moreover, government departments themselves became cultural producers, creating titles that served their policy agendas but that would also appeal to urban consumers. The Department of Commerce, for example, produced a magazine that promoted internal tourism, once an elite activity, but now available to a wider catchment of citizens. Entitled *Thongthiao Sapda* [*Tourist Weekly*], this magazine made the claim that by following the work of the bureaucracy, and by earning an income within the expanding wage economy, the individual could fulfil the necessary desires that came with modern life. It also suggested that the government would support this entry into modern notions of personhood. As the magazine explained in 1939, 'making a trip, changing one's location, taking oneself out of one's routine environment, is something which lifts our spirits and cheers a human soul'. For a working person, it explained, going for a trip was an activity 'that is very important' for human life in the new world today'.[25]

Another obvious example of how the new government promoted itself through a narrative about private consumption habits was evident in state-sponsored spectacle, in particular the annual Constitution Day Fair. Attracting large crowds, this event soon emerged as an important arena for the marriage of government ideology with an urban lifestyle characterised by consumption. During the fair, an event that lasted about 10 days during the first two weeks of December, Bangkok was transformed into a vast network of high streets.[26] All the major agencies of the new government had stalls where they promoted their activities. Yet there were also stalls run by private companies where importers of the latest consumer goods could display their most recent collections. These stalls were able to provide the thousands of visitors with access to large quantities of products at reduced prices, in turn confirming the individual's personal sense of belonging to the event, as well as to the new society more generally. As an advert for one such stall explained in 1934, 'if you're going to visit the Constitution Fair then you need to buy some clothes or other consumables that will improve the way you look'.[27] Bicycles, which were vital for getting around the fair, were available, and in large writing in the middle of the advert, visitors were reminded to buy their coats at 'knock down prices'. Another private advertisement published during the 1938 Constitution Day festivities said that 'if you see somebody wearing something you like, you can come to us and we can find it for you'.[28]

Casting the whole event as a stage upon which urban Thais might parade the latest fashions, government-sponsored events such as the Miss Thailand contest, and dress competitions that judged the best day wear, evening wear or holiday wear reinforced the central role of consumption and social advancement at the fair. Facilitated by the state, such competitions supported individual efforts to gain an understanding of what was in fashion, and how

60   In and out of Vogue

hard-earned wages should be spent to maintain personal civility. It was also an event that required participation, not only for those seeking to enter one of the competitions, but for all who attended. In the weeks leading up to the celebrations, special services were offered that sought to both stimulate and capitalise upon conversations happening across the city. Adverts would promise customers exclusive access to the most recent styles so that they might look and feel their best at the fair. As an advert published in December 1938 stated, 'for those who are making their new dress, or have nearly finished it, there are two places you now need to visit'.[29] *Sairung*, it explained, had a vast range of accessories including handbags and hairpieces, while *Sumali* would take care of your hair. For those who wanted to create their own garments, another offered women a short and easy course by an expert in 'skirts and shirts'.[30]

However, the revolution's strong connection with consumer-driven views of progress also presented a number of significant challenges and problems that were increasingly introduced to Bangkok's urban consumers as stumbling blocks to development. On one hand, harnessing individual aspirations toward a modern lifestyle suited state assertions that it was overseeing the birth of a 'new' Siam. On the other, the model for development that followed 1932 had imposed certain limitations. While vital in securing the regime's legitimacy, this 'middle stratum' remained a tiny minority of the overall population of the country, and it was soon understood that activities focused on nation building needed to embrace a much wider constituency. By focusing on the bureaucracy as the principal body for the expansion of opportunity and the wage economy, the new government had placed a practical limit upon the extent and speed with which it could change the country's situation.

In particular, new educational opportunities were focused largely upon supporting entry into the government bureaucracy, and did not cater the vast majority of Thais. This, it was felt, was creating a limit upon the state in spreading notions of citizenship. In December 1937, a newly elected MP from the province of Chachoengsao explained that the education system must seek to foster a greater sense of everyday attachment with the state, something that could be achieved only through the expansion of state-sponsored employment opportunities:

> Siam needs more citizens, but the problem in increasing citizenship is that citizens need employment, they are not just people. To put it simply, it is not about quantity [of citizens], it is also quality. Education is at the heart of what it means to be a citizen.[31]

The timing of the MP's comment was apt. Since the revolution, economic policy, which ultimately sought to improve the status of the local Thai population, had focused primarily on dismantling the economy dominated both by the royalists and the Western powers, and in particular on ending the still unequal treaties that restricted the country's autonomy in economic matters. Between 1935 and 1938, Pridi Banomyong put considerable effort into renegotiating

In and out of Vogue 61

Siam's status in the international system in order to secure fiscal autonomy and end the extraterritorial rights offered to the Western powers since the middle of the nineteenth century.[32] By the end of 1937, with the renegotiation of such treaties well under way, the country's leaders began to focus more urgently upon what could be achieved internally.

Over the following year, policies such as increased tariffs on imported goods were implemented to improve the conditions of local industry. Now, however, with focus on the international system lessening, internal reasons for the country's fundamental economic weaknesses dominated. As a result, the latter half of the decade saw attention more firmly focused on ending what were perceived to be 'Thai' weaknesses, combined with reducing the control of ethnic Chinese communities over the internal economy. In particular, it was seen as vital that local Thai populations reduced their dependence on cheap foreign imports, bought through the export of locally grown rice. For the aforementioned MP, the need was for schemes that diversified the economy in these areas away from rice production by linking the expansion of urban consumption with the local production of high quality and affordable products. Just as had already happened in his own province since 1935, co-operatives set up to stimulate local industries such as textiles should now be established across the country. With the support of the central state, such projects, it was suggested, would provide a practical way of bettering the lives of all Thai people and would also improve the status of the nation internationally.[33]

Over the following year, as tension in Europe rose, the Bangkok press became increasingly fixated upon such ideas, promoting the implementation of a rapid national progress based on encouraging rural communities to take on new economic identities and embrace their status as citizens of the Thai nation. As an editorial in *Prachamitra Daily News* from April 1939 demonstrated, this need became attached to the urgent desire to re-craft Thai character to suit the needs of the present moment.[34] In the past, the writer explained, the Thai had tended toward the maintenance of an internal self-satisfaction and general stagnation. This, in turn, had encouraged an acceptance of, and reliance upon, dominant market systems over which they had little control. In the case of cloth, for example, 'we hardly feel the need to weave cloth to wear ourselves when we can buy cheap cloth for a few satangs in the market'. Yet in the context of the 'new era', these old ways were no longer acceptable. The reason was that 'the world is striving ahead and we feel we need to keep up with the outer world'. If the country was not to progress, the article explained, 'we will wake up one day to discover that the world has passed us by. We have now come to the time when we must stir ourselves and revise our situation to suit that of the rest of the world'.

> When we look around us we find that international politics are not carried out in an honest and happy fashion. We see governments which are not Just; we see minorities oppressed; we see unannounced wars carried out with great loss of life; we see such an organisation as the League of Nations become of no effect; we see nations arming themselves more

62   *In and out of Vogue*

than ever before; we see solemn treaties treated as mere scraps of paper; we see the white and yellow races creating and encouraging hatred of one another.[35]

As a solution to the problem, the article concluded, the Thai needed to adapt their behaviour and work together, so that the nation might progress with speed. 'Always on time, always speaking the truth, always hustling', Thais must realise 'the truth of the saying that we are invaded by aliens commercially, educationally, and politically'.[36]

These assertions, made in the context of a rapidly worsening international situation, were also in line with state thinking, which had become increasingly clear under the country's new Prime Minister, Phibun Songkhram. Yet it was only on Nation Day, on 24 June 1939, that such ideas were formalised through state policy, when Phibun announced that the government would now actively seek to re-mould the character and behaviour of the Thai people so that they could better serve the needs of the developing state. These 'cultural edicts', to be disseminated through bureaucratic channels, were intended to act as a direct appeal to the national population, encouraging them to consider themselves part of the 'new' era. Labelled *ratthaniyom*, the literal translation of which would be 'stateism', these declarations were first introduced to the country via a radio speech in which it was explained that the government established in 1932 was entirely different from what had gone before, and that the change required the direct involvement of the Thai state in the day-to-day lives of the population. 'Thai people', Phibun explained, 'must grow in order to develop the personal characteristics that can work within the new system of government.'[37]

On the day before Phibun's speech, the name of the country had been changed from Siam to Thailand, representing the intention of the government to seek a wider participation, reaching beyond the borders of the current territory through a radical claim to represent all peoples of 'Tai' ethnicity. It was also intended to re-align the country internationally. Siam, the nationalist rhetoric went, had been a name imposed by foreigners, and in its maturation as a nation of the world, the country must now be recognised as home to a society free from that influence. When the *ratthaniyom* were introduced a day later, they were thus promoted as the formal awakening of the Thai people as citizens of both a nation and the world. Luang Wichitwathakan, in his treatise on the *ratthaniyom* that was also broadcast to the nation, explained how the population needed to realise their status as 'real' Thais, meaning first they had to be self-reliant, and second that Thai culture needed to be appreciated fully by the international community.[38]

There is no doubt that the *ratthaniyom* represented a powerful and in many ways extraordinary intervention into everyday Thai life. Particularly in relation to dress, the edict that all Thais must observe appropriate standards was highly prescriptive, and demanded public awareness of the state and its ideology. Promulgated on 15 January 1941, 'Thais', the edict explained, 'should not appear in public, populous places, or in municipal areas without proper clothing, for instance wearing only underwear (drawers), no shirt or with loose shirt-tails.' As Maurizio Peleggi has explained, these prescriptions were illustrative of a political system that was both authoritarian and increasingly militaristic. They were also illustrative of a state that sought to 'standardize bodily practice' in order to create a disciplined citizenry, and in many ways 'followed in spirit and content the attempts by the fascist regimes of Italy and Germany, for whose dictators Phibun expressed open admiration, to mould the body politic through mass regimentation and propaganda'.[39] As Thamsook Numnonda, has also explained, the *ratthaniyom* were, 'aimed at arousing and mobilizing the consciousness of the whole nation' with the specific intention of creating a 'psychological feeling among Thais that their country had entered a new era'.[40]

Yet it is also important to recognise that the *ratthaniyom* were not disseminated to Thai communities without a clear assertion of the state's rationale, and that a primary element of this was the context of an international system that was rapidly breaking down. The hope that had been placed in the League of Nations, and in Siam's membership of it, was no longer a realistic avenue for asserting the place of the Thai nation as equal to the 'great' nations of the world.[41] In June 1939, war in Europe seemed increasingly inevitable, and it was widely acknowledged that the war would almost certainly transform the international order. A sense of historical imminence dominated developments everywhere in the world, and this was repeatedly expressed as both a problem and an opportunity for the Thai government, and the Thai people more generally. With this in mind, it is vital to recognise that, while the enforced wearing of certain clothes, and particularly the wearing of hats, might have been the subject of ridicule for critics of the Prime Minister, the underlying ideological commitments that such new dress styles asserted were more than just those of Thai racial superiority. They were intimately connected to the much more long-standing priority of the post-1932 government to commit the country to a path of progress that would win independence for the Thai economy.

Dress and development in the 'new' Thai nation[42]

As Siam's primary import commodity, from the start of the revolution textiles had been singled out as a major concern of the revolutionary government.[43] As documents distributed by the finance ministry explained in 1936, the country had long produced cotton. As it stood, however, this cotton was being sold to 'foreigners' only to be sold back to the internal market as finished garments or ready-woven cloth.[44] It was not that the Thais didn't know how to spin yarn, or to weave it. The problem was that they were unable to produce it in sufficient quantities or of suitable quality to be sold in a competitive urban marketplace. Earlier, in December 1933, it was explained that the populations of Isan, who were particularly adept in the 'ancient' techniques of garment production, were unable to access the national market because of the difficulty they had in distributing their products.[45] Isan was virtually cut off from

64 *In and out of Vogue*

Bangkok, it explained, with the train ticket to the capital prohibitively expensive. Even if the producers did get there, the price of products in the city's markets were too competitive for it to be worth their while.

With textile imports for 1937 estimated at a potential 20 million baht, the decision was thus made to develop a textile industry that would curtail the Thai dependence on cheap foreign imports.[46] However, it was also noted that, unlike in India and China, where intense nationalist feeling had been successfully channelled to promote the purchase of locally made textiles, there was little appetite in Siam to sacrifice a high quality import for a more expensive local alternative. To compete, therefore, it was decided that the government must develop a textile industry with a high emphasis on quality. Taking the lead from previously mentioned experiments in Chachoengsao, the decision was taken to expand the creation of textile production co-operatives across the country. By 1941, the Finance Ministry suggested there had been a slow but steady growth in the internal sale of Thai cloth. From 1937, when the total production of Thai cloth had been worth just over 10,000 baht, by 1940 it had reached close to 180,000. With plans now under way to roll out the programme to every province, it was predicted that the figure could only improve.[47]

However, it was clear that Thai products remained a fraction of the total textile market, a reality blamed on the ongoing limitations placed upon the Thai industry by the international system. Since 1934, Japan had become responsible for 60 per cent of the country's imports, overtaking Britain as the primary importer.[48] With Thai leaders keen to cultivate friendship with the Japanese regime, fostering Thai distrust of Japanese goods was not an option. At the same time, any boycott would have aligned the government to Chinese political motives, the very group whose influence the Thai state was intent upon limiting. This was made particularly clear from 7 July 1937, when war broke out between Japanese and Chinese forces not far from Beijing. In protest, Chinese business leaders in Bangkok sought to show their solidarity with their homeland by planning a new boycott of Japanese goods. This soon led to an internal conflict within the Chinese community as business leaders turned on those traders who it felt to be unsympathetic to its political aims. The outbreak of violence within the Chinese community provided the Thai government with the pretext for a repressive crackdown, leading to the shutting down of a number of Chinese-language newspapers and the arrest and deportation of thousands of local Chinese.[49]

The events were to provide powerful narratives with which to consolidate anti-Chinese, and thus pro-Thai, sentiment. However, by allying itself with an anti-Chinese stance similar to that of the Japanese, the Thai state also made appeals to anti-foreign rhetoric an unsuitable vehicle for the promotion of the Thai textiles. Even attempts to boycott Chinese merchants were inappropriate because it was largely Indian communities that dominated the internal trade.[50] Instead, the promotion of Thai textiles was to focus on the development of public relations activities intended to spread awareness of the industry, and to associate the purchase of such products to a 'new' and 'modern' nationalist Thai identity. Throughout the country, Nation Day and Constitution Day were increasingly used as platforms to promote the use of Thai-produced textiles, while in Bangkok the government produced publicity material that attempted to inform urban consumers of the new products.[51] Presenting the new industry as a government project embedded in establishing modern industrial techniques, it also sought to encourage consumers to associate buying Thai-made textiles with a modern identity. As an advert made clear in 1939, 'Those who are not shaped by the new era can't call themselves modern', and 'at the moment Thai men and women are all using Thai products. Are you using Thai cloth yet?'[52]

Yet, such propaganda also sought to complicate the purchase of cotton in the minds of consumers, by associating the activity with a test of the individual's commitment to the nation. In an article published in *Thongthiao Sapda* entitled 'When Thais manufacture and sell textiles', the reader was explicitly asked to help support the growth of the internal textile industry to help the country compete on a level playing field with foreigners.[53] Setting out the argument by describing the need to industrialise, the article went on to clearly establish the fact that at the present time the government was unable to act independently. It also explained that the government had to act quickly to establish the economic freedom of the nation. In terms of textiles, the article lamented that before global industrialisation, Thais engaged in textile production without question, but that now this had changed. To solve the problem, it went on, the government had established new institutions, such as a Ministry of Economic Affairs, to rectify the problem of the nation's dependency on foreign products. Since then, they had worked tirelessly to find ways of securing the availability of essential goods, but ultimately only full industrialisation would achieve this endeavour. In the meantime, the article pleaded with readers to support the industry nonetheless:

> It is necessary for Thais to help each other and work together in order to support the textile industry, to change our ways and use Thai textiles for our clothes. The result of this will get the nation to where we want it to be. When the majority of Thais have a desire to achieve the same objective ... to see the nation modernise, then it will no longer be a dream, but will be close to a reality.[54]

In this example it is clear how state ideology, while remaining focused upon the urban consumer as the central figure in the building of the nation, was by the end of the 1930s increasingly attempting to connect the urban centre with the national periphery. It also identifies how, with the world slipping toward war, and with the newly named Thai nation on an increasingly authoritarian trajectory, sacrifice was now becoming a central theme in the harnessing of national consciousness. Underlying that shift was a clear desire to reprimand the urban consumer who failed to grasp the significance of their purchasing power. As a cartoon published in the more militant government mouthpiece,

66   *In and out of Vogue*

Sang Ton-eng, proclaimed in 1941, those who wore Thai textiles could be proud even if they didn't look as good as those who wore clothes made with foreign imported materials.[55] Speaking to her partner as they passed a couple walking the other way down a busy high street, the woman expressed concern that the other two looked better than they did, reassured only when her husband said that they could be proud because 'we are wearing Thai cloth'. Once again, the message was that Thai consumers must recognise their personal responsibility for supporting the development of Thai industries being established in rural areas if they were to consider themselves true nationalists.

Dress under Phibun, therefore, while recognising the power of urban consumers in determining the success of the nationalist project, was also increasingly focused on challenging their commitment to support the betterment of their fellow citizens. This was also true of the *ratthaniyom*, which by dictating what all Thais should wear, explicitly sought to break down the class distinctions that attitudes to dress had created. As Kullada Kesboonchoo Mead has argued, since the end of the nineteenth century dress had been an important social marker, not only of elite identity, but also of those who had made the transition from 'commoner status' to an elevated social standing within the wage economy.[56] Now, however, while wearing a 'suit, socks and shoes' was still regarded as vital in asserting social standing, it was also recognised to be having a negative effect on national unity, something that the cultural edicts on dress were intended to address.

It is important to understand how, in the aftermath of the proclamations on dress on 15 January 1941, assertions were subsequently made to illustrate their universal nature and their ability to cut across class distinctions. Perhaps the most obvious example came during the aftermath of the successful Thai campaign to 'liberate' territories from the Vichy French regime in Indochina, when dress was seen as an important tool to integrate the local population into Thai culture. As a public relations memo outlined, the 'liberated' people who lived in these territories needed to see themselves as 'equals' both to the French from whose repression they had been freed and to the urban Thai centre under whose authority they now existed. 'In line with our victory against French forces', the memo explained, 'and in the spirit of fairness and equality', these people must 'dress properly.'[57] While they should, if they wished, be allowed to maintain traditional styles, they must also understand what was not appropriate in a civilised country. They must grow their hair long, and they must wear more than just one piece of cloth to cover their bodies. This, it was clearly hoped, would help the new population feel a part of the nation, and in turn reduce their sense of inferiority to the European powers. However, it was also clearly intended to encourage those in Bangkok to view them as equally deserving of citizenship status. Indeed, back in Bangkok, state media disseminated images of these new members of the Thai community as evidence that the nation was successfully disseminating its superior culture (Figure 2.1).[58] It also affirmed strongly that, for the Phibun government, nationalism must include everyone, and that how to dress was crucial in establishing that.

Figure 2.1 Thongtiao Sapda (Bangkok, 13 March 1941) presented young female populations from the newly 'liberated' territory as members of a now larger national community, and therefore now free to dress properly

By the end of the same year, in a memo from Phibun to the Fine Arts Department, the Prime Minister sought to reinforce the point.[59] In it, he claimed that some people were openly criticising the new directives on dress, arguing that at a time when the country was facing economic tightening and with the world now engaged in war, there were more important things to worry about than dress. Phibun's response was categorical, emphasising that concerns about dress were not simply ideological, but explicitly connected to an individual's commitment to the development of the nation as a whole. Certainly, Phibun's argument was committed to civilisational arguments about the Thai race. He made clear that foreigners took no pleasure in seeing Thais dressing well, but that Thais should learn to dress well in order to assert their cultured status on the world stage. 'Encouraging people to think about how they dress', he explained, 'is important because it helps them to feel as if they are a people with culture, unlike people such as those who live in Africa.'[60]

However, he also sought to see changing attitudes to dress as representative of a society committed to breaking old class distinctions, a process inherently connected to tracking the progress of the nation under the new government. The world was at war, and Thailand was in a perilous condition. As a response, the government was working hard to establish industries to support peace. But this had to be done to 'provide the Thai people with a living, so that for all of those people who believe in fairness, it becomes evidently clear that we must do all we can'. As a result, those who argued against the enforcement of specific dress codes for all were driven by an instinct to disenfranchise the worse off; 'it is like saying the poor should not be considered a part of the national community' and 'such a view is to look down on the poor'. 'If someone is poor', he went on, 'then you need a way to get out of that condition, and dress is an important such way.' If someone wants to participate in

68   *In and out of Vogue*

national life, 'then they will either save, or they will find some extra work in order to buy new clothes'.[61]

The extent to which Phibun was actually responding to public criticism about the *ratthaniyom* is impossible to gauge. Yet the polemical nature of his argument is important because it shows how the context of the global war was used to support his claims. It is also clear that, before the country had formally entered the war on the side of the Axis powers, there was a growing implication that those who failed to recognise the importance of a mass cultural mobilisation should be viewed as unpatriotic and unsympathetic to the notion of a united national population. When the Japanese invaded in December, themes of sacrifice and unity became more prevalent as the Thai government continued to emphasise culture as a way of asserting their right to be treated as 'equal to those with whom we are in alliance'.[62] However, so did the assertion that Thais needed to recognise the right of their fellow citizens to the same fashions that such cultural parity spurned.

Dressing for war, imagining the future.

If the theme of sacrifice had become central to Thai propaganda prior to the Japanese invasion, it was unavoidable following Thailand's formal entry into the Second World War. In the initial aftermath of Thailand's entry into the war, textile imports quickly collapsed, from 14,200 metric tons of cotton cloth in 1941 to a mere 800 in 1943, leading to a rapid rise in prices and the expansion of an unregulated black market trade.[63] Highlighting the urgency of the developing situation, the Department of Commerce explained in June 1943 that the price of cloth in the country's markets was 'rising sharply every day', angering the population that was increasingly finding daily life untenable.[64] For those Thai who sought to maintain a high standard of dress, life became incredibly difficult. After the war, those who recalled the period spoke of households having to share one outfit amongst multiple family members.[65] For many who had grown used to wearing white imported cotton, and who couldn't afford the price of such goods on the black market, the only option now was to wear the low quality unbleached Thai cotton spun on local looms (*pha tip*). This material, which despite its material similarity had none of the political con- notations of its Indian equivalent, *khadi*, was unable to overcome its function as marker of poverty. As a result, during the war, dependency on the material represented the rapidly declining economic status, not only of individual citizens, but the nation itself.

Yet, while the strain of rising prices and limited supply continued throughout the war, the Phibun government remained committed to issuing strong and increasingly complex directives about the way people should dress in order to maintain dignity and honour for the nation. At the forefront of the campaign to maintain high standards in dress throughout these harder years was the title *Suphap Satri* [*Cultured Woman*]. This magazine was edited by Phibun's wife, Laied Phibun Songkhram, who was also head of the Institute for Women's

In and out of Vogue   69

Culture, and was focused on serving the community of women who were either married to members of the bureaucracy or who were themselves working in the new institutions of government. It was particularly focused on urban life, and bore a clear resemblance to fashion magazines such as *Vogue* and *Glamour*. It was also, like those American titles, heavily ideological and steadfastly attached to the state's propaganda agenda. In an article on how to dress, published in September 1943, the magazine explored the need to dress correctly in distinctly civilisational terms, claiming that how a country's citizens dressed distinguished a nation with culture from a barbarian community. Now, however, in the context of an increasingly militarised society, the article explained that how Thai people dressed in public was equally important as the uniforms people wore to work. 'You shouldn't have to think about the fact that [these standards in dress] are enforced', the magazine exclaimed, because this should be considered normal; and 'when all the citizens of a nation, every one of them are dressing appropriately, only then can that nation expect to receive the respect of other nations'.[66] In a separate edition of the magazine, a standalone message announced that 'dressing properly according to culture is how you help the country become preeminent; it also asserts our independence'.[67]

Other articles sought to explain the different terminologies associated with a dress code, explaining what was meant when the Prime Minister referred to different types of dress. In one detailed account, 'universal dress', it was explained, referred to 'wearing a dress, in either two pieces or one', while 'Thai dress' meant either 'wearing something that has been made in Thailand' or something that has a 'distinctly Thai character'.[68] Normal dress, or 'whatever you should wear on a day to day basis', was then split into three separate parts. 'Day wear', it explained, should be in the universal style, suitable for going to the market or meeting people, and should not be too dazzling. 'Afternoon wear' should also be in the universal style, but should be of a better quality than daywear, and should be worn for eating out or attending a marriage. Gloves were recommended but not obligatory. Finally, 'night wear' could be either an evening dress, down to the floor, perhaps with an open neckline, or sometimes, if the host allowed, it could be a short skirt; again in the universal style. The only place where Thai dress was mentioned was in relation to palace ceremonies, most of which where now defunct.[69]

There is little question that *Suphap Satri*, perhaps more than any other magazine, sought to harness urban aspirations. Yet in the context of a world at war, the magazine also sought to establish a commitment to dress as connected to the global war in which Thailand was now involved. It also continued to assert that the adoption of high standards of dress should be considered a universal right of citizenship. In one of the more subtle examples, the front cover of the magazine for August 1943 included a picture of a young woman in a rural setting, feeding turkeys and wearing a blouse with a hat (Figure 2.2).[70] In stark contrast to the prejudiced vision of a primitive rural Thailand that had been so prevalent prior to the revolutionary era, here a new vision of rural life was being posited.[71] Turkey, goose and other poultry were regularly

Figure 2.2 Front cover, *Suphap Satri*, 22 August 1943

featured inside the magazine as foodstuffs to be desired in the new society. Here, however, a market for that food was providing a livelihood to a rural family, allowing it to follow the universal cultural practices associated with global citizenship. The vision here was also of a nation where the old distinctions between rural and urban, in civilizational terms at least, had been dismantled.

However, while such ideological assertions might have upset urban sensibilities, ultimately it was the growing distance between urban desires and the ability of the government to fulfil those aspirations that best explains why the

Phibun government's ideological message began to falter. By 1944, the Thai commitment to support Japan was costing the country vast sums, with loans made to finance Japanese military operations costing 45 million baht a month. This in turn forced the Thai government to print money, leading to even higher levels of inflation. At the same time, the completion of the Thai–Burma railway had made Bangkok a more important strategic target for allied bombing, bringing the war more directly into the daily life of the capital's residents. With plans being actively pursued to abandon the city and move the capital to the north, the government was rapidly losing credibility. In this context, it is easy to see why such propaganda messages about how Thais should dress came to be viewed as increasingly out of touch with reality and would undoubtedly have contributed to legitimising the removal of Phibun from power in August of the same year.

Yet the removal of Phibun did not mean that urban communities lost interest in maintaining high standards in dress. As has been established, state propaganda following 1932 had from early on sought not to craft urban life-styles, but to harness them. Knowledge of fashion and of appropriate dress styles was not simply state-led, but was well embedded in urban life, and in pre-existing notions of social betterment. What was unique about cultural production during the Phibun era, therefore, was not the lifestyle that such dress represented, but the claim that this lifestyle should be expanded to include a national population. As a result, the collapse of the Phibun government in 1944 did not curtail the urban desire to conform to the social mores that had been long established as central to the nation. It was just that in the post-war period what constituted eveningwear or daywear was to be re-affirmed as part of a more specifically urban identity. In Bangkok's complex post-war political environment, new magazines such as *Phap Khao Sayam Nikon* might have sought to establish the period as new and distinct for Thai consumers. Yet, invariably, the mark of this new era was framed as a return to the aspirational society of urban imaginations.

Dress and Bangkok's post-war media: chasing elusive abundance

Overall, therefore, while internal textile production did increase during the war, the context in which it happened only served to identify the inherent weakness of state-led messages about the viability of indigenous manufacturing capabilities. Moreover, as the purchase of Thai material was increasingly associated with necessity rather than choice, Thai consumers became ever more sure of the undesirability of local fabrics over imported equivalents. As a result, when the war came to an end, they once again looked to foreign imports to replenish their wardrobes. At the same time, however, the desire for high quality clothes was combined with a strong interest to re-engage with an international community from which the country's urban consumers had felt largely isolated during the war. It was in this climate that a new form of cultural media began to emerge which, in serving a market of urban readers, aimed to reflect these

72   In and out of Vogue

wishes. Crucially, such publications continued to focus on everyday consumption habits as fundamental markers of a collective Thai identity. In a similar guise to the wartime media that they replaced, these magazines also remained committed to informing readers about international fashions, associating Thai knowledge of the new styles as a mark of the Thai ability to participate in an international consumer culture.

Expensive to produce and to purchase, *Phap Khao Sayam Nikon* [*Siam Nikon Photo News*] was one of the earliest such publications, becoming a principal commentator on the life of the nation and its place in the world. Sold as a magazine with pictures from both inside and outside the country, it updated readers on the latest cultural news, and focused principally on connecting Bangkok to the outside world. Routinely concerned with what it described as 'society', meaning a rather loosely defined urban society based almost entirely in Bangkok, the magazine continued to narrate the cultural life of the nation. A notable difference from wartime publications, however, was the privileged status given to America as the most important centre of international culture. There was a particular focus on news from Hollywood of the latest stars and movie news, combined with the assertion that with the war now over, Thailand would soon be back on their travel itineraries. In the June edition of 1947, for example, an article proudly informed Bangkok that 'in the past they have come from Hollywood to visit Thailand, stars and producers of the movies, known throughout the world', and 'not long from now we can expect them to return'.[72]

In preparation for the Hollywood invasion, other articles discussed new fashions from abroad, in one example noting how Thai women were now wearing long dresses, in keeping with international trends. It also introduced the latest ideas about dress from the editor of the American magazine *Modern Screen*, a woman who, according to *Phap Khao Sayam Nikon*, was among those most qualified to discuss such issues.[73] Quoting from the American publication, it stated that a woman's sense of fashion – knowing what to wear and when to wear it – was crucial to securing a happy and functional life for her and her family. In Thailand, the magazine reassured Thai readers, that knowledge of the international standard was well understood by experts such as Mom Kopkaeo, and Thai women would be able to learn not only how to dress well, but also the subtleties of what constituted evening or daywear. To accompany the article, a picture of a woman dressed in her new long dress and looking directly at the reader clearly asserted the ability of the Thai to present a confident cultural face to the world.[74]

In another of the early issues, the magazine proudly proclaimed that the 'cultural life of the nation had returned', and was developing fast, 'after a period when it had been quiet, elevating the spirit of the people who are recovering from the effects of the war'.[75] Announcing the return of an annual celebration organised by the newly reinstated Institute of Culture, the same arm of government that had been responsible for the cultural edicts of the wartime era, the magazine reassured readers that once the Prime Minister had opened it, 'there are sure to be plenty of beautiful girls, dressed correctly in accordance with culture (but without the hats!)'. With Phibun back on the political scene, and only months away from once again becoming the Prime Minister for a second period, the magazine asserted that the country was now in a new era. Repeatedly, the assertion that the enforced wearing of hats was no longer government policy was used to establish the distinct nature of the moment. What remained was the emphasis on dress as something that could track modernity and progress.

The image presented of Bangkok, therefore, was of a city getting back on its feet and engaging confidently in global culture. The message was that new fashions, such as the swimming costume, had been fully accepted by Thai women, who were portrayed as not only open-minded and engaged with the new trends, but in some cases better suited to them than 'Westerners'. In a regular look at fashion from Chulalongkorn University, which was repeatedly emphasised as the centre of Bangkok's social scene, the writer commented on photographs of students modelling the costumes noting that 'in these cases in particular, it is very hard for the Westerners, who have in the past been famous in this regard, to compete, and by looking at these images, it seems clear they would lose'.[76]

A notable absence from such magazines, however, was any of the universalising rhetoric that had presented dress as a liberator during the war. Indeed, while the magazine sought to reassure readers that high society remained intact, there was little attempt to provide direction as to how the individual reader might participate in that society. Free from the practical support to self-betterment that had been such a feature of cultural media during the war, the individual reader was thus reduced to a position of either observer or participant in a cultural world defined by access to modern styles, and knowledge about how to wear them. At the same time, a constant reference to the United States as a new centre of the fashion world was disorienting, providing a constant sense of time moving forward, and emphasising the idea that there was a renewed need to 'keep up' with an ever-moving target. In another Thai-language magazine that began production in 1950, entitled *'Daily Mail' Pictorial News*, it remained common for coverage to focus exclusively on high society figures as evidence that Thais were more than capable of participating in the now rapidly changing world culture. Here, pictures of small groups of well connected and wealthy girls, often explicitly described as 'Bangkokonians', were depicted in the most modern fashions of the day.[77] In one feature titled 'Modern design', numbered pictures of different women in the most recent fashions interspersed high society Thai socialites with pictures of American models.[78] In another, a high society trip of young girls to the beach at Bang Sean was depicted as an impromptu fashion show (Figure 2.3).[79]

Another distinct difference between these magazines and their wartime equivalents was the lack of interest in viewing the state as a guarantor of modernity. As has already been explained, the context of Thailand's deteriorating economic situation had done significant damage to the view that the state could sustain Bangkok's consumption habits. Thus, while such magazines

Figure 2.3 'Fashion Show', *'Daily Mail' Pictorial News*, November 1953

sought to represent the rehabilitation of Thailand's urban middle class as a relevant consumer society, they rarely discussed state policy. The return to more stable economic conditions would not truly begin until the Korean War set off a mini economic boom from the start of the 1950s. Yet the immediate desire to return to pre-war consumption habits had already created a sense amongst Thailand's better off families that life was improving. Economic data from the period show that despite the weakened economic position of Thailand, personal debt rose rapidly as urban consumers, who had lost faith in the inflated wartime currency, clamoured for access to products that were not available under wartime conditions. As Alexander MacDonald described Bangkok in the immediate post-war period:

> As poor and as ravaged as such a country might be, immediately peace came the people wanted luxury goods. They wanted lipsticks, refrigerators, automobiles, and electric fans; wanted them at any price. That was why in Bangkok import–export firms were being born almost as fast as signboards could be painted. Everyone wanted to bring in that first shipment of streamlined fountain pens and cosmetics.[80]

While magazines such as *'Daily Mail' Pictorial News* promised optimism about the Thai ability to participate in global consumption practices, the Thai state was now far more involved in determining, and in many cases restricting, access to that world of high consumption. Immediately after the war, the country had faced a number of economic problems: the need to rebuild infrastructure such as railway lines and communications, to fulfil international obligations in the sale of rice, to replenish spent foreign currency reserves, and to curb inflation.[81] As a result, the post-war Thai state became highly involved in managing foreign trade, and as part of that had sought to actively restrict imports of goods considered 'extravagant'. Cars, for example, were subject to a quota system, which meant that between 1946 and 1950 just over 6000 were granted permission to be imported and sold. When a private importer of Ford argued in 1951 that the increased import of new, cheaper models would bring down the price and thus make cars more available to the people, the decision was that the quota should remain. Later, as the economy began to stabilise and the controls were relaxed, the experience of these post-war years nevertheless left a powerful legacy, identifying how, just as state actors might support consumption, they could also act to restrict it. For those who hungered for consumer goods from abroad, denied to them during the war, an awareness of the state as the principal force in determining access was increasingly acute.

Conclusion

Throughout the 1950s, *Phap Khao Sayam Nikon* was joined by a number of similar titles, some of which would cease production almost as soon as they begun, and others that would continue well into the 1960s. In a competitive media marketplace, editors struggled to attract readers, and often talked openly with their audience about what were the best images to represent both the nation and modernity. This trend, for photo magazines to act as primary commentators about the state of Thai society, was indicative of a community deeply concerned with issues of representation, both internally and in relation to the international community. The focus on dress was understandable. For over a generation, the Bangkok media and increasingly state propaganda had focused on dress as a key identifier of what it meant to be a member of a modern citizenry. Now, however, the economic conditions had made that far harder to achieve. At the same time, confidence in the Thai state to secure a consumer society had been reduced, and the end of state guidance about what people should be wearing was replaced with a raised interest in new fashions from abroad.

Yet uncertainty about those fashions also led to confusion, and overall the post-war interaction with a changing international situation was to have a significant impact. While the initial meeting between *Vogue* and urban Thailand could be largely characterised as one of cultural misunderstanding, over time repeated American interest in Thai dress was to raise new perspectives over what should be considered a specifically 'Thai' dress. Particularly after the release of *The King and I* (1951) in New York, the emergence of Thai silk as a product sought out by American visitors began to have an effect on the fashion scene

76   In and out of Vogue

in Bangkok (see chapter 1). Increasingly, fashion shows featured in Bangkok's photo media began to include displays of the latest dresses made in Thai silk as well as the usual cotton. Aware of the growing demand, new silk producers emerged, and market traders in Bangkok began to stock silk for Thai residents to incorporate into their latest dresses. While by the mid-1950s this trend was still extremely marginal among Thai consumers, a growing interest in Thai silk amongst Bangkok high society would eventually help to build narratives of interaction with Americans that would create an important sense of commonality and relevance between elite Thai and American communities.

However, early displays of Thai silk to a Thai audience would, unlike American narratives in the magazines of Condé Nast and Time Life, focus promotion of the product on its 'newness', emphasising both its quality and suitability as a material to make high-end dresses. Put on by the Association of University Women 'in view of promoting the silk industry in the country', one such show was, according to the government publication *Thailand Illustrated*, 'greatly appreciated by the women audience'. Featuring a display in which high society Bangkokonians wore billowing long dresses as well as low-cut Hollywood styles, the message was clearly intended to convince the crowd of the viability of Thai silk as a premium material.[82] However, at this early stage, no mention was made of the product's connection to an ideology of development. Rather, the silks were generally promoted in rather simple terms, as high-cost Thai products that had fostered a level of international interest.

What was also lacking in the way Thai silk was promoted to a Thai audience was any sense that the material represented something historic, or that it could be used to assert a distinctive Thai style. As can be seen with the *Vogue* coverage of India, and the later Condé Nast interest in Thailand, a sense of historical commitment to colour and to distinctive styles were viewed as an important means to distinguish India, and to foster interest from American society. Set within the context of a world shaped by the reality of decolonisation and Asian independence, evidence of a harmonious and stable society that was distinct, but not hostile, to the American centre was reassuring to American readers. By emphasising the Indian commitment to traditional costumes and materials, *Vogue* was able to present the country as a potential partner, in a relationship that reinforced America as a modern centre. Yet, for Thailand, existing attitudes to dress had made it much harder to depict the country in such a way, meaning they had to be almost entirely imagined or constructed by American writers.

That is not to say that from the 1930s through to the early 1950s urban Thailand was not interested in marking what might be described as 'traditional' styles of dress. From the very start of the Miss Thailand competition in the aftermath of the 1932 revolution, the wearing of historic dress was often regarded as integral to any display of Thai culture. Yet the trend following the revolution, to historicise and memorialise the past in order to project a modernising society, meant that significant effort was always made to distinguish the past from the present. While, during the Second World War, such an emphasis had been tempered by the Phibun government as it sought to focus more on expressions of modernity and bodily perfection, at the end of the war there was a clear attempt to re-integrate historic forms of dress into expressions of Thai culture. Once again, however, such displays would invariably be clearly differentiated from the wearing of modern fashion. At the 1954 Constitution Day Fair, the Miss Thailand contestants were depicted in *Thailand Illustrated* as 'among the beauties of the world with their creamy soft skin, dazzling teeth, and appealing eyes', while displays of historical dress were consigned to a display of manikins, put on by the Woman's Culture Bureau.[83] Moreover, while magazines such as *'Daily Mail' Pictorial News* and *Phap Khao Sayam Nikon* did on occasion feature young girls in historical Thai dress, it was generally made explicitly clear that these were fancy dress costumes.

While Thais at the end of the Second World War were therefore keen to reintegrate into the world of international fashion, they struggled to find cultural narratives that supported their ambitions. The next chapter looks at how, by ignoring the recent past and emphasising the cultural uniqueness of the Thai, American cultural producers, and in particular area specialists, were to have a deep impact on how Thai publications came to present the nation. In doing so, it looks more closely at how notions of what it meant to be an urban Thai began to change as a result of the country's re-integration into the international community. Building on the analysis of dress in this chapter, it looks at how ideas emanating from the United States that sought to re-create a psychological profile of the Thai were increasingly appropriated in the search for a confident and globally relevant notion of national citizenship in a new era.

Notes

1 *'Phuying'* [Women], *Phap Khao Sayam Nikon*, December 1947. Early editions of the magazine did not always have specific dates of publication, meaning that referencing here is not consistent.
2 Ibid.
3 NA ST 0701.9.5.1/16 [3], Chancheun Kambhu, Royal Siamese Embassy, Washington to Office of the Prime Minister, Bangkok, 13 June 1947. *'Kho amnuai khwam saduak lae chuailuea phoeiphrae watthanatham knong chat'.*
4 Ibid.
5 NA ST 0701.9.5.1/16 [3], Bartlow Underhill, Office of International Information and Cultural Affairs, Department of State, New York to Major Chancheun Kambhu, Royal Siamese Embassy, Washington, DC; 22 May 1947.
6 NA ST 0701.9.5.1/16 [3], Condé Nast Publications to Major Chancheun Kambhu, Royal Siamese Embassy, 23 May 1947.
7 Ibid.
8 Siam was renamed Thailand in 1939 by the nationalist government of Phibun Songkhram. After the war Phibun's political rivals, under pressure from the British, returned to the older name, but in 1947 the country was once again named Thailand, as it still is today.
9 'The Colour of India', *Vogue*, December 1 1948, p. 107.
10 Ibid.

78 *In and out of Vogue*

11 Ibid.

12 Fancy dress was prolific in Bangkok both before and after the war. Photo magazines would regularly feature Bangkok citizens parading in a vast range of fancy dress, including what were described as traditional 'Thai' outfits and 'peasant' costumes.

13 Photographic evidence from post-war Bangkok confirms that this was the case. Also, Kobukua Suwannathat-pian confirms that this was a lasting legacy of the Phibun era. See Kobukua Suwannathat-pian, *Thailand's Durable Premier, Phibun Through Three Decades, 1932–1957*, Singapore: Oxford University Press, 1995, p. 119.

14 Maurizio Peleggi, 'Refashioning civilization: dress and body practice in Thai nation building', in Mina Roces and Louise Edwards (eds) *The Politics of Dress in Asia and the Americas*, Eastbourne: Sussex Academic Press, 2010, pp. 65–66.

15 Chris Baker and Pasuk Phongphaichit, *A History of Thailand*, Cambridge: Cambridge University Press, 2005, pp. 116–121. In recent years, existing accounts of the 1932 revolution, which cast it as a coup performed by a small group of marginal, foreign-educated individuals, has come under serious scrutiny. It is now accepted that the move to end absolute monarchy was more of a popular revolution than has previously been considered. Influential studies that have supported this shift in emphasis include Scott Barme, *Man, Woman, Bangkok: Love, Sex and Popular Culture in Thailand*, Lanham, MD: Rowman & Littlefield, 2002; Matthew Copeland, 'Contested nationalism and the 1932 overthrow of the absolute in Siam', PhD thesis, Australia National University, 1993; and Nakarin Mektrairat, *Khwamkhit khwamru lae amnat kanmueang nai kanpatiwat sayam*, Bangkok: Fa diaokan, 2003. For a more recent discussion that provides a certain nuance to current thinking, see Arjun Subrahmanyan, 'Reinventing Siam: ideas and culture in Thailand, 1920–1944' PhD thesis, University of California, 2013.

16 As Matthew Copeland has noted, widespread critiques of absolute monarchy portrayed the institution as a 'museum piece' when compared with the other nations of the world, and were focused on the winning of equal rights and political privileges. Matthew Copeland, 'Contested nationalism and the 1932 overthrow of the absolute monarchy in Siam', p. 62.

17 Scott Barme, *Man, Woman, Bangkok*, p. 2.

18 Ibid., p. 9.

19 Ibid., p. 2. Matthew Copeland has argued that critiques of the absolute monarchy portrayed the old system as a 'museum piece' when compared with other nations of the world. See Matthew Copeland, 'Contested nationalism and the 1932 overthrow of the absolute monarchy in Siam', p. 62.

20 Ibid.

21 Chris Baker and Pasuk Phongphaichit, *A History of Thailand*, Cambridge: Cambridge University Press, 2005, pp. 121–124.

22 Kobkua Suwannathat-Pian, *Kings, Country and Constitutions: Thailand's Political Development 1932–2000*, Abingdon: Routledge, 2013, pp. 78–79.

23 *Prachachat*, 13 December 1935, p. 21.

24 *Prachachat*, 10 December 1935, p. 2.

25 '*Utsahakam kanthongthiao nai ngae setthakit*' [The tourist industry from an economic perspective], *Thongthiao sapda*, 16 August 1938, p. 25.

26 Chatri Prakittanonthakan, *Khanarat chalong ratthathmmanun: prawattisat kan mueng lang 2475 phan sathapattayakam 'amnat'* [*Celebrating the People's Constitution: A Thai Political History of Architecture following 1932 through 'Power'*], Bangkok: Arts and Culture, 2005, p. 134.

27 *Prachachat*, 9 December 1934, p. 15.

28 *Prachachat*, 9 December 1938, p. 14.

In and out of Vogue 79

29 '*Kon ngan chalong ratththammanun*' [Before you go to the Constitution Day Fair], *Prachachat*, 15 December 1938, p. 21.
30 *Prachachat*, 10 December 1937, p. 21.
31 '*Wa sariphap pen yot pratthana khong manut lae cha sanapsanun kansueksa yang temthi*' [Freedom is the great desire of all humans and I totally support education], *Prachachat*, 9 December 1938, p. 3.
32 Chris Baker and Pasuk Phongphaichit, *A History of Thailand*, Cambridge: Cambridge University Press, 2005, p. 123.
33 *Prachachat*, 9 December 1938, p. 3.
34 'Thailand is heaven', *Prachamitra*, 27, 28, 29 April 1939. Obtained in translation from Wheaton College Archives. Illinois. Margret and Kenneth Landon Papers, Series 4, Subseries 7, Box 153, Folder 16, 'Translations from Chinese and Thai newspapers'.
35 Ibid.
36 Ibid.
37 NA ST 0701.29/4, 24 June 1939, Announcement from the Office of the Prime Minister concerning the *ratthaniyom, Rang prakat samnak nayok rattamontri wa duai ratthaniyom: raksa marayat nai thi chumnum chon lae hai kiattiyot kae phu chuailuea ratchakan* [Directive to look after the manners of the community and to honour and support the government].
38 NA ST 0701/29/4, 1939, '*Ratthaniyom*' *doi Luang Wichitwathakan* ['*Ratthaniyom*' by Luang Wichitwathakan].
39 Mina Roces and Louise Edwards (eds), *The Politics of Dress in Asia*, p. 73.
40 Thamsook Numnonda, 'Phibunsongkram's Thai nation building programme during the Japanese military presence 1941–1945', *Journal of Southeast Asian Studies*, 9(2) (1978): 235.
41 For more on the importance of the League of Nations to Siam's national development, see Stefan Hell, *Siam and the League of Nations: Modernization, Sovereignty and Multilateral Diplomacy, 1920–1940*, Bangkok: River Books, 2010.
42 This section contains a number of paragraphs and remarks that have been previously published in *South East Asia Research*. See Matthew Phillips, 'Crafting nationalist consumption: public relations and the Thai textile movement under the People's Party, 1932–1945', *South East Asia Research*, 21(4) (2013): 637–655. Republished with permission from the publisher, with thanks.
43 James C. Ingram, *Economic Change in Thailand Since 1850*, Stanford, CA: Stanford University Press, 1971, p. 113.
44 NA (2) SR 0201.22.2.5/1, 1936. Department of Commerce to the Office of the Prime Minister, '*Khrongkan songsoem utsahakam thopha*' [The project to promote a textile industry].
45 NA (2) SR 0201.22.2.5/1 Department of Commerce to the Office of the Prime Minister, '*Banthuek rueang tua rongngan chak sendai nai phak isam*' [The project to build a textile factory in the northeast region].
46 NA (2) SR 0201.22.2.5/1, 1936. Department of Commerce to the Office of the Prime Minister, *Khrongkan songsoem utsahakam thopha*' [The project to promote a textile industry].
47 NA (2) SR 0201.22.5/4, 1941. '*Rai laiat kandamnoen ngan kong utsahakam*' [Details of the progress of the industry].
48 William L. Swan, *Japan's Economic Relations with Thailand: The Rise to 'Top Trader' 1875–1942*, Bangkok: White Lotus, 2009, p. 56.
49 William G. Skinner, *Chinese Society in Thailand: An Analytical History*, Ithaca, NY: Cornell University Press, 1957, p. 265.
50 Department of Overseas Trade, *Economic Conditions in Siam, 1933–34*, London: Department of Overseas Trade, 1935, p. 11.

80   In and out of Vogue

51 NA (2) SR 0201.22.5/4, pp.199–208, *Sathiti ngan songsoem fai nai 1941*, [Statistics on the promotion of cotton in 1941], 1943.
52 *Thongtiao Sapda*, August 1940, p. 41.
53 *Thongtiao Sapda*, June 1940, p. 1.
54 Ibid.
55 *Sang Ton-eng* [*Make it Yourself*], Bangkok, 15 September 1941. Thanks to Arjun Subrahmanyan for alerting me to the existence of this magazine in the National Library of Thailand, Bangkok.
56 Kullada Kesboonchoo Mead, *The Rise and Decline of Thai Absolutism*, London: Routledge Curzon, 2004, p. 119.
57 NA SR 0701.29/17, 14 March 1942, p. 3. *'Kham wingwon khong than nayok ratthamontri fak wai kae phi nong satri thai' chak krom khosanakan* [Directive issued by the Prime Minister for the women of Thailand, distributed by the Publicity Bureau].
58 *'Satri thai chao nakhon champasak sueng batni yu nai khwam khum khrong khong thai laeo'* [Thai women from the District of Champa, which is now part of Thai territory], *Thongtiao Sapda*, Bangkok, 13 March 1941.
59 NA SR 0701.29/15, p. 2. Prime Minister to the Director of the Fine Arts Department, 16 October 1941. *'Khwam samkhan nai kanbamrung watthanatham khong chat'* [The importance to nurture the culture of the nation].
60 Ibid.
61 Ibid.
62 This was often mentioned as an issue when considering cultural policy during the formal alliance with Japan.
63 James C. Ingram, *Economic Change in Thailand*, p. 121.
64 NA (2) SR 0201.11.1.5/9 Department of Commerce to the Office of the Prime Minister, 8 June, *'Kan khuap khum kan kha pha'* [Controlling the price of textiles].
65 There are a number of instances where the post-war media mention the issue. For one such case, see *Khon Muang*, 9 March 1956, p. 118.
66 *'Kantaengkai'* [Dress], *Suphap Satri*, 29 September 1943, p. 13.
67 *'Kham naenam kiaokap kantaengkai khong ying'* [Advice on how to dress for women], *Suphap Satri*, 25 April 1943, p. 30.
68 *'Rabiap kantaengkai'* [How to dress], *Suphap Satri*, 13 June 1943, p. 6.
69 Ibid.
70 *Suphap Satri*, 22 August 1943.
71 'The others within: travel and ethno-spatial differentiation of Siamese subjects 1885–1910', in Andrew Turnton (ed.) *Civility and Savagery, Social Identity in Tai States*, Richmond: Curzon, 2000.
72 *'Khao khoei ma… lae cha ma mueng Thai'* [They came before… and will come to Thailand], *Phap Khao Sayam Nikon*, June 1947.
73 *'Thatsana thi kiaokap… phuying thai rao'* [The outlook for… our Thai women], *Phap Khao Sayam Nikon*, June 1947.
74 Ibid.
75 *Phap Khao Sayam Nikon,* early 1948.
76 *'Sujin ta klong khong rao trawen rop sa sanam Chulalongkorn'* [Sujin, Our photographer takes a wonder around the Chulalongkorn swimming pool], *Phap Khao Sayam Nikon*, December 1947.
77 This is a specific reference to an article that appeared in the magazine about a group of Thai high society girls leaving to study abroad. In it the magazine noted 'that Thailand's smart girls go to continue their studies abroad is no news to all of us here, because a great many Thailanders have already attainted a status of millionaires'. See *'Daily Mail' Pictorial News*, August 1950. Note that this is a

Thai-language magazine, with small paragraphs in English. The title is in English and Thai. The magazine does not include page numbers.

78 Ibid.
79 *'Daily Mail' Pictorial News*, November 1950.
80 Alexander MacDonald, *Bangkok Editor*, New York: Macmillian, 1949, p. 12.
81 Puey Ungphakorn, *Economic Development in Thailand 1950–1962*, Bangkok: 1963, p. 1.
82 *Thailand Illustrated*, No. 26, December 1954.
83 Ibid.

3 If not 'Great', then what?

Rethinking Thainess in post-war Bangkok

In November 1946 a 'foreign observer', writing in the English-language newspaper *Democracy*, pleaded with Thai readers to recognise that, for them, the world had fundamentally changed. 'You', he exclaimed 'have just come through a world struggle during which through no real fault of your own you backed the wrong side.' Now, with that conflict over, he continued, the Siamese people needed to 'awake', and understand that they had little to fear from the 'Great Nations'. From now on, the powers that had previously dominated global systems would no longer be engaged in expansion, but would instead be educating new nations in the ways of peace and efficient administration. Siam, meanwhile, should accept in this changed world that it was 'fantastic for a small country like yours to possess an army, a navy, an air force as large as you maintain?'. In a world with new technologies in tank production, aeroplanes, rockets and 'of course the atom bomb', it was obvious that Thailand would have no chance fighting the major powers of the world. As a result, the Thai people must accept defeat graciously, and at the same time recognise that the country should never again imagine itself as a member of the club of 'Great Nations'. If this was done, the article promised, the country would not be held accountable for its 1942 declaration of war.[1]

Illustrative of the tone through which Thailand's re-integration into the international community was negotiated, the message was clear. Speaking directly to the Thai people, rather than to the country's political leaders, the assertion was that the decision to go to war had revealed a fundamental weakness in the Thai national project. Not only did the article cast the Thai as subservient to the Japanese, it also assumed that the declaration of war had been entirely unrepresentative of popular Thai sentiment. It dismissed the Thai state as envisioned by Phibun Songkhram, in which a Greater Thai Kingdom would dominate the Southeast Asian mainland, and assumed that the Thai people held little sympathy for the form of chauvinistic nationalism that such a policy had exhibited. More subtly, it assumed the Thai to be fundamentally peaceful and free from any of the ambitions toward greatness that had dominated international relations in the pre-war period.

Yet, whereas for 'foreign observers' the offer might have seemed generous, the truth was that coming to terms with Thailand's diminished international status was to have profound implications for urban Thai society. As explored

Rethinking Thainess in post-war Bangkok   83

in chapter 2, while peace promised the return of consumer goods that defined life in the city, high inflation and government import restrictions meant that any saved baht would not go far. At the same time, the practical costs of Thailand's re-admittance into the international community were generally understood as symptomatic of the country's reduced status in the region and the world. In particular, the seceding of territories gained from the French in 1941 was viewed as a humiliation and an injustice. As one newspaper exclaimed in October 1946, 'the plea for the return of these four *changwats* (provinces) is based on the desire to establish peace in Southeast Asia', but what 'is the foundation for this peace if it is established by the loss of one side of territory rightfully belonging to them'. It concluded by assuring the international community that 'we Siamese will retain this act in the depth of our heart'.[2] In another newspaper, it was claimed that everybody who was in the government recognised that 'these territories belonged to us since olden times and had been acquired by sacrifice and through the efforts of our national brethren in those territories', but that now 'the tide of history had turned' and the country must 'turn over the page of history to the next one, which may bear the promise to be fair'.[3]

Forced to give up territories won in Indochina, and for over a year unsure about the extent to which the country would be punished for its declaration of war on Britain and America, Thailand's post-war experience was defined by anxiety and uncertainty. In the years that followed, Asian decolonisation, and ongoing concerns about the Thai economy, heightened fears that the country was rapidly slipping down the global hierarchy of nations. At the same time, ravaged by factionalism and episodes of sporadic violence, Thai politicians seemed to offer little hope that they would be able to halt the decline. Acutely aware of Thailand's vulnerability to international assertions about how the nation should be understood internationally, the period quickly became defined by a broad and complex discussion about what it meant to be Thai. With many keen to establish distance from the wartime culture that had taken Thai primacy for granted, new ideas about Thai culture competed and converged as different groups sought to stake a claim to the future direction of the nation. In the background of those discussions, however, remained the fact of Thailand's developing relationship with the United States and the Cold War. While these discussions were not to establish a dominant narrative, they were nevertheless to see new ideas emanating from an American centre contributing significantly to the creation of new frames of reference and subjectivities.

Thai culture and behaviour

One legacy of the Second World War in the United States was the mobilisation of academics behind the ambitions of the American state. In an ideological climate where being non-partisan was not an option, and where the morality of the conflict seemed clear, during the war many US academics helped to provide intellectual support to the state's aims and objectives. For those who were successful, the rewards in the post-war world were great. Stimulated by

84 *Rethinking Thainess in post-war Bangkok*

enormous funds, made available through federal channels and philanthropic organisations such as the Ford Foundation, universities 'not only cooperated with government authorities; they now depended on them'.[4]

The introduction of area studies onto US campuses was a symptom of this marriage between government policy and academia. Both during and then following the war, policy makers in Washington recognised that there was a dearth of knowledge about those regions outside Europe with which they desired a deepening relationship. As a result, they were to place a significant value upon accounts of 'peoples and places' that offered simple narratives of large populations in foreign lands, and that explicitly offered concrete advice to the government. Motivated by the vast amount of funding made available and an ideological commitment to the Cold War, many academic institutions were from the late 1940s re-structured to promote an agenda of common problem solving in regard to topics of 'pressing national security concern'.[5] By mobilising their considerable resources, funding bodies were also to elevate the position of the behavioural sciences into one of the primary disciplines for those who sought academic advancement. Rejecting the existing disciplinary divisions, these 'behaviouralists' held central command in the new university system, producing 'provocative, multidisciplinary, yet often whimsical intellectual concepts for government consumption'. They also drove the area studies revolution, translating 'culturally distant people and events' into 'measurable ideal types, mostly by fostering a series of primitive pictures of the Other'.[6]

While clearly influenced by previous colonial projects of classification, area studies also secured a new language and set of theoretical frameworks that were in keeping with changes happening within the regions they sought to understand. As a result, the study of 'distant peoples' was often located quite explicitly within a multi-national world, where the importance of ideas such as freedom, independence and sovereignty was given primacy. Moreover, race was rejected as a legitimate category to group large numbers of people together. Instead, it was through the work of a new school in anthropology, which through the early part of the century had built its reputation upon the study of villages and their social structures, that the new discipline was based. Drawing on Freudian ideas about human psychology, such studies would seek to understand traditional social structures and relations, such as child rearing or sexual roles, as instrumental in the formation of a community's 'pattern of culture'. This in turn was used to map a community's personality, as well as common behaviours shared by all its members. Importantly, the focus on the village as the site of a pure cultural heritage would often side-line local narratives of modernity, or indeed the deep inter-connectedness of such societies with global cultural flows and change. As Lenora Foerstel and Angela Gilliam have described, 'members of the school of "personality and culture" placed 'less emphasis on world events and more on psychological theory', focusing 'their studies of third world cultures through the lens of Western Individualism'.[7]

It is in this light that, both during the Second World War and in its aftermath, the ideas of anthropologists Ruth Benedict and Margaret Mead, both founding members of the personality and culture school, came to occupy a central role in American society. With Mead enthusiastically writing accounts of American personality as unique, both in books and in magazines such as *Vogue*, Ruth Benedict worked for the Office of War Information.[8] The national character studies that she was commissioned to write sought to establish simple narratives about the 'enemy', offering direction to US policy, and providing those who would deal with the respective countries upon their defeat with straightforward information about the people they would encounter. On one hand, her studies recognised the primacy of the nation state as the legitimate form through which such societies should be governed. Yet by reducing such societies to the status of an individual, these studies also framed ideas of self-determination in terms that emphasised cultural distinctiveness, and ultimately submissiveness, to Western forms of political and social control.

Her most influential work, which was published in 1946 as *The Chrysanthemum and the Sword*, but had been distributed to US servicemen before the end of the war, was an account of Japanese culture from a distance. In it, Benedict largely ignored the political and economic context of the war. She failed to recognise the country's industrial revolution, and the state's anxiety about resource management prior to the war. Instead, the text outlined the cultural narratives that made it a nation ready for war, namely its militaristic cultural traditions. It also, however, identified those elements within the culture which were deemed 'unaggressive', 'aesthetic', 'polite' and 'adaptable', seeking to account not only for who the enemy was, but also for which psychological conditions could be liberated during the country's post-war occupation.[9] According to Mari Yoshihara, Benedict did this by focusing on the dominance of male spheres of life, and by emphasising the undemocratic, anti-individualist nature of this cultural world. By associating the military defeat of Japan with a victory of American ideals, Benedict presented the cultural battle as one that would release the country from a dominant masculine character, and replace it with a revitalised, yet peaceful, Japanese way of life under American tutelage. As Yoshihara explains, Benedict 'emasculates and feminizes Japan ... by suggesting that Japan's masculinist ideology will surrender in the face of the Western spirit of freedom, democracy and independence'.[10]

It was in the same manner that Benedict's lesser-known study of *Thai Culture and Behaviour* constructed a narrative about the 'Thai' that was conducive to the re-integration of the country into an American-centred world order. While not published as a book, the document was written specifically 'for those who will deal with them after the war', and was to become instrumental in establishing ideas about Thai society and culture among American military officials and academics alike.[11] It was also to form the basis for the many readings into Thai culture that emanated out of area studies departments over the following years. In particular, scholars who formed the Southeast Asia program at Cornell University during the 1950s continued to place a great value upon this initial work, often regarding it as the formative study upon which their extensive investigation of Thai culture rested. As one such scholar, Herbert

86 *Rethinking Thainess in post-war Bangkok*

Phillips, later clarified, Benedict's essay was 'a clear landmark in Thai studies', being 'the first serious attempt to penetrate aspects of Siamese character'.[12]

Unlike its sister study about Japan, *Thai Culture and Behaviour* did not seek to explain the Thai declaration of war against America in cultural terms, but rather as a consequence both of elite contact with European culture and of a misguided modernisation project which had nothing to do with the 'genuine' culture of the people. Instead of reporting Thailand's recent past as the primary tool for understanding how Thai notions of citizenship had emerged, it presented an alternative vision of the Thai based upon an analysis of 'the whole culture', including its 'sociological as well as its psychological aspects', and rooted in a 'centuries-long continuity unknown in Western cultures'. Developments within 'officialdom' or 'the upper classes' were deemed of only peripheral importance, and the 1932 revolution was noticeable only because of the very little interest shown in it by the majority of the population. Benedict did concede that some changes, which had for the present generation 'been enacted by legislation', meant that many of the customs outlined were 'no longer general'. Yet she felt that the conditioning of youth and the influence of the past meant that the existing practices must be given precedence. Importantly, the only reference to the war was that the alliance with Japan was the inevitable consequence of a nationalist movement that had been led by 'university and foreign-trained Thai'.[13]

By removing from the cultural equation urban society, the political classes and the recent past, and by reducing the alliance with Japan to the responsibility of a marginal and largely foreign-trained Thai polity, the image of the Thai that Benedict portrayed replicated the imperialist views of European orientalists from which most of her material was drawn. However, by fusing existing notions of Siam as a 'land of smiles' with psychological analysis, the Thai became more than just a carefree population. They were, for Benedict, measurably and scientifically unique when compared with her own. Unlike Western society, which was referenced through its many psychoses and taboos, the Thai were described as living with a 'psychic security' which guaranteed a life of 'cheerfulness, easy conviviality, and non-violence'.[14] They were, for example, untroubled by their sexual identities, a result of an upbringing where little emphasis was placed upon sexual differentiation and where a person's age was more important in governing relationships. As they grew, behaviours such as toilet training were left unenforced, and would be learnt at a child's own pace, and from observing others.[15] Also, 'no attention is paid to the boy baby's play with his genitals, or to any erection', meaning that Thai men were not weighed down by problems with their sexual identity. This childhood, its length and the lack of direction given, meant that for Benedict, Thai society was not governed by complexes of guilt as they were in the West. Rather, the Thai were portrayed as having 'no cultural inventions of self-castigation'.[16] Without an authoritarian family in the Western sense, without disciplining parents, Thais, according to Benedict, therefore grew up to accept a reverence for hierarchy, developing a 'remarkable permissiveness' that fundamentally shaped their adult identities.[17]

Distinguishing the Thai as secure in an identity that gained its sustenance from village life, and from a lack of contact with Western sexual taboos, Benedict's depiction of the population supported the view that the Thai people were peaceful by nature. In doing so, she cast the declaration of war against America as something that was not in accordance with Thai behaviour. Instead, she presented it as a purely political decision that had little to do with the true cultural identity of the people, whom the government were presumed not to represent. When Bangkok fell to Allied forces, it was a perspective that was often repeated, and went a long way to securing the American argument that Thailand should be rapidly re-integrated into the international community. Bruce E. Reynolds has explained how Britain, as head of Southeast Asia Command, wanted to punish the Thai, seeking to reduce economic and military independence and impose conditions that would 'facilitate the reestablishment of the British position in Southeast Asia'.[18] American policy, on the other hand, was to secure a 'free, independent Thailand, with sovereignty unimpaired and ruled by a government of its own choosing'. This, it was hoped, would ensure a partnership between the Thai political classes befriended by the USA during the war and an American state that had been largely responsible for defeating the Japanese.[19]

Culture, politics and 'American friends' in post-war Bangkok

The sense of urgency that had brought down the Phibun government, and the late decision by leading political figures in the wartime administration to abandon their Japanese allies, had left a complex legacy. In 1944, when the civilian faction of Pridi Banomyong had manoeuvred to remove Phibun from power, Pridi had recognised that royalist groups exiled in England, imprisoned, or simply marginalised from the political system following the 1932 revolution, could provide him with powerful support. As a result, he had invited them back, promising that they would be allowed to participate fully in the post-war government. He had also invited Seni Pramoj, a figure with royal lineage who had been Ambassador to the USA upon the declaration of war, to become the country's first post-war Prime Minister. Having refused to deliver the declaration of war, Seni had instead worked with the State Department to establish a resistance to the Thai government and its alliance with Japan. Labelled the *Seri Thai* [Free Thai], this group was supported by the US government through the Office of Strategic Services (OSS), which worked closely with Seni to topple the wartime administration in Bangkok. In a government that remained dominated by revolutionaries from 1932, yet which sought to avoid punitive measures from the wartime enemy, Seni's appointment was a clear recognition of the importance placed on winning international friends in the aftermath of the conflict.

From early on it became clear, therefore, that Thailand's most valuable international friends were from the United States. With Britain's post-war focus fixed primarily on re-occupying European colonies in the rest of Southeast

88 *Rethinking Thainess in post-war Bangkok*

Asia, British representatives in Bangkok spent the final months of 1945 working toward securing a settlement that would reprimand Thailand for its declaration of war. However, with the Thai government already forced to pay for the British presence, and made responsible for re-building British-owned buildings damaged during the war, the prospect of further reparations had by the end of the year created a significant amount of ill feeling amongst certain sections of Bangkok society. At the same time, reassurances from Americans that the US government sought to spare Thailand bolstered confidence amongst the Thai leadership that Thailand could avoid the harshest of punishments. Throughout the period, British officials in Bangkok frequently informed London of how Americans on the ground, working through informal channels, were undermining British efforts to secure a settlement. In particular, they pointed to the way the Thai leadership was successfully playing off the two countries against each other, and showed particular disdain for the 'Americanophile' Prime Minister Seni Pramoj, who they believed was working with the Americans to challenge British authority.

While the concerns were in many respects as much to do with British anxiety as Thai political savvy, it is nevertheless clear that in the immediate aftermath of the war, American servicemen based in Bangkok became closely connected to a Thai establishment dominated by figures associated with the *Seri Thai*. It is also clear that, generally speaking, the two groups shared a relatively specific view about the Thai people and the wartime government. In particular, there was little sympathy for the ideals of the 1932 revolution, and certainly for the universal view of the Thai people promoted by the Phibun government from 1938. Rather, the ex-Prime Minister was viewed as a figure of ridicule, and events in Bangkok over the past decade were cast as irrelevant to the majority of the population.[20] At the same time, the views of both groups tended to complement the account of Thailand put forward by Ruth Benedict, in that they would generally distance the Thai people from the government's declaration of war. They would also tend to emphasise the view that the Thai people were governed by traditional and conservative values, rather than ideas of universal progress.

Incidental reporting of discussions between early American residents and their Thai 'friends' thus expressed considerable commonality over how to understand the country and its people. Underpinned by the political realities governing these exchanges, in which both understood the importance of the other to their joint political future, the congeniality was often used to narrate experiences of revealed insight about the Thai nation. In one such example from 1946, Chavala Sukumalanandana, who had been a student in the USA and was now pursuing a career in journalism, explained to ex-OSS officer and founding editor of the *Bangkok Post*, Alexander MacDonald, how he saw the country. Recounting a trip to Ayutthaya, MacDonald explained how Chavala described Thailand as 'a land of eighteen million, and seventeen million are these happy, simple folk of the soil'.[21] Recounting the 'short trip away from Bangkok', Alexander MacDonald went on to explain how his guide helped

Rethinking Thainess in post-war Bangkok 89

him to question more fully how much the 'city people', 'the politicians, the officers, and the merchants – worry about the people out on the farms?'.[22] Portraying both himself and his guide as individuals outside the current political establishment, but as people who were clearly interested in the welfare of the majority population, the trip was illustrative of the tone through which many of these post-war exchanges took place.

At the same time, media that sought to service elite society, such as the English-language newspaper *Democracy*, would often present an image of the nation that castigated the previous decade's claim to universality, emphasising Thai peculiarities and reinforcing the idea of the 'West'. The column, 'Random Jottings', regularly lamented the failures of the wartime culture and spoke of the need for renewal. On 21 December 1946 a column on 'customs, ceremonies and national costumes' argued that 'the wanton discarding of these aspects of national life in this country is a sad mistake and is gradually tending to dissolve that national unity that is so essential'. These customs and ways of dressing, the writer went on to explain, were 'gradually evolved and adapted to suit our peculiar needs', and that 'by casting them off we have cut one of our sheet anchors'. Importantly, the column spoke about the 'danger in blindly imitating others', claiming that while 'the West has much to teach us', it 'does not mean that we must ape Western culture in all its aspects'.[23] In an earlier column on a similar topic, the writer claimed that 'one of our brightest hopes for the future lies in a closer study of the past'.

> Every country has, or at least ought to have, a character of its own. In the East where civilisation flourished for many centuries and where spiritual values were at a premium, each country developed along its own lines. Gradually and not without mistakes it evolved a culture which was peculiar to it, and which suited the temperament of its people. Customs and habits were formed which had their origin in the mystic past, but which were found necessary and were faithfully followed by generation after generation.[24]

Once again, the message was that the recent past had seen much of what was 'good' about the Thai nation dismissed for the sake of progress, which was seen as coming almost exclusively from the West. Instead, the view of the writer was that the Thai needed to find a way to resurrect those elements of its past that had helped develop a strong and unified culture, in order to secure a more stable future. Written almost exclusively for an elite Thai audience and their Western friends, this vision clearly illustrated the sense of rejection many such individuals felt toward the notions of citizenship put forward following the 1932 revolution. It also represented the views of those royalists who had returned to the political scene and who now sought to re-establish their authority. In the coming years, the return of these groups to positions of power would have a significant impact on official approaches to culture and cultural policy. Following a decade where cultural production had been focused on destabilising notions of hierarchy inherited from the system of

90 *Rethinking Thainess in post-war Bangkok*

absolute monarchy, the emphasis now shifted to the resurrection and maintenance of historical cultural practices. In relation to music, for example, the wartime production of rousing nationalist songs and accompaniments gave way to the promotion of more 'classical' forms associated with an historical Thai past. In terms of theatre, new productions that had sought to historicise the past and foster a collective sense of nationalism up to the end of the war were replaced with a return to the purist, traditional forms of performance that had been popular prior to the 1932 revolution.

Writing in 1946, the Director of the Fine Arts Department, Phya Anuman Rajadhon, explained that the thinking behind the new cultural policy was to recognise the need to 'separate arts that are from the present, with arts that are of the nation (traditional art)'. 'Present arts', he explained, should not be dismissed, because they were concerned with developing the conditions of the nation and could not be changed. 'The way we dress, or the things we eat', for example, had permanently altered people's lives. But at the same time, he continued, 'while we might not be able to return to the past, we must nevertheless make sure we don't discard our character and remain the Thai nation'.[25] The focus therefore should not be on a full rejection of imports from outside, but upon preserving and in some cases restoring cultural practices that had become subsumed by the previous decades' clamour for progress. At the same time, however, it was made clear that protecting the country's cultural heritage would be an important way of restoring the country's international reputation.

As Patarawdee Puchadapirom has explained, cultural policy in the period following the Second World War was governed by the return of royalists to the Thai political arena combined with the re-integration of Thailand into the international community.[26] Set up in the aftermath of the war, the United Nations Educational, Scientific and Cultural Organisation (UNESCO) soon became the primary global body concerned with recognising important markers of national culture. For the post-war Thai government, early participation was viewed as vital if the country was not to 'fall behind' the rest of the world. As a result, work started almost immediately to catalogue the country's cultural heritage, with considerable effort spent on recognising what was appropriate for international recognition. While the emphasis remained focused on elite forms of culture, there was also an interest in ensuring that the art presented was recognisable to an international audience as 'high art' or 'classical'. This required considerable thought, not only to investigate and decide upon what was an appropriate form of art to present to the outside, but also to compile considered and well informed explanations to foreigners about why those forms should be considered of cultural importance. Increasingly concerned with ideas of 'national heritage', UNESCO thus provided an important means through which to embed the new emphasis on resurrecting cultural forms from the past.[27]

In Bangkok, however, private American individuals tended to maintain a looser attitude toward what constituted Thai culture, relying more on assumptions learnt during the Second World War, and on dialogue between themselves and Thai colleagues. They also tended to view the need to understand the

Thai people with a parallel desire to present America as a 'friend' in this new era. In the years that followed 1945, as the US military presence in the country wound down, ex-OSS officers came to lay the foundations of American society in the city, establishing themselves as the principal expatriate community. While some continued to work for the American state, most relied on an informal network that connected them to a diverse group of policy makers and cultural producers back at home, as well as to influential members of Thai society in the city.[28] Fuelled by the same idealism that governed US engagement with the world more generally, most of these projects explicitly sought to re-integrate Thailand into the international community; orienting the Thai public not only politically and economically, but also culturally and psychologically, to a world in which the USA was undeniably the principal power.

The setting up of the *Bangkok Post* in July 1946, a publication that would for much of the early Cold War remain the only English-language daily newspaper in the country, marked an early victory for this American presence.[29] Having outbid the British Information Service for use of the country's only rotary press, the newspaper maintained a strong pro-US line, keeping readers up to date with international news that maintained a distinctly American flavour.[30] It would also include updates on the activities of other ex-OSS officers who had made the city their home. People such as Jim Thompson, who was struggling to get his silk production off the ground, or Teg Grondahl, who had become country director of the United States Information Service (USIS). When Teg left in March 1949, the *Bangkok Post* lamented the loss, noting his skill in informing hundreds of Thais 'something about America', 'demonstrating to them by word, music and film, how people can live and work together while sharing a nation's bounty'.[31] At the same time, the *Bangkok Post* provided an avenue for the dissemination of American media itself, becoming the sole distributor of both *Time* and *Life* magazines in the city.[32]

Yet, while this physical presence was consolidated in the coming years, the initial success of the American community in integrating into Bangkok society was tempered by political and economic developments. While the initial partnership between Pridi and the royalists had opened up new avenues for political participation, it had also led to a period of unprecedented instability. Factionalism was rife, and alliances were regularly made and broken. Moreover, at the end of the war those who had opposed Phibun and joined the Free Thai movement had access to a vast supply of weapons, provided by the Allied forces to defeat the Japanese. Emboldened by this, the new government took a position directly opposed to the army, redrawing the constitution in order to ban those with military positions from occupying political office. They also sought to humiliate those military leaders who had joined the Japanese alliance, openly accusing ex-prime minister Phibun Songkhram of being a war criminal, and charging the army with having 'lost the war'.[33] In a world with nuclear bombs, such political groups even questioned whether or not the country needed an army at all.

92 *Rethinking Thainess in post-war Bangkok*

To counter the smear campaign, Phibun and his political allies mounted their own attack. In June 1946, King Rama VIII had been found dead in his bedroom with a gunshot wound to the head, and over the next year and a half, insinuations that Pridi and the Free Thai were Communists and had committed regicide were used to fuel distrust of the post-war government. Deals were struck with the more conservative royalists, and on 8 November 1947 a coup was launched that received widespread backing from a Bangkok public who had become frustrated with the *Seri Thai*-dominated administration. After a short period when Khuang Aphaiwong, the civilian head of the new *Prachathipat party* [The Democrats], led the government, there was a second coup on 6 April 1948. This time Phibun, who in November had been welcomed back to Parliament on a wave of popular support, was restored to the position of Prime Minister.

It was a change that was to significantly reduce the influence of Americans in the city. Following the coup, Pridi fled the country with help from the American and British ambassadors, and many OSS officers, including Jim Thompson, helped other close friends escape.[34] Bitterly opposed to Phibun's return to power, they pleaded with Washington not to acknowledge the new regime. Viewing it as a step away from democratic government, they also recognised that their support of Pridi could place their own position in the city at risk. As Joshua Kurlantzick has explained, 'Jim Thompson and his allies, like the Ambassador in Bangkok, Edward Stanton, fought Phibul with the desperation of men who knew that if they lost, they might have no future in the country.'[35] In the aftermath of the affair, Thompson found that he was under almost constant surveillance, worried about even stopping at a friend's house 'for fear of casting suspicion on them, too'.

Yet, unlike his American neighbours, Phibun had understood the changing dynamics of Cold War politics well. Recognising Truman's speech to Congress on 'Block Communism' in March 1947 as a crucial turning point in post-war international politics, the former Prime Minister was careful to frame his return in the context of the Cold War, calling for stricter anti-communist laws in the country. When Phibun came to power, therefore, American fears that he was both a war criminal and a fascist quickly diminished, replaced by recognition of his credentials as a staunch anti-communist. Toward the end of the decade, as American policy makers increasingly saw Asia as a front line in the fight against Soviet power, and following the success of the communist Party in China, Phibun became fully accepted as both an ally and a friend.[36] For those who remained in Bangkok, accepting the new administration became a prerequisite to maintaining good relations with Washington, and for some was to create a permanent schism.

While in many respects, therefore, Phibun's return to power represented a small victory for the American position globally, the impact was also to fuel tension in Bangkok. In terms of cultural policy, Phibun did not seek to reverse the shift in official emphasis dramatically. Despite returning to the position of Prime Minister for a second time, his position now was far weaker than in

1938, and as a result he was forced to accommodate the return of royalist power and ideology. He therefore allowed for the continued resurgence of elite Thai culture, providing impetus and funding for the promotion of classical Thai music and theatre, and expanding the professionalisation of handicraft and artisan activities. In line with the global move toward promoting heritage through global bodies such as UNESCO, such activities continued to be presented as evidence that Thailand had a strong and civilised national culture that deserved respect from the international community.

Yet, in more subtle ways, Phibun's return to power presented a clear challenge both to the royalist position in the country and for the cultural integration of Thailand into an American-centred view of the world. While Phibun accepted the return of elite cultural practices as markers of Thai national culture, he nevertheless remained committed to a constitutional arrangement that limited royal power politically. His promotion of the arts, therefore, was as much about claiming state ownership over such royal symbolism as it was about promoting a royalist revival. Moreover, in relation to the international community, Phibun remained keen to ensure that it was the Thai state that remained in control of determining the country's image on the world stage. Public relations campaigns focused on foreigners therefore continued to project Thailand as a modern nation state populated by citizens who appreciated their status within the political system. While certain cultural forms from the past were now embraced once again, the focus continued to be upon historicising and memorialising the period before the 1932 revolution.

Kukrit Pramoj and the 'democratisation' of Thainess

While support for the 1947 coup illustrated a distrust of the post-war government, the coup was not to end the sense of disillusionment with the political establishment. A new constitution, passed in 1946, had appeared to usher in a period of greater democratisation, opening up electoral politics to members of the royal family and barring permanent government officials from holding political office. Yet in truth, the very opposite seemed to be the case. Liberal commentators, who had held high hopes for the new administration, complained bitterly about a system through which members of the powerful Senate were elected by the House of Representatives, meaning that its members included no opposition figures, and lacked in ability. Fuelled by a growing frustration with a government that seemed both ineffective and unrepresentative, it was charged that the democratic experience in Thailand had been a failure, an argument that legitimised the royalist/military-backed coup in late 1947. When the new government took office, only to be headed by an unconvincing civilian government and then replaced by Phibun himself in 1948, the sense that the Thai state was an only obtuse arena for elite power struggles intensified.[37]

Throughout the early 1950s, as the Phibun government consolidated power and further centralised state authority, such concerns about the overall future

94 *Rethinking Thainess in post-war Bangkok*

of the country remained. With the government committed to reducing the influence of potential political rivals, those who might have otherwise sought a greater role in the state instead began to establish themselves as public intellectuals. Operating as private citizens in a public arena, cultural themes were increasingly used to offer such figures access to narratives that, while avoiding settling on a particular ideological system, were nevertheless able to recognise the readers' search for an alternative vision of nation. In this climate of widespread disillusionment with what Kasian Tejapira has described as 'the staleness and waning appeal of hitherto underachieving political systems in post-war Thailand', Kukrit Pramoj, younger brother of the ex-Prime Minister and a key supporter of a royalist revival in the country, was to become an increasingly important figure.[38]

Unlike his brother, Kukrit Pramoj had not been in the USA during the war. Having completed a degree at Oxford, where he graduated in modern greats (philosophy, politics and economics), he returned to Thailand just after the 1932 revolution. He spent his early career working in the government bureaucracy, in the Revenue Department of the Ministry of Finance, before moving to the Siam Commercial Bank. Under Phibun Songkhram, he served as a corporal in the campaign in French Indochina, and during the remainder of the Second World War, worked at the Bank of Thailand as a special officer in charge of the Governor's office. When his brother returned to the country as Prime Minister, Kukrit also went into politics, elected as a Member of Parliament on 6 January 1946. Significantly, he did so as a member of a new political party, which he himself established, the first since the People's Party.[39]

In April of the same year, his brother, along with former Prime Minister Kuang Aphaiwong, joined with Kukrit's Progress Party to create the Democrats. As a key member of the party that supported the 1947 coup, Kukrit was elected in early 1948, only to be forced out of the government nine months later. Now in opposition, his political career soon came to an abrupt end over a disagreement about a proposed increase in MPs' salaries to 1000 baht a month. Kukrit opposed the idea, claiming that it was not appropriate in light of the continued economic difficulties facing the country, and resigned on 1 January 1949.[40] The affair was to prove valuable to Kukrit, who in the following years would emerge as the single most important public intellectual of the post-war era. Establishing him as a man of high moral standing, the affair also drew on an increasingly well versed view about politicians and their actual interest in the welfare of the people. Charges of hypocrisy and of self-interest were widely disseminated in the post-war period, by all sides of the press, and would sustain much of the political debate in the following decade. By taking up a teaching post at Chulalongkorn University in 1948, and by ordaining as a monk for 50 days in 1950, Kukrit further distanced himself from the political world, establishing a public identity as a teacher, or guru, who could speak with authority about the issues he felt were most pressing to understand the demand of modern Thai life.

Rethinking Thainess in post-war Bangkok   95

When Kukrit established a newspaper on 25 June 1950, it was from the very beginning used to promote his own persona as a charming, charismatic and moral figure. The *Sayam Rat* adopted a markedly different style from the majority of newspapers of the time, tending to refrain from the more sensationalist headlines and instead claiming to offer a more intellectually informed analysis of the current state of the country.[41] As a figure with a British education and with royal lineage, and who in Thailand had been a teacher, an economist, a monk and a politician, Kukrit was to adopt the position not merely of an editor, but of a political and social sage. By emphasising his knowledge of international relations and of the political movements occurring around the world, he also presented himself as someone who could explain the changing world to his largely urban readers.

Central to Kukrit's public persona was a daily conversation with his readers in which the most pressing problems facing Thai citizens were discussed. Located under a section entitled *Panha pracham wan* [Problems of Everyday Life], these would be addressed to Kukrit himself, who would respond to the questions. He would, however, make clear attempts not to be too dogmatic in his answers, leaving space for his readers to themselves contemplate the problems and their possible solutions. Placed in this public forum, he explained that 'the value of the 'Problems of everyday life' is with the problem itself, not with the answer'.

> Problems printed come from all over Thailand, from people of a different class and employment, from children to adults .... These problems are therefore a collection of opinions, suspicions, and desires of all Thai people, which we put into the newspaper because it is important knowledge. By reading the problems of others, at the time that they are having them is useful, because it allows us to know what it is that interests all Thai people; of what kind of things they are suspicious or fearful about. Those who read the *Problems of Everyday Life* therefore participate in a movement of opinion, of people who are friends; brought together permanently by fate and by the nation.[42]

The letters were therefore established as representative of a diverse set of ideas which, when brought together, might be considered to be a general presentation of the nation as a whole at a particular point in time. They were also established on a developmental trajectory, the idea being that as Thais better understood each other, and as the political and economic status of the country became clearer, the problem pages would contribute to a better conception of the nation.

This meant that while the discussion was, in the early years at least, presented as non-partisan, 'Problems of Everyday Life' did present a clear impression of the country, namely that the ideological basis through which life had previously been understood was now undefined and needed to be re-clarified. Letters would invariably revolve around a discussion about a

96 *Rethinking Thainess in post-war Bangkok*

society in disarray, still struggling to understand the real meaning of the Second World War and not yet able to comprehend the world that had emerged from it. They were also deeply concerned in understanding the ideological and political movements shaping the lives of nations and peoples throughout the world, and clearly identified readers as a community in search of answers. Short questions, such as 'what is the difference between culture and civilisation?', or 'how is Thailand being governed right now?', sought clarification in a new era.[43] They also indicated a presumption that the means by which they had previously been explained could no longer be correct. While there is no reason to question the authenticity of the letters published, editorial selection, combined with the clear requirement that readers respond to the central question posed by the paper, meant that from the beginning the column was distinctive in both character and style.

Specific questions revolved around a number of themes that continued to deal with Thailand's changing fortunes. Still seeing the world as a community of competing nations, Asian independence was regularly referred to as problematic in situating the Thai nation within an international context. Confusion over the speed of Asian decolonisation, and the apparent ability of those new states to function independently of the 'Great Nations' on which they had depended for so long, was heightened by the fact that at the same time Thailand was struggling. In one letter, published on 5 October 1950, the reader sought an explanation as to why the Thai economy was failing to recover, and more importantly, why other, newly independent countries were not struck by the inflationary pressures of the baht.[44] It questioned why countries that had only just become independent, such as India and Burma, could begin printing their own money without serious problems, whereas in Thailand the value of printed money was decreasing rapidly; 'items such as cloth, oil, gas, firewood, and agricultural equipment, are all getting more expensive', the reader explained, suggesting that having a longer history as an independent country was actually putting Thailand at a disadvantage.[45] In another letter, this time looking at the political impact of decolonisation, and signed by 'a person who wants to know', the writer questioned why 'countries which received their independence after us', nevertheless 'have good clear policies that are clearly their own', while Phibun, 'who always makes quick decisions', is 'sometimes in my opinion wrong'.[46]

In a particularly long letter concerning when Thailand should hold its national holiday, the reader felt that the country's unique position in Asia, having not been colonised, meant that its existing national holiday lacked a clear declaration about the nation's identity.[47] The current day was inappropriate because it marked the 1932 revolution, and therefore held meaning only for those who had participated in that event. He also felt that choosing the right day was made even more difficult due to the fact that in recent years the Philippines, Indonesia, Laos, Burma, India, Pakistan and Sri Lanka had all received their independence, and celebrated that moment as their national holiday. He therefore felt that in Asia, this was being increasingly recognised as the day upon which the nation came into full existence, and although it was hard to understand, it required the Thai to become better informed as to why they did not celebrate such a day. In relaying his experience at an Independence Day event held at a foreign embassy in Bangkok, he recalled how a foreigner had asked him when Thailand celebrates its independence. Unable to answer, another foreigner had helped him, explaining that Thailand had 'been independent for a very long time', freed from the Burmese by King Naresuan in the sixteenth century. Shocked at the superior knowledge of a foreigner, the reader felt that Thai people should be taught more about their own history and their own identity. He also, however, felt that while the day of freedom from the Burmese, 3 May, should be recognised as a national holiday, it was nevertheless hard to understand the attraction of celebrating a moment that drew attention to the fact that the nation was once 'enslaved' by another, as he concluded:

> The Thai people should take on the responsibility of explaining to visitors from foreign countries how we ourselves gained independence, so that they know it was a long time before the others. That is why we should develop this day as a special day of the nation. But, if the Thai choose it as the important day of the nation, the Burmese will be very satisfied and feel very proud.[48]

Other letters indicated a growing interest in America, which in the beginning at least displayed a rather simplistic attitude to the country. Most referred to an American standard, in terms of political and economic freedom and social unity, with which the Thai were struggling to compete. The gulf, for example, that existed between the support Americans gave their politicians compared with the Thai, as noted in a letter published on 18 October 1950: why is it that American citizens never seem to damn their politicians with any real severity?[49] It was, he felt, a feature of American politics that seemed to be 'the complete opposite of Thai politicians, who receive nothing but abuse from the public'.[50] In another example, a reader relayed a conversation that he had had with an American scholar, who had told him that Thailand was not yet a free country because the constitution did not guarantee religious freedoms.[51] Kukrit put him right, explaining that this American was both wrong and ill mannered. There was also anxiety that the world was once again heading toward war and that Thailand was again being drawn into a potentially dangerous alliance. Published on 9 September 1950, the writer wondered whether, 'if there was to be a Third World War, would Thailand have to save itself again like it did before?'.[52]

Early in the newspaper's life, the impact of such interactions with America, when placed alongside other letters, reinforced the notion of a society in turmoil, and failing in the face of increased international competition. At the heart of these anxieties, however, remained the continued struggle to maintain a life of consumption, and a strong commitment to the discourse of civilisation and developmental time that had been a defining feature of Thai

98   *Rethinking Thainess in post-war Bangkok*

nationalism since the 1932 revolution. As a result, Thailand was seen as a society in stagnation at a time when others were presenting new and confident faces to the world, and where America was experiencing unprecedented prosperity. As one reader exclaimed to Kukrit in April 1951, 'Do you believe, that the Thai are standing and dying because we have to use expensive stuff?'. 'Bad quality', 'fake' and 'low grade products', he explained, were being sold at inflated prices, meaning that 'those who make fake stuff are getting rich, while we are stuck in the same place ... dying because of money'.[53] 'Why is it', other readers exclaimed, 'that the economy is in free-fall, unlike other nations of the world ... are we developing or going backwards compared to other countries of the world?'[54], 'what will the future hold?' and 'what is ideology anyway?'.[55]

Such existential interest in what entailed ideology heightened over the following years, as readers gained a greater understanding of the Cold War and of their role within it. Following the outbreak of the Korean War, American interest in Thailand intensified. From an initial aid package in 1950 of $10 million, the shift of interest to Asia meant that policy makers in Washington placed greater emphasis on maintaining a strong relationship with the Thai state, its military and its police force. Over the coming years, aid was to rocket, in 1953 amounting to $53 million and making the Thai state increasingly a client of American power, supporting clandestine operations into northern Burma and allowing American officials to embed themselves in the Thai political system.[56] While the full scale of this involvement might have been kept from the Thai public, it is clear that many felt uneasy about the increased American presence, sensing subservience rather than partnership. Published in 1952, one letter wanted clarification, noting that considering 'our country is receiving such an enormous amount of help from America, what do we have to provide in return?'.[57]

The Korean War also saw Thai troops return to military action, this time on the side of the United Nations. While some readers questioned the move, wondering what Thailand gained, others for the first time began to seriously question the ideological basis for the Cold War.[58] One such letter, signed by a reader from Thonburi, who 'likes to know, and likes to see', asked 'what kind of ideology is Communism?', complaining that at the moment, 'we are fighting the communists, and the people are getting angry and scared of Communism, but it is like children afraid of ghosts without knowing what they are or what they look like'. This, the reader felt, was odd and lacked rational insight, for as he continued, 'if Communism is so bad, and is something to fear, or is such a despicable ideology, why is it that all of Russia, China, North Korea and so many other countries and so many millions of people support Communism?'[59] Kukrit, who on the subject of Communism at least was clear, explained to the reader that the ideology was far from a popular movement of the people, and instead was a despotic system of government that banned freedom of speech and religion. Despite Kukrit's rare display of an explicit ideological position, such letters continued to support the view that 'Problems of Everyday Life'

Rethinking Thainess in post-war Bangkok 99

represented a broad range of opinion, and therefore that regular readers would be able to form an independent set of ideas about the future of the country through a regular reading of the contributions.

'Problems of Everyday Life', in a climate in which political participation was highly restricted, thus appeared to offer a broadly democratic conversation. Fuelled by the moral stance of Kukrit, who would often seek to distance himself from political life in his responses, the impression was that not only were people disillusioned about the current generation of political leaders, but that politics itself was riddled by dishonesty and a lack of interest in the welfare of the people. In particular, it was widely assumed that the revolutionary group of 1932 continued to dominate politics, but that they did so to benefit themselves rather than the nation. One such letter, signed off by a reader called 'South Star' and published on 8 November 1950, questioned whether the revolution had brought true democracy to the people, and if so, what kind of democracy?[60] He sought clarification as to whether it was the kind of democracy where 'politicians take a monthly wage, while local government is unable to afford tables and chairs for children to be able to study', and he wanted to know if this was 'English style democracy, American democracy, or unique Thai democracy'. Scathing in his attack on the political classes, he went on to ask how important religion was, and whether or not 'if we don't respect religion, it will have a negative consequence for the nation?'. He asked about those politicians who served in government for whom corruption was their principal interest, whether they 'respected religion or not', and if they did then 'what kind of religion?' Kukrit's response was to say that they worshipped money, 'money is their god, and their religion'.[61] These two critiques, first that the political system remained immature and inauthentic when compared with the Western democracies, and second, that the political classes had failed to adhere to even the most basic characteristics of Thai citizenship, were common threads.

By the time the Korean War had come to an end, such assertions continued to resonate. After years of discussion about Thailand's changing status in the world, the letters published continued to display a frustration with the state and an ongoing confusion about what a 'good' political ideology would look like. In his responses, Kukrit had only served to fuel this debate, displaying an inconsistency in his political views which meant that for one reader who had spent 'many years watching' him, it was impossible to know where he stood ideologically: 'you sometimes seem like a conservative, sometimes a socialist, and sometimes a liberal'.[62] Yet Kukrit's elusive political identity served the objective of the problem pages well, allowing him to participate more freely in a debate that sought to understand what it meant to be Thai in an era of anxiety and confusion. As Saichon Satyanurak has identified, Kukrit's interest was in a broad investigation of 'Thainess' as an identity that might emerge out of the need to solve the various problems facing Thai identity.[63]

What this meant, however, was that the 'open' conversation tended to look for solutions in conceptual spaces outside contemporary experience, be it in

100 *Rethinking Thainess in post-war Bangkok*

nostalgia for the past prior to the 1932 revolution, or in the idea that being Thai was not a political identity at all, but a simple feeling that all Thais were presumed to share. Echoing strongly the words of Margaret Mead in *Vogue* during the war about what it meant to be an American, and in line with Ruth Benedict's treatise on Thai culture, Kukrit argued in December 1953 that for him, being Thai meant something quite simple: 'I have been born as a type of human being that we call Thai, I live a life that is close to other Thais for my entire life, and this closeness allows me to have a knowledge and understanding about who I am.' Not governed by biology, and certainly not dependent upon a relationship with the state, Thainess was for Kukrit something which came about through the fate of birth and the environment, social or physical, within which a person grew up. Two months later, one reader asked Kukrit to elaborate, asking whether or not he would 'like the ideology of nationalism once again to return to Thailand?'. Kukrit's response was long and emphatic.

> If that nationalism means that we see our nation as the best in the world, that there isn't anyone as good as us, and that we have the right to stand on the heads of others. If that nationalism means that we have to love the nation so it consumes our eyes and our ears or if someone can say, 'this is for the nation', and we have to let them do it without seeing any reason because if we protest or disagree, we will be told we don't love the nation. Or if Nationalism translates as having to let one person or one clique reign over us for ever, because they were the ones to start the ideology, and the nation has to be theirs, and we have to do as they order, and not do those things that they prohibit. And if that nation means that we have to go crazy upon hearing the word nation, so that we don't know what is for real ... I don't want this to return here again.
>
> However, if a nationalist ideology means we love where we live and get our food, sincerely loving the land, and respecting everybody as its owners, never trying to extort each other ... If we love our sense of being Thai, our art, our tradition; always knowing our responsibility to the land upon which we live: Having ideas about how to develop the land so that it is a pleasant place to live and full of peace and fun, while at the same time as protecting it from enemies outside, and from dangers presented by enemies inside. While at the same time knowing our rights and our responsibilities, not allowing for anyone to come and trick us. If nationalist ideology means loving our fellow human beings, joining hands with other nations and other languages, bringing peace and understanding. If this is what a nationalist ideology means, I would like to see this to arrive in Thailand as soon as possible.[64]

Kukrit's vision was therefore of a new type of nationalism, based not upon constructed notions of citizenship, but upon a commonly held spirit, which simply needed to be fully realised. Explicitly against a resurrection of the wartime ideology, this nation sought to present the Thai as a community for whom the nation was an emotional entity. Its enemies were simply those who sought to upset that balance, and international alliance was perfectly acceptable as long as it was not to threaten the intra-personal bonds that brought the nation together. At the same time, Kukrit's nation had nothing to do with the state or with political representation, and it certainly was not determined by economic advance.

Thus, as urban Thais continued to worry about their diminished status on the world stage, and as they searched for a way to return to the aspirational lifestyles that had given such initial impetus to the nation-building project, Kukrit was able to appropriate apparently banal ideas about a traditional Thai way of life as important markers of citizenship. In doing so, he was able to offer a narrative through which problems about political participation and disillusionment with the government were displaced by a search for new forms of cultural representation, alluding to possible alternatives without directly promoting them. Perhaps most important, however, was the way that Kukrit's appeals about the new nation, made directly to his readers, bore a striking similarity to American views as to how the urban citizen should conceive of their Thai identity in the context of the Cold War.

'The fields are full of rice': area studies and the re-thinking of Thainess

Released in 1953, by Time incorporated, the documentary *Oasis on a Troubled Continent* had also presented an idealistic picture of the Thai nation that fundamentally rejected political and economic markers of national citizenship. Uninterested in the complex concerns that had struck Thai society in the aftermath of the war, the American documentary made no mention of the Thai declaration of war on the United States, or of the nation-building projects that had unravelled in the years following the country's re-integration into the international community during the early Cold War. Rather, the country portrayed was one in which a centuries-long way of life remained intact, and where the population lived in peace and harmony.[65]

To illustrate this, the documentary took the viewer on a trip. Following an American tourist, the announcer explained that Thailand was different from other nations in Asia because, unlike those deprived areas, the Thai remained well fed due to a bountiful supply of rice, making it an ideal place to visit. Here 'the even tenure of life' went on unabated and remained unaffected by the concerns of populations elsewhere. The American woman who was travelling through Thailand did so without having to engage directly with the problems of the Cold War, but instead came to view a country that America had befriended, and which she wanted to know more about. She began her trip on the banks of a Bangkok canal, from which point she travelled into a world that must have seemed both quaint and exotic to the American audience. Important, however, was that sitting beside her was a young Thai woman, ignored by the commentator but in clear view of the audience.[66]

102   *Rethinking Thainess in post-war Bangkok*

Recognisable from the front pages of Thai magazines for a generation, a young woman dressed in the latest international fashions sat neatly between one world and another, mediating an alien way of life through an internationally intelligible set of stories. Situated in a position as cultural interpreter, she was presented as proud of her nation but at the same time able to form a close friendship with her American friend. While global political developments might have been a topic of conversation, they were not issues that directly affected the people they had both come to observe. Here, strange and exotic fruits, or the way that Thai people conducted their daily lives on a *klong*, demonstrated the life of the nation far more effectively than images of high society parties or fashion shows. Moreover, free from the burden of the country's wartime ideology, the story here was one in which the status of the Thai nation in the international order could be accepted with little anxiety. In one scene in the motion picture, the Thai woman acts as a guide to her glamorous American friend, an informant to a culture that exists all around. Unlike her fellow countryman, who stood behind them, steering the boat and wearing no top, the Thai woman was perfectly manicured and her hair impeccably styled. Communicating with the tourist, no doubt in English, she provided the insights needed to make sense both of exotic fruits, and of an alien but charming people.[67]

As explored in chapter 1, *Oasis on a Troubled Continent* was one of a number of films about Thailand, released in the aftermath of the Korean War, that characterised the Thai as a peaceful and happy people. In doing so, they reflected many of the assertions made by Ruth Benedict in her wartime study, not least that the Thai people were privileged holders to a psychic security that came about due to their simple way of life in an underdeveloped environment. Yet, while such films were made principally for an American audience, they also reflected a very real engagement with Thailand in the decade that followed the end of the war. Toward the end of the 1940s, as much of Asia remained in a state of conflict, Bangkok had emerged as a hub for regional activity. In 1949 the United Nations had made the city its Asian headquarters, and at the same time, an increasing number of US businessmen had established a presence there. Bangkok was buzzing with international representatives, many of them Americans. High-profile international conferences were becoming increasingly regular, and the city's hotels were often fully booked with groups of foreigners who, working with organisations such as UNESCO, the Food and Agriculture Organization (FAO) or the Economic Commission for Asia and the Far East (ECAFE), travelled to Thailand to discuss 'development' in the name of 'peace' and 'security'.[68]

Yet it was the stream of area specialists from US university campuses who arguably had the greatest impact in cultivating new ideas about what it meant to be Thai during the period. After receiving funding from the Rockefeller Foundation, the Cornell Research Center was set up in Bangkok toward the end of the decade, and served as a base from which to study both the country and the region. Studies conducted from the centre were varied, but by far the most significant was the psychological profiling of a rural Thai community

Rethinking Thainess in post-war Bangkok   103

that lived around a temple called Bang Chan, about 30 km from Bangkok. Beginning in 1948, the early architects of the project demarcated a community of around 1,600 people who were to be studied as part of a project to understand the cultural impact of 'facilitating the introduction of agriculture, industrial, medical and other innovations into areas where such technologies were wanted but were deficient by modern standards'.[69] In line with the view that, in the post-war period, the United States had emerged as the most advanced nation on Earth, the study of Bang Chan was thus interested in understanding 'cultural transfer, cultural continuity, and cultural change' within a society that was yet to industrialise.[70]

The Bang Chan project drew heavily from theoretical developments on American campuses which, in the context of the Cold War, sought to 'move beyond racist and ethnocentric definitions of Western progress' and instead view development as an issue of modernisation alone.[71] It was a theoretical paradigm in which the progress of nations was re-drawn so that it might assert modernisation as a 'series of one-way transitions from tradition bound subsistence economies to technology-intensive, industrialised economies; from authoritarian political systems to participant-orientated systems; from religious beliefs to secular, scientifically based values'.[72] Bang Chan, as a community close to the capital, was thus set up as a human laboratory where such processes could be measured, and where conclusions could be made. In turn, it was hoped, the village would act as a model from which to understand not only changes happening in Thailand as a whole, but to a certain extent village communities throughout Southeast Asia. The project's early embrace of modernisation theory, or convergence theory as it was otherwise known, thus located it firmly into an American narrative about the Cold War. By promoting evolutionary as opposed to revolutionary change, the hope was that these theories could be used to oppose Communism.[73] They might also draw the non-aligned world into a US-centred research agenda.

Indeed, while the basis for modernisation theory sought to undermine notions of fundamental difference between peoples, researchers nevertheless arrived in Thailand with highly prescribed ideas about development and national identity. The principal question that such researchers posed was to understand how 'the ramifying influences of the present, most of them stemming ultimately from the Atlantic civilization, affect the future of peasant communities and of the agrarian societies of which they are a neglected part?'.[74] Presuming the primacy of Western modernity and its influence in determining the 'present moment', researchers such as Lauriston Sharp and Lucien Mason Hanks, recognised the villagers as a group of people who existed in an entirely different temporality, where time itself was considered an intrusion from the outside. As a result, scholars who travelled to Thailand would tend to view the country as a unified field of enquiry that presumed distance from the subject people, and however favourable a picture they drew, invariably did so from the perspective of an outsider looking in. Viewing modernity as a historical force which came from a Western centre, they thus looked at the village as a prism

104 *Rethinking Thainess in post-war Bangkok*

through which, if they looked hard enough, they might be able to create a likeness of a true Thai way of life.[75]

Arising from the assumed developmental superiority of the West, and from the idea that cultural change came as a result of interactions with enlightened Western societies, the area studies intervention thus reinforced the idea of distance between what were presumed to be globally informed citizens and the 'native' populations they studied. Significantly, among those who lived in Bangkok during the same period, early converts to the behaviourist agenda were quite open about the fact that their shift in interest resulted from interactions with foreign observers. Phya Anuman Rajadhon was one of the most important figures in promoting the social sciences in Thailand, and was quite clear that his interests had emerged through dialogue with outsiders. As he explained in 1949, 'originally I never thought of collecting old customs, because I had no interest in learning about them' but 'later when I had read books on customs written by foreigners, I came to see from those books that customs are an important feature of a society'.[76] Strongly echoing Ruth Benedict's assertions about the value of such descriptions of Thai society, he saw old customs 'like a mirror reflecting the life and minds of the majority of the people of the nation'. Importantly, he also recognised that for him, knowledge of such customs was hard to come by:

> I feel regretful that when I became interested in learning about old customs of the Thai, not so very long ago, and thought of asking this person or that, in some cases it was already too late, because many of those who had known about these old customs were already dead. Some customs must be investigated in localities where they are understood to still be extant, but I had no opportunity to go there because I was busy with my work.[77]

A son of part-Chinese ancestry, Phya Anuman Rajadhon was already deeply connected to the nation-building projects of the previous decades. An early proponent of the need to develop the manners and etiquette of individual Thais, he had worked closely with both Luang Wichit Watakhan and Phibun Songkhram to establish the national ideology of the late 1930s. He had also worked on the language-simplification projects that had sought to make the project to establish universal citizenship a more manageable prospect. Perhaps more important, however, was how he had become a key proponent of the need to change the attitudes of the Chinese urban minority so that they might feel a greater commitment to the Thai nation. In doing so, he had developed an elaborate theory which asserted that Chinese migrants who had travelled to Thailand came from regions with a Thai heritage, and that showing a respect for Thai culture could therefore help them to understand their essential identity. While never at odds with Phibun over the pro-Thai policies of the wartime government, his focus upon the urban Chinese meant that he had, at the end of the war, developed a specific perspective on matters of culture. In

Rethinking Thainess in post-war Bangkok 105

particular, he had developed a strong commitment to the idea that there was a Thai essence that could be viewed most explicitly in the countryside.[78]

In the post-war period, Phya Anuman Rajadhon therefore became a champion of the idea that developing an understanding of traditional ways of life was vital to those who were interested in learning about an authentic Thai nation. Moreover, his personal orientation as an urban Thai citizen with Chinese ancestry placed distance from the countryside at the heart of his ideas. In line with the analytical position of area specialists, he therefore supported the view that there should be a re-alignment of Thai cultural identity, which had previously been governed by an urban lifestyle, in order to place the lives of rural communities at its centre. Yet, rather than identifying America as the centre of developmental time, he placed 'the city' as the 'centre of progress', a place where life was fundamentally different from the rural areas, which he viewed as committed to a way of life rooted in the past. As he explained, 'whatever country people have done and believed in the past with satisfactory results, they continue to do and believe, not changing readily'.[79] By placing the rural Thai in a different temporality, he thus emphasised the view that the countryside acted as a repository of knowledge about a Thai way of life in which, until now, the urban dweller paid little attention.

With the economic hardships and political humiliations of the post-war period continuing to restrain consumption, his affectionate writings about a Thai way of life became increasingly relevant and popular. At a time when most urban Thais were struggling to sustain their lifestyle, his gentle lamentations at the loss of traditional self-sufficiency were easily juxtaposed to a life in the countryside where 'the fields are full of rice, the water is full of fish'. As he explained, 'We', meaning the urban dweller, 'have only just recently gotten away from making things for our own use and providing our own amusement, and so we do not feel the great value of making things for our own use and providing our own amusement like farmers'. However, while this urban population might not actually want to return to that way of life, it was important that they recognised the spiritual value it offered its adherents, who were 'not adventurous, not progressive, not wealthy and not powerful'.[80]

As his popularity grew among Thai readers, he also became recognised by Americans as a unique individual, making his writings relevant to the ideological logic of the post-war period and to the emergent Cold War. William Gedney was one of the most prolific and influential of the American academic community in Thailand following the war. Initially provided with a scholarship, he had refused to return to America upon its conclusion. He had become a resident expert in Thai language and often helped with translations for Willis Bird, who was working for the CIA. He also became instrumental in fostering relations between Thai intellectuals and the American area studies community. For him, Phya Anuman Rajadhon was an enormously important figure, having done the most 'to introduce and popularize Western learning among the Thai', while at the same time making an unparalleled 'contribution to the study of traditional Thai culture'.

106   *Rethinking Thainess in post-war Bangkok*

What is perhaps most significant, however, is that Phya Anuman Rajadhon failed to recognise the inherently ideological premise of the social sciences during this period. Instead, by emphasising the passing of time as having distanced urban dwellers from the country's cultural heritage, his ideas about what made up Thai culture were seen to transcend existing framings of the nation and unify disparate urban identities. Throughout the 1950s, his latent inferences that gently reprimanded the city for losing its cultural identity were increasingly exploited by groups that, politically, would have disagreed profoundly about the future of the country. For those who supported the rehabilitation of the monarchy, such as Kukrit, nostalgia for the period before 1932 and derision over the wartime commitment to a universalisation of cultural practice emanating from the city were powerful tools in re-imagining a national image with the King at its centre. At the same time, progressive intellectuals, who sought to undermine elitist notions of a subservient majority population, also recognised the value of re-aligning Thai cultural identity with the customs and practices of people who had little knowledge of a cosmopolitan lifestyle. In all cases, it is important to recognise how resident experts from abroad, who took an interest in culture alone, were rarely criticised, but were regarded as allies in establishing the fact that ideas about the nation were up for negotiation. As Prince Dhani, president of the Siam Society, confirmed in 1956, co-operation between the Cornell Research Centre, UNESCO and the Thai people had meant that 'in modern days knowledge too has become democratic and within layman's reach'.[81]

It is certainly true that the lack of any real form of democratic representation had a significant impact on the formation of a radical tradition at the time, and that demand for such a tradition came out of the desire for an 'untainted-because-untried political system'.[82] It is also the case that, because of the fact that Thailand had not been directly colonised, such material was focused on undermining internal power structures, rather than those imposed from the outside. As Craig Reynolds has explained, during the post-war period 'there is no question that certain members of the urban based Thai-intelligentsia, drawing on Soviet and Chinese revolutionary models, sought to inspire a radical and distinctly non-militaristic nationalism for Thailand', which 'with no colonial masters to attack and displace' ... 'was directed at the indigenous power elite, and at Phibun in particular'.[83] What is interesting, however, is the reluctance of even those on the political Left to recognise the power of modernisation theory as a tool to frame Thai identity within a US-centred worldview. Instead, leftist intellectuals would tend to accept the view that American interest in Thai culture was relatively banal.

Illustrative of this was Jit Pumisak, who, while developing a public identity as a radical, during the early 1950s also spent much of his time in the company of William Gedney, translating Communist texts for American Intelligence.[84] A linguist and a historian, Jit Pumisak held a disregard for the elitist version of the Thai past which for him had promoted the idea that it was 'great' leaders who had determined the nation's historical development. For him, Thai history needed to be re-written as a story of all the people. As Sopha Chanamul has explained, Jit's focus was largely on the stories of local people, as well as the ancient art and material culture that had ultimately produced the Thai nation.[85] He also, however, criticised previous histories of the country for their aping of the West, claiming that in the past 'we have looked down at ourselves, and have studied the story of ourselves from the works of the *farang* and the English'.[86] In doing so, Jit contributed directly to the area studies assertion that was at the same time engaged in reinforcing the binary between Western and Asian societies, promoting the idea that the Thai in their recent past had failed to understand themselves, and that they now had to form an autonomous history. In a climate where much of the Bangkok media was shifting toward the Left, these views were to promote a powerful narrative that on one hand supported the sense that Thai society was engaged in a democratic debate about the future, while at the same time rejecting much of the recent past as a suitable place to find answers with which to solve the country's problems.

Re-consuming Thainess

By the middle of the 1950s, a plethora of new publications sought to put forward a new vision of the Thai nation. Editors who were keen to recognise the sense of crisis felt by many of their readers would frequently speak of the need to re-educate society in light of the country's post-war situation.[87] One such magazine was *Khon Muang*, a Chiang Mai-based publication which began in 1954 and was sold exclusively to the northern population. A region that had for generations relied on cultural flows arriving from Bangkok, *Khon Muang* was the first publication in which the primary interest was in telling the story of 'northern' culture. Here, while value continued to be placed upon universal consumption practices, contributors also sought to educate the readers about local cultures and ways of life that apparently remained protected from the world economy. The front covers, while continuing to feature women of the nation, now dressed them in local costumes rather than in the latest fashion (Figure 3.1), and inside, Chiang Mai's reading public were often given tours of local communities.

In an early edition of the magazine, an article entitled 'Made in America' reported on a conversation with someone who worked for an organisation under contract for the United Nations in the country.[88] In it, the writer reported how this member of the expatriate community felt disappointed with the lack of interest Thai people had shown in 'things which were Thai'. Focusing explicitly on a Thai fascination with foreign imports, he lamented that all Thai houses would rely on imported tinned food rather than on fresh produce from the land. Thailand, he explained, was an abundant country which had all it needed, but the current generation, he lamented, 'see no value in things that are Thai' and are interested only in festivals which have been borrowed from foreigners. This, he felt, was because of the country's history,

Figure 3.1 Front cover of *Khon Muang*, July 1954

for while the people might have been comfortable for a long time as their neighbours became colonised by the West, this meant that the Thai 'became less interested in your own tradition'. Now, at diplomatic ceremonies, 'those from India, Burma, Laos, Indonesia, Cambodia, dress in distinctive ways, so you know where they have come from'. In the face of Western colonialism, 'they have worked hard to maintain their own national symbols'. Such articles thus encouraged readers to view themselves as lacking because they had failed to recognise themselves as distinct from the modern nations of the

Rethinking Thainess in post-war Bangkok   109

West, and because they were failing to assert a clear and coherent identity to the international community.

Khon Muang, more than any other title of the time, remained fixated both upon America and upon the culture of local people. Each month, features focused on traditions that were yet to be displaced by modernity, such as the life of men in Lampang who depended on the horse and cart for their living.[89] Uninterested in Bangkok, the magazine presented Chiang Mai as a cultural centre, where traditional costumes, foodstuffs and industries had been maintained regardless of a diminishing interest. As elsewhere, the magazine gently castigated urban Thailand, in one article questioning why during the war, when cotton had been so hard to find, 'we hadn't started wearing locally produced fabrics'. Yet it also celebrated the fact that, in Chiang Mai at least, access to such products meant they now could. In another example, the magazine covered the work of a wood carver who was an expert in making elephants. In doing so, it encouraged a greater interest in such products, which it made clear 'were distinctly Thai' and therefore added a great deal to a discerning home.[90] Importantly, the magazine emphasised that buying such an item not only showed respect for local culture, but also involved participation in a global consumer culture. Accompanied by an image of a young Thai Chiang Mai consumer sitting in an expansive and modern-looking front room, the text explained that 'this is one decoration for your house that you can place in your living room, or in any corner of your house, which help to improve the sophistication of the room', because 'the wood carvers of Chiang Mai, in one year, are able to sell many of these pieces, both to foreigners and other visiting Thais'.[91]

Distancing urban readers from a Thai subject, the articles in *Khon Muang* thus presented Thailand as a set of images and related stories that were both distant from existing conceptions of the nation and, at the same time, deeply relevant to the construction of the country's post-war identity. With the Thai economy now beginning to improve, it encouraged readers to once again become consumer citizens, not in order to compete with the great powers, but in order to join them. Presenting consumption as an activity through which Thais could once again become nationalists, it was now a nationalism that left room for the consumption of American, European or Japanese imports. Moreover, it was also a nationalism that could only prosper through an interaction with academics both from abroad and increasingly from inside the country; *farang* who had travelled in search of what it meant to be Thai. As was reported in a series of images in 1956, when the Siam Society visited Chiang Mai to view the city's cultural life, the northern region, 'Lanna', was a city of culture, where the past had been preserved, and therefore a place that 'visitors' from Bangkok came to understand themselves.[92]

Back in Bangkok, *Phap Khao Sayam Nikon* also attempted to recognise the shift, and in late 1953 engaged in a major process of re-branding. Since the late 1940s, the magazine had explicitly modelled its brand identity on *Life*. Now, however, in the changing cultural environment, the magazine aimed to present the cultural nation as its primary narrative. It redesigned its front cover, replacing the standard red-on-white with an older-looking Thai script. It also ended the practice of featuring pictures of young modern Thai women, but instead sought to display new scenes that were directly relevant to the issues being raised in Thai society. Inside, it featured stories of rural Thais for whom a life harvesting the land or fishing the sea was the way of life upon which the city relied. At the same time, while it often displaced the city as the centre of Thainess, the magazine continued to view it as the heart of civilisation, a place where transnational narratives emanating from America were translated into overt displays of a 'free' and 'independent' nation. Thus, when the newly styled magazine featured a trip to Bang Chan, it came close to replicating the image that had featured in the earlier *March of Time* documentary (Figure 3.2).

Figure 3.2 Front cover, *Phap Khao Sayam Nikon*, December 1953

Rethinking Thainess in post-war Bangkok   111

Now, however, the image reversed the roles, depicting a Thai student travelling away from Bangkok in a boat, this time with the American acting as guide, into what the corresponding article described as the 'enlightened tradition of the countryside'.[93]

Proudly explaining that Bang Chan was only one of four corresponding projects in the world, the story emphasised the very real value foreigners felt Thailand held for them. It also, although perhaps less overtly than *Khon Muang*, alluded to the idea that, for those Thais who took on the role of cultural informant and who gained an ability to explain peculiar cultural practices, they might once again be able to participate in a global culture.

Initial response to the rebranding of *Phap Khao Sayam Nikon* seemed positive. In a letter printed at the front of the January edition 1954, a reader celebrated it as a triumph because the magazine had finally found a distinctive character that differed from the previous attempt to model it on *Life*.[94] He raved that the 'magazine now has a character of its own, a Thai character, it is unique and I plead with you to keep it like this for ever, because if you stopped, I would be terribly upset'. In another letter, published in May the same year, the reader praised the editors, saying that they were now including new colourful photos that 'had a meaning about the real life of the Thai', and the magazine now had the potential to be 'the standard publication of Thailand' (Thailand written in English).[95] Yet other letters indicated dissatisfaction: as another reader claimed, the publication had become 'too civilised', including pictures that held 'too much meaning'.[96] He felt that many of those who bought the magazine continued to want to see images of a lively looking 'cultured woman' on the front, rather than an attempt to say something special. Others asked why pictures of the countryside, rather than the people who lived there, had stopped being printed.[97]

In response, the magazine sought to explain that the reader was wrong. The countryside hadn't disappeared from the magazine, it was there, 'in the last issue, in this issue, and in the issue to come':

> The countryside isn't just coconuts and beaches, it isn't just rocks and waterfalls. It isn't just blue sky and fluffy clouds. The countryside has people in it; people who grow coconuts and fish, who mine the rock and use the waterfalls and who have houses with roofs and fields. The Thai land has life in it, as well as nature both beautiful and ugly which is worthy of interest.[98]

Castigating the reader for what was deemed a misguided view, the magazine thus sought to reconstruct the understanding of what an appropriate representation of the nation should be. In doing so, it asked the reader to include in his mental picture images of people who had not been included in the past. The magazine also assumed that the existing portrayals lacked authenticity, the staid infatuation of a national community that sought to airbrush reality and live in a state of denial.

112   *Rethinking Thainess in post-war Bangkok*

While the rebranded magazine had been popular among some, *Phap Khao Sayam Nikon* was unable to convince enough of its readers that such a view of the nation should be given primacy, and by the end of 1955 it had reverted back to a style even more similar to *Life*. Once again, the magazine presented uncomplicated images of Bangkok as a cosmopolitan city through which glamorous representatives of the international community travelled, and where Thais aspired to global participation. Yet the unsuccessful rebranding of *Phap Khao Sayam Nikon* had nonetheless served an important purpose, articulating a debate about representation that had come to preoccupy urban society. Struggling to understand how they fitted into the international community, and unclear as to what a Thai political identity looked and felt like, a conspicuous gap had opened up since the end of the Second World War between rhetoric and reality, undermining confidence in the ability of Thai politicians to provide the answers sought. Old assurances that had promised an expanding citizenship through internal development now seemed bankrupt, and Phibun Songkhram was increasingly viewed as the man who had taken Thailand into a war from which it was yet to recover. Moreover, he was also unable to rein in a government bureaucracy riddled with corruption and self-interest. The lack of faith in the government bureaucracy was accentuated by fear that US money, now flowing into the country in ever greater proportions, was only serving to support a political system that was fundamentally unable to represent the interests of the people.

In 1955, such concerns came to a head when leaders from much of the decolonised world travelled to Bandung in Indonesia for the first conference of nations that had established a position of neutrality in the Cold War. Organised largely at the behest of Sukarno, Nehru and U Nu, the conference revealed the clear distance between the Thai political tradition and emergent political philosophies developing elsewhere in the region. Confident assertions about a third way in the global conflict between America and the Soviet Union, and promises of a solidarity amongst the newly independent nations, raised serious questions about Thailand's international standing. Once the only sovereign nation in the region, the fear was that Thailand was languishing as other political systems seemed to be offering new and dynamic responses to the Cold War. Pictures of Sukarno receiving the popular support of his people were accompanied by articles about Indonesian economic policy, outlining how it was still possible to develop trading networks that were not dependent on the old powers. Moreover, this new crop of political leaders engaged in a new kind of charismatic diplomacy, not only talking about independence, but illustrating their commitment to the nation on the world stage through their costumes and behaviours, carefully adorning their suits with accessories associated with a national iconography.

In this climate, Phibun became a figure of ridicule, associated with an out-of-date political philosophy and holding delusions of grandeur in a world far removed from the one in which he had built his legitimacy. By the middle of the 1950s, the anxieties and ambiguities that had contributed to an uncertainty

Rethinking Thainess in post-war Bangkok 113

about what it meant to be Thai following the Second World War were heightened, culminating in a period where the search for an alternative Thai politics came to dominate the popular press. Forced to recognise the change in fortunes, the state response was to reinvigorate state propaganda with new messages that better reflected both the international situation and Thailand's place within it. With a particular focus on state spectacle, this public relations response to these challenges is the focus of the following chapter.

Notes

1 A Foreign Observer, 'Siam Awake', *Democracy*, 17 November 1946, p. 2.
2 Editorial from *Siang Thai*, republished in *Democracy*, 17 October 1946, p. 2.
3 Editorial from *Siam Daily*, republished in *Democracy*, 17 October 1946, p. 2.
4 Jeremi Suri, *Henry Kissinger and the American Century*, Cambridge, MA: Belknap Press of Harvard University Press, 2007.
5 Ibid., p. 94.
6 Ron Robin, *The Making of the Cold War Enemy, Culture and Politics in the Military–Intellectual Complex*, Princeton, NJ: Princeton University Press, 2001, pp. 6–7.
7 Lenora Foerstel and Angela Gilliam, *Confronting the Margaret Mead Legacy, Scholarship, Empire and the South Pacific*, Philadelphia, PA: Temple University Press, 1992, p. 59.
8 For examples of Mead's work in *Vogue* see Chapter 1.
9 Ruth Benedict, *The Chrysanthemum and the Sword, Patterns of Japanese Culture*, New York: Mariner Books, 2005, p. 2.
10 Mari Yoshihara, 'Re-gendering the enemy, orientalist discourse and national character studies during World War II', in Nancy Lusignan Schultz (ed.) *Fear Itself, Enemies, Real and Imagined in American Culture*, New York: Purdue University Press, 1999, pp. 167–185.
11 Ruth Benedict, *Thai Culture and Behaviour, An Unpublished Wartime Study Dated 1943*, New York: Cornell, 1953, II.
12 Herbert Phillips, *Thai Peasant Personality: The Patterning of Interpersonal Behaviour in the Village of Bang Chan*, Berkeley and Los Angeles, CA: University of California Press, 1966, p. 49.
13 Ruth Benedict, *Thai Culture and Behaviour*, p. 13.
14 Ibid., p. 44.
15 Ibid., p. 29.
16 Ibid., p. 24.
17 Ibid., p. 44.
18 Bruce E. Reynolds, *Thailand's Secret War: OSS, SOE and the Free Thai Underground During World War II*, Cambridge: Cambridge University Press, 2005, p. 369.
19 Ibid., p. 370.
20 Alexander MacDonald describes Phibun as the man who 'allowed the imperial army to walk into the kingdom, and he declared war on the Allies', explaining how he 'ruled the kingdom with a tighter and tighter grip'. Placing 'petty restrictions... upon the people' and passing laws that meant 'no woman could be seen in the streets without a hat. Anyone entering a public building must wear coat, hat and shoes'. See Alexander MacDonald, *Bangkok Editor*, New York: Macmillan, 1949, pp. 82–84.
21 Ibid., p. 35.
22 Ibid.
23 'Random Jottings', *Democracy*, 6 November 1946, p. 2.
24 Ibid., p. 2.

114 Rethinking Thainess in post-war Bangkok

25 Quoted in Patarawdee Puchadapirom, *Watthanatham banthoeng nai chat Thai kan plian plaeng khong watthanatham khwam banthoeng nai sangkhom Krung Thep Maha Nakhon pho.so. 2491–2500* [Entertainment Culture in Thailand: Change in Entertainment Culture in Bangkok Society, 1948–1950], Bangkok: Samnak phim matichon, 2007, p. 91.

26 Ibid., pp. 77–94.

27 Ibid.

28 See Arlene Nehrer, 'Prelude to the Alliance: the expansion of the American economic interest in Thailand during the 1940s', PhD thesis, Northern Illinois University, 1980.

29 The two other post-war English-language newspapers, *Democracy* and *Liberty*, were Thai-owned, and had both closed by the end of the decade.

30 Prasit Lulitanond, *A Postman's Life 1910–1997*, Bangkok: Post Publishing Company, 1999, pp. 62–66.

31 *Bangkok Post*, 14 March 1949, p. 1.

32 Regular adverts in the *Bangkok Post* promoted itself as such.

33 Kasian Tejapira, *Commodifying Marxism, The Foundation of Modern Thai Radical Culture, 1927–1958*, Melbourne, Kyoto: Kyoto University Press, 2001, p. 81.

34 Joshua Kurlantzick, *The Ideal Man: The Tragedy of Jim Thompson and the American Way of War*, Hoboken, NJ: John Wiley & Sons, 2011, p. 79.

35 Ibid., p. 79.

36 Chris Baker and Pasuk Phongpaichit, *A History of Thailand*, p. 142.

37 Kasian Tejapira, *Commodifying Marxism*, pp. 75–92.

38 Ibid., p. 92.

39 Saichon Satyanran, *Kukrit kap praditthakam 'Khwam pen Thai' lem 1 yuk chomphon Po Phibun Songkhram* [Kukrit and the construction of Thainess book 1: The era of Phibun Songkhram], Bangkok: Samnak phim matichon, 2007, p. 21.

40 Steve Van Beek and Vilas Manivat, *Kukrit Pramoj, His Wit and Wisdom, Writings Speeches and Interviews*, Bangkok: Duang Kamol, 1983.

41 Early readers of the newspaper noted this fact, as a letter to the paper asked in 1950, 'why does your newspaper not indulge in sensationalist stories and quarrels?'. Surat Wannakun *thueng* Kukrit Pramoj, *Sayam Rat*, 18 September 1950, in Kukrit Pramoj, *Panha pracham wan*, Bangkok: Rong phim sin akson, 1956, p. 59.

42 Kukrit Pramoj, *Panha pracham wan*, Rong phim sin akson, 1956.

43 The first question was published on 3 February 1951, *Watthanatham kap arayatham tang kan yang rai? Khai koet kon?* The second was published on 20 April 1951, *Prathet Thai diao ni khao pokkhrong kan baep nai?* Kukrit Pramoj, *Panha pracham wan chut thi* 2(1956): 11, 180.

44 *Samachik Uttaradit thueng* Kukrit Pramoj, *Sayam Rat*, 5 October 1950, *Panha pracham wan*, (1956), p. 95. Another letter, printed on 20 April 1951 revolved around a similar theme, asking whether 'the current situation of the Thai economy is developed or falling behind when thought of as a country in the world'. The writer went on to ask 'what will the future hold?', *Panha pracham wan chut thi* 2(1956): 181.

45 *Panha pracham wan* (1956), 95.

46 '*Khon yak ru' theung* Kukrit Pramoj, *Sayam Rat*, 9 September, in *Panha pracham wan* (1956). The convention of signing letters with a name that indicated confusion and deference to Kukrit was common. Such names included '*khon ngo yak chalat*' [an idiot who wants to be clever]. On other occasions, letters made further statements about their identity and the nation through the name they used, examples of which included 'Anuchon khong chat' [youth of the nation]; '*Phu klua communist*' (someone who is scared of the Communists); '*Seri*' [free]; '*Rak Thai*' [love Thai]; '*Ekkarat*' [independence].

47 *Samachik mai lek 1 theung* Kukrit Pramoj, *Sayam Rat*, 20 May 1952 in Kukrit Pramoj, *Panha pracham wan chut thi* 4(1958): 188–195.

48 Ibid., p. 192.

Rethinking Thainess in post-war Bangkok 115

49 Thongchai Waeowiset *thueng* Kukrit Pramoj, *Sayam Rat*, 18 October 1950, *Panha pracham wan* (1956), 135.
50 Ibid.
51 *'Phu yak ru' thueng* Kukrit Pramoj, *Sayam Rat*, 4 November, 18 October 1950, *Panha pracham wan* (1956), 183–189.
52 *'Khon yak ru' theung* Kukrit Pramoj, *Sayam Rat*, 9 September 1950, *Panha pracham wan* (1956), 37–39.
53 *'Khon ngo' theung* Kukrit Pramoj, *Sayam Rat*, 11 April 1951, *Panha pracham wan chut thi* 2(1956): 162–164.
54 *Sathit Suttarot thueng* Kukrit Pramoj, *Sayam Rat*, 19 April 1951, *Panha pracham wan chut thi* 2(1956): 177–179.
55 *'Nu Lampang' theung* Kukrit Pramoj, *Sayam Rat*, 20 April 1951, *Panha pracham wan chut thi* 2(1956): 180–181.
56 Daniel Fineman, *A Special Relationship*, p. 131.
57 *"Wang prat" theung* Kukrit Pramoj, *Sayam Rat*, 2 April 1952, *Panha pracham wan chut thi* 4(1958): 70–73.
58 *Ratsadon khon mai theung* Kukrit Pramoj, *Sayam Rat*, 22 March 1952, *Panha pracham wan chut thi* 4(1958): 42–45.
59 *'Chop ru chop hen' theung* Kukrit Pramoj, *Sayam Rat*, 8 April 1952, *Panha pracham wan chut thi* 4(1958): 84–87.
60 *Dao tai theung* Kukrit Pramoj, *Sayam Rat,* 8 November 1950, *Panha pracham wan* (1956), 197–200.
61 Ibid.
62 *Nakhon Phanomphan theung* Kukrit Pramoj, *Sayam Rat*, 23 December 1853, in Kukrit Pramoj, *Panha pracham wan chut thi* 7(1958): 1–2.
63 Saichon Satyanran, *Kukrit kap pradicthakam 'Khwam pen Thai' lem 1* [Kukrit and the construction of Thainess book 1], p. 11.
64 Kukrit Pramoj, *top khamtham chak 'chao khao khon krung',* *Sayam Rat*, 19 February 1954, *Panha pracham wan chut thi* 7(1958): 151–154.
65 *March of Time, Oasis on a Troubled Continent* (1953).
66 Ibid.
67 Ibid.
68 Patarawdee Puchadapirom, *Watthanatham banthoeng nai chat Thai*, p. 81.
69 Lauriston Sharp and Lucien Mason Hanks, *Bang Chan: Social History of a Rural Community in Thailand*, Ithaca, NY: Cornell University Press, 1978, p. 26.
70 Ibid.
71 Ron Robin, *The Making of the Cold War Enemy*, p. 30.
72 Ibid.
73 Harry Harootunian, *History's Disquiet, Modernity, Cultural Practice, and the Practice of Everyday Life*, New York: Columbia University Press, 2000, p. 33.
74 Lauriston Sharp and Lucien Mason Hanks, *Bang Chan*, p. 26.
75 Ibid., p. 39.
76 Preface to 'Customs connected with birth and the rearing of children', 22 February 1949, in Phya Anuman Rajadhon (ed.) *Life and Ritual in Old Siam: Three Studies of Thai Life and Customs*, translated by William Gedney, New Haven, CT: Hraf Press, 1961, p. 101.
77 Ibid.
78 Saichon Sattayanurak, *Phraya Anuman Rajadhon: Prat saman chon phu niramit 'khwam pen Thai'*, Bangkok: Samnak phim matichon, 2013, pp. 58–105.
79 Phya Anuman Rajadhon, *Life and Ritual in Old Siam*, p. 9.
80 Ibid., p. 53.
81 H. H. Prince Dhani Nivat Kromamun Bidyalabh, Introduction, *The Social Sciences and Thailand: A Compilation of Articles on Various Social-Science Fields and their Application to Thailand*, Bangkok: Cornell Research Center, 1956, p. 1.

116   *Rethinking Thainess in post-war Bangkok*

82 Kasian Tejapira, *Commodifying Marxism*, p. 91.
83 Craig Reynolds, *Thai Radical Discourse: The Real Face of Thai Feudalism Today*, Ithaca, NY: Cornell Southeast Asia Program, 1994, p. 26.
84 Wichai Napharatsami, *Lai chiwit Jit Pumisak* [The Many Lives of Jit Pumisak], Bangkok: Fa diaokan, 2003, pp. 111–116.
85 Sopha Chanamool, *Chat thai nai thatsana panyachon jua kao na*, pp. 245–267.
86 Ibid., p. 260.
87 Ibid., p. 271.
88 'Made in U.S.A.', *Khon Muang*, July (1954), 128.
89 '*Rot ma lampang*' [The horse carts of Lampang], *Khon Muang*, October 1955.
90 '*Fak faen*' [A souvenir for your partner], *Khon Muang*, January 1955.
91 Ibid.
92 '*Dinner baep khantok*', *Khon Muang*, February 1956.
93 '*Phum thamma chonnabot*', *Phap khao sayam nikon*, December 1953, p. 31.
94 Thanu Charuchinda, '*Yak hai den!*', sent to *Phap Khao Sayam Nikon*, January 1954, p. 4.
95 Chiwit Khurusin, '*Khwam tong kan thi pho patina dai*', sent to *Phap Khao Sayam Nikon*, May 1954, p. 4.
96 Dusit Watthanasiri, '*Yang mai civillis pho*' [Not yet civilised enough!], sent to *Phap Khao Sayam Nikon*, May 1954, p. 4.
97 Inthiyot, '*Tong kan phuen phaen din Thai*' [I want Thai land], sent to *Phap Khao Sayam Nikon*, May 1954, p. 5.
98 Response to letter '*Tong kan phuen phaen din Thai*' [I want Thai land], published in *Phap Khao Sayam Nikon*, May 1954, p. 5.

4 Cultural spectacle, political authority and the subversion of Thai modernity

Between 1932 and 1945, state spectacle had been re-invented to incorporate new ideas about state and society. As a result, powerful cultural symbols, such as the elaborately decorated royal barges that had been such iconic markers of the country's cultural landscape, remained tied to their moorings.[1] Associated with a past in which the Thai monarchy had fashioned itself as the country's primary institution, the constitutional regime that had deposed absolute monarchy in 1932 avoided employing the symbolic capital of the boats.[2] Instead, the new civilian leaders established forms of state spectacle that distanced the regime from the recent royal past and fostered a popular nationalism by encouraging broad social participation. The most important of these was the Constitution Day Fair, a week-long event that took place annually during the month of December both in Bangkok and across the country. An exhibition of the power and prestige of the new bureaucratic regime, it was also a location in which the population was encouraged to recognise the positive role of the government in shaping their day-to-day lives. By harnessing the urban hunger for a modern way of life, the state sought to promote the consumption of Thai products as a principal way of forging the everyday practices of a national Thai community. As a result, the Constitution Day Fair became a primary location from which the exploration and performance of Thai identity could be facilitated by the state.

In the post-war era, however, the meaning of Constitution Day was to be repeatedly undermined as political instability and economic austerity meant that it was a number of years before the event could be fully reinstated into the social calendar. When it was, the fair was soon drawn into the ideological politics of the Cold War. Throughout the early 1950s, Constitution Day became a site not only for the dissemination of Thai propaganda, but also for the Soviet Union and the United States to compete for the hearts and minds of the local population. Seeking to overwhelm the Bangkok public with displays of American or Soviet modernity, stalls at the fair were to become a model for the respective countries' public relations activities internationally. They were also, however, to heighten the concerns of the Thai population over its status in the world. In 1954, in particular, the US attempt to beat its Soviet rivals left some in Bangkok concerned about their own government's

118   *Cultural spectacle and Thai modernity*

continued commitment to state-led development. Paling in comparison to the glittering displays that presented the USA as a consumer's paradise, the idea that Thai products could ever compete was seen as ridiculous. Moreover, for most, access to an American-centred consumer paradise was still highly restricted, so that the pitiful displays of Thai products only served to emphasise the distance that now existed between the Thai people and those figures who were benefitting from the international alliance with the United States.

Overall, the Constitution Day Fair only contributed to the collapse in ideological unity that had disturbed Thai state power since the end of the Second World War. In response, Phibun embarked on a public relations campaign that was intended to rejuvenate his premiership and regain popular support for the state and its ministries. Following a trip to the United States in the middle of 1955, he returned to announce that Thailand would become a full democracy. The media would be invited to participate in regular press conferences where Phibun and his principal ministers would be put under scrutiny, and in 1957 elections would be held in which he would put himself up for election. At the same time, the Prime Minister tied his fate to a religious revival, focusing his attention on the promotion of Buddhism and the rebuilding of ancient temples. The 1957 elections were to be held in February so that they would precede the May celebrations for the twenty-fifth centennial year of the Buddhist calendar. Using the opportunity to tie a political revival with a spiritual one, the Prime Minister also used this event to distance state propaganda from the country's international alliance with America.[3] Moreover, having cancelled Constitution Day in 1955, the centenary was to be a new kind of spectacle that sought to fuse aspirational political and economic messages with nostalgia for state traditions that few in Bangkok could now remember.[4]

Years in the making, the Twenty-fifth Centenary was both ambitious and truly national. On 13 May 1957, at 6:00 am, the nation's radio stations picked up a live government broadcast of the opening ceremony in Bangkok where 2500 monks, representing every year since the Buddha had achieved enlightenment, were ordained before making chants as 2500 Buddha images were cast. Then, representatives of Buddhist countries from across the world, including monks from Japan and Prime Minister U Nu of Burma, joined a crowd of 7000 at Sanam Luang. Across the country the proceedings were played out on loudspeakers in town and village temples, while guards banged drums outside factories and sirens were sounded at air bases. For the rest of the day, crowds in the capital looked on as parades of carnival floats made their way along a route that took them from Rachadamnern Avenue to Saphan Phut Bridge.[5]

The first royal barge procession in a generation began the following day, in Nonburi at 8:30 am, when a procession of royal barges began their one-and-a-half-hour journey toward the heart of the old city. At 10:00, when the boats had arrived at the royal landing outside the Grand Palace, large crowds greeted them from the opposite side of the bank, at Wat Arun. After a day

Cultural spectacle and Thai modernity 119

spent moored up, the festivities continued in the evening, when the crew of the boats performed ceremonial paddling and chanting. For the following two evenings, the most famous of the boats, the *Suphannahong* (Boat of the Golden Swan), and two others once again took to the water, remaining close to the bank where the crowds could look on. After the final acts of worship, in which candles were lit in front of an image of the Buddha positioned in a pavilion towards the back of the *Suphannahong*, fireworks lit up the sky.[6]

Unlike anything Bangkok had recently seen, the celebrations nevertheless failed to save the Prime Minister. Anger toward him and his government continued to rage in the press as political opponents sought to undermine the event. Both during the celebrations, and then after, the claim that the government was unable to represent the people was used to challenge the integrity of the celebrations, which were openly referred to as a cynical political ploy rather than a genuine reflection of the religious identity of the people. The purpose of this chapter is to understand how an event that sought to project national unity was transformed into one that reflected ideological bankruptcy. In particular, it looks at how publications that covered the event were able to draw upon cultural narratives in order to undermine the legitimacy of the government and put forward the need to find an alternative political system. In doing so, it seeks to provide insight into how popular support was galvanised for a coup that in September of the same year would permanently remove Phibun from power.

State spectacle from World War to Cold War

While the production of spectacle had long been a central part of the Thai state's public relations activities, it was the coming to power of Phibun Songkhram in 1938 that saw a transformation in both the scale and impact of such events. In support of his broader nation-building projects that sought to transform the daily lives of the population, such spectacle was used to regulate space and time in order to draw the Thai people into a relationship with the state. Events, small or large, were highly choreographed, with arrangements made well in advance as to how the principal participants, citizens employed by the state, should behave and compose themselves. What was an appropriate dress, and even how people should travel to such events, was disseminated to all ministries with the intention of ensuring that attendees projected a unified national community. Supported by a state media that regularly presented government bureaucrats as the principal national community, society at large was encouraged to participate in such events through their close adherence to state guidelines on how to behave. In doing so, the government was able to frame the bureaucracy as a community of role models to whom society should aspire.

Heavily tied to an ideological commitment to nation building, the events also made the projection of the state as the guardian of Thai progress and modernity their primary objective. Nation Day, celebrated annually on 24 June to mark the 1932 revolution, was under Phibun to be marked by a procession

120 *Cultural spectacle and Thai modernity*

that celebrated the regime. Floats that wished to enter, Phibun made clear, should 'show the importance of Nation Day, or show the progress of the nation under the constitutional system, or promote the state edicts, or show an example of consumables made in Thailand'. For government ministries and departments, the floats must 'show the progressive activities being made by the said institution', and private establishments should use the opportunity to display their products, but only 'those which have been produced in Thailand'.[7] Overall, Phibun made clear, Nation Day was to represent the incessant march of the Thai nation and its people toward a better future.

Similarly, the Phibun regime invested heavily in making the Constitution Day Fair an extravaganza that would impress attendees with the progress of the nation. As with Nation Day, the Constitution Day Fair provided both state and private actors with the opportunity to promote their work. All who participated would have to comply with regulations that enforced a commitment to incorporate the iconography of the new regime into their various displays.[8] It was also a site of competition, where those who attended were encouraged to think about how the nurturing of cultural identity contributed to the formation of a political affiliation with the state. As Chatri Patiknonthakan has explained in regard to the annual art competition, held by the Fine Arts Department for the first time in 1937, the production of such artefacts was to be valued principally for their ability to reflect the aspirations of a national community that sought a globally relevant cultural identity. 'Over the last 20 years', the Fine Arts Department explained in 1938, 'for those countries that have organized themselves under a new political system, it has become accepted that art is a crucial tool in stimulating a love of the nation and to help educate the people to look toward their respective governments.'[9]

With the Phibun government firmly in power, the 1939 Constitution Day Fair was the most extravagant yet, extending through a larger section of Bangkok than ever before, a train was built to take visitors around the displays. Also, with state-led construction projects already under way, government exhibits embraced the modernist and art deco architecture that was becoming such a permanent feature of the capital. Other stalls propagated the idea of a greater Thai Kingdom, including territory lost to the French at the end of the nineteenth century. At a separate stall, Asia's other 'great' empire and an increasingly important ally, Japan, was represented with an elaborate stall entitled 'the light of Asia'.[10] Echoing the themes of international fairs and exhibitions of the period, the fair presented the world as a community of competing nations. The message was that, as those respective nations jostled for supremacy, Thailand too might taste victory.

The Constitution Day Fair continued to be held annually until 8 December 1941 when, just hours before it was due to open, Japan invaded Thailand from the south. Although it was only hours later that a ceasefire was called, the invasion still put an end to the celebrations. The following year a large flood submerged the capital under water and, with Bangkok under attack from allied bombings, Constitution Day was once again cancelled. It did not

Cultural spectacle and Thai modernity 121

return until 1947, but was never again able to mobilise or promote the ideological power of the Thai state as it had before. With the cost of living an endless concern in the press, the expense of the event was used by political opponents to criticise the Phibun government. Also, by the early 1950s, Constitution Day was increasingly becoming a battleground in a fierce propaganda war being fought between the Soviet Union and the United States. As the American Embassy explained to Washington in December 1953, the annual fairs were seen as ideal locations from which to promote American power. Moreover, with a rising anxiety about the growing influence of Soviet propaganda efforts, it was believed that America needed to respond, as the ambassador reported:

> One of the most outstanding features of this year's Constitution Fair held in Lumpini Park, Bangkok, was the Soviet Union's display of manufactured goods. Curiosity was the chief characteristic of the people who visited the Soviet pavilion and every action taken by the Russians from the moment the 'SS Stavropol' docked at New Harbor to their offer at the end of the Fair to donate the pavilion to the city of Bangkok was followed by newspapers. The building itself was striking and attractive in appearance and the tall central shaft tipped by a red star dominated the section of the Fair in which it stood. At night streams of people passed through, making it one of the most popular exhibitions. Although it might be thought that the United States was sadly outclassed by this display and its popularity, it should be remembered that the Constitution Fair is not primarily a trade fair despite the Russian, Japanese and commercial companies displays.[11]

Using the example of a Russian success, the United States Information Service (USIS) and the US Embassy in Bangkok managed to secure funding from Washington to outdo the Soviet Union the following year, making the 1954 fair one of the US government's most sophisticated propaganda efforts during the Cold War.[12] Spending a total of $400,000, the American exhibit featured twice nightly, free-of-charge film showings on a vast Cinerama screen; a fashion show put on by the New York department store Macy's, displaying the latest fashions and synthetic fabrics from America; and a complicated train ride around the displays of American products and cultural exhibits.[13] Also, by displaying a vast number of American products, from companies as large as Coca-Cola and Caltex Oil to those products imported by Willis H. Bird, it also played directly to the ideological worldview being put forward in America.[14] *Business Week* reported a 'Propaganda triumph at Thai Fair', while *Life* announced 'America triumphs at Bangkok Fair'.[15] The *Life* article went on to explain to its American readership how 'the Soviet Union has been using the world's trade fairs to peddle its politics with exhibits that are shrewd mixtures of commerce and Propaganda', but that 'last month the US abandoned its snooty attitude and moved actively into combat in Bangkok, Thailand'.[16]

As a result, the American stall dominated the Thai press. The newspaper *Khao Pannit* [*Commercial News*] explained that the erection of the Cinerama

122   *Cultural spectacle and Thai modernity*

screen was the first time it had been seen in the East, let alone Thailand. The article explained how, 'for the whole two hours that you watch it, it is entertainment from start to finish, so that you really do feel like you are watching a bull fight in Spain, or that you are at an Opera in Milan, or on the nose of an airplane' ... 'all of those who go and see this new kind of cinema will see what civilization at this time really looks like and at just how glorious it is'.[17] In *Khao* [*News*], another Thai-language publication, the American and Japanese stalls were juxtaposed to the Thai ones. It complained that despite the cost of the event, many of the stalls were disappointing when compared with the previous year. Many had not even updated their displays, and there was a decidedly shabby feel to it all. In particular, it pointed out that the Ministry of Industrial Production had little to show and that, while the Department of Science had a lot of products on display, it did not have the capability to produce anything in large enough quantities.

> Take the example of a drink that looked so good that it could have almost been compared to a product from a foreign country, but when you look into it, it couldn't be sold on the open market because they didn't have a factory as big as if they were a private company. It just seemed a real waste of the skill of those who work at the Department and the Ministry of Industrial Production, that they already had succeeded, but because there isn't a factory to produce the products they had created, it would only ever be consumed by other bureaucrats.[18]

The message to Thai readers was clear, that however they felt about the Thai–US relationship, America was the most modern nation on the planet and the Thai nation was unable to compete. In contrast to the description of the Cinerama screen and its impact on visitors to the fair, the Thai stalls were a tired reflection of a regime losing its grasp on facilitating progress. For the American ambassador, the Cinerama screen was also a clear highlight. Writing to the President of Cinerama, Inc., Ambassador Peurifoy wrote that the display had made a 'profound impression on Thai people, both because it represents American leadership in technical development, and because of [the] content which has [an] ideal blend of the American story and general culture'. He went on to thank the President for his help at a 'moment when we are engaged in a struggle for men's minds in this part of the world'.[19]

US psychological strategy and the search for an alternative politics

From 1949, the escalation of US aid to Thailand had served to illustrate US support for the Thai state, but it had also served to draw the United States into a complicated set of political relationships that had strengthened authoritarianism in the country.[20] Up until 1951, civilian politicians continued to provide opposition to the 'coup group' in parliament, and the potential return of Pridi to the political scene sustained the idea that there might be an alternative

Cultural spectacle and Thai modernity   123

politics in waiting. In June of that year, however, the Manhattan rebellion had undermined such hopes, when a number of Pridi's supporters, with help from the Navy, had attempted to take power. Despite successfully kidnapping Phibun, it was a failure. Apparently willing to sacrifice the Prime Minister, the boat on which he was held was bombed by government forces and he was forced to swim to safety before it sank. As a result, the rebellion served to identify that the real power was held by the military, in particular by Field Marshal Sarit Thanarat and by the police, by then headed by Phao Siriyond. Both were already independent recipients of US support, Sarit acquiring military aid from January 1951, and Phao through the CIA following a covert operation against Chinese nationalists in northern Burma from November 1950. Over the course of the following years, this aid would provide the two figures with the patronage needed to maintain important networks in a fine balance of power where Phibun was increasingly a figurehead.

By the end of 1951, the Thai state was viewed by much of the Bangkok public as corrupt, self-interested and undemocratic. In the crackdown that followed the failed rebellion, the military had engaged in a violent suppression in which over 1000 people in the city, including many civilians, had been killed. In November the following year, when the Democrats and the military had continued to battle for space in government, a coup was launched by Phibun and the army that brought an end to opposition politics. The so-called 'silent coup' returned the country to a slightly amended version of the 1932 constitution and saw the cabinet occupied by a majority of military personnel. With Phibun looking weak, and with the royalists now removed from power, Leftist intellectuals were already focusing on the heightened disillusionment with the Thai political system and with the government's US patrons. By the end of the year, Leftist dissidents were holding increasingly conspicuous meetings under the banner of a worldwide peace movement based in Stockholm, and were engaged in a number of publishing enterprises that were ever more focused on presenting Phibun as the puppet of a power structure secured by American money.[21]

In Washington, fears that Communism might spread in Southeast Asia were heightened by these developments, and there was a concern that the long-term strategy for Thailand needed to counter the potential for Communist thought to permeate the public sphere. While the payment of aid to the Thai government was recognised as an important part of the US effort to oppose the Communist threat in Southeast Asia, it was also understood that this should be only one element in a successful campaign. In late 1952, it was thus noted that anger toward the Thai government was widespread, and that US aid was being interpreted by many Thai as responsible for propping up the regime.[22] Since the end of the Second World War, it was correctly recognised that the majority of the Thai press had been anti-government and that, fuelled by the absence of a legitimate opposition in the form of Pridi, such distaste for the current regime was increasingly Leftist in its inclination. This, it was made clear, needed to be countered by a campaign that focused particular

124   *Cultural spectacle and Thai modernity*

attention on acquiring the support of 'opinion moulders', who were currently swinging 'perceptively in a pro-communist direction'.[23]

Moving forward with caution, it was nevertheless decided that USIS strategy should focus principally on influencing these Thai 'opinion moulders' who, it was claimed, numbered something close to 1500 people and were all based in Bangkok. 'Profit from legitimate job-printing contracts' and 'payments for editorial and translation services', it explained, 'can go a long way in making fence-sitting journalists more friendly and in making large circulation news-papers more accessible to placement by USIS of both attributed and non-attributed materials'.[24] US staff in Bangkok should engage themselves in the 'personal cultivation' of key individuals. They should entertain regularly, and they should make sure that such figures, even if suspected of a Leftist leaning politically, 'be given priority consideration for leader grants and graduate student grants'. Noting that such opinion moulders were more 'monitaire than doc-trinaire', the USIS report put forward the view that American resources could be used not only to buy government support, but also to provide private citizens with a sense of debt to American friends. The budget for the publication of USIS material, it made clear, 'will be used for two purposes: (1) to influence key newspapers, individuals, and groups within the important "opinion moulders" target, and (2) to carry out standard press and publications activity'.[25]

In terms of material printed, it was vital that US interest in Thailand was seen to be concerned with the 'well-being of people of Thailand and avoid giving the impression that the United States supports any particular govern-ment group or party'.[26] US propaganda should recognise the fact that US aid was 'being regarded as partially responsible for the many unpopular acts of the government', and that it was associated with supporting a state riddled with corruption. It also recognised that poor roads, limited radio facilities, low lit-eracy and limited knowledge of English undermined the real value of American support. It should instead, therefore, make it clear that 'American economic and military aid is not given for imperialistic purposes, but is directed toward strengthening the economy and security of Thailand as an independent nation in the family of Free nations.' It was also made clear that, in securing American interests in the country, it must exploit the 'myth of traditional freedom' which gives the Thai a sense of 'independence and separateness not felt by neighbour-ing peoples who have experienced decades of colonisation'.[27] Recognising the high value that the Thai placed upon economic security and the maintenance of a high standard of living when compared with neighbouring countries, the Thai should be encouraged to see themselves as unique and unified through a common past and strong cultural identity. 'The psychological climate', it was explained, 'is unified, stabilized, and "conservatized" by traditional Thai attitudes toward king, country and religion.'[28]

While US aid to the Phibun government continued to rise, therefore, American propaganda sought to distance the USA from the current regime, recognising that the aspiration of Thai communities to political and economic independence was deeply embedded. Instead, the psychological strategy was focused on

Cultural spectacle and Thai modernity 125

fostering a popular nationalism based upon emphasising a traditional set of 'myths' about the Thai nation that gave its members a sense of superiority, and might therefore protect them psychologically from establishing a commonality with Communists in neighbouring countries. In 1953, these attitudes were tempered, following fears that France was failing to formulate a counter strategy to what was considered the 'psychological harassment' of Southeast communities at the hands of Communist forces. Remaining one of the most favourable regimes to US influence, Thailand, it was decided, should be viewed as 'politically and geographically the most suitable base in which to initiate and develop a substantial U.S. counter effort'. Once again, this strategy was to include economic, political, military and psychological programmes, which would 'prepare the minds and emotions of the people to collaborate' with American personnel in Bangkok. It would also recognise that the current regime was authoritarian, that corruption was rife, and that there was a distinct lack of political opposition. For now, however, the United States, it made clear, was 'receiving from Thailand most, if not all, of the varieties of cooperation and assistance which it desires'.[29]

This slightly revised US confidence in the Thai government had come as a result of a crackdown on Leftist activity that began on 10 November 1952, when over 1000 individuals, deemed to be of Communist sympathy, had been arrested.[30] Mainly members of the Sino-Thai community that had long been regarded as the country's principal Communist group, the arrests had also included 37 Thai citizens, including a number of journalists and members of the Communist Party of Thailand. At the same time, the country's main Leftist newspapers were closed down, leaving both a dearth of radical literature and a climate of fear around its dissemination. What remained, however, was a number of popular newspapers that continued to feed the general enthusiasm for a critique of Phibun and his government. Heavily satirical, these publications became expert at using innuendo and double-speak to communicate their distaste for the Prime Minister. To Phibun they also emphasised how, despite his success in winning the confidence of Washington, he remained unable to use the relationship to serve his own internal public relations objectives. With the Bangkok press lacking ideological coherence, by the middle of the decade it was nevertheless gaining confidence in its presentation of Phibun as a weak and ageing fascist whose power relied upon his relationship with America.

Throughout 1955, a string of events were to fuel this depiction. The formation of the Southeast Asia Treaty Organization (SEATO) in February and then the Bandung Conference in April provided the most forthright expression of Thailand's position internationally. With the first serving to significantly reinforce the profile of Thailand's alliance with the USA, the second was to raise serious questions about the value of that relationship. It was also to reinforce the idea that while Thailand had tied itself to the USA, other nations in Southeast Asia were articulating confident international identities that were far less interested in establishing an alliance with the 'great powers'. Then, in May, with many in Bangkok talking about the benefits of a neutral foreign policy,

126 *Cultural spectacle and Thai modernity*

Phibun travelled to the United States for the first time.[31] In contrast to the foreign policies of both Nehru and Sukarno, Phibun's trip to America was portrayed in the Bangkok press as the act of a leader who had become dependent upon a polemical framing of the Cold War. While there, he had spent time meeting leading business people and speaking words of encouragement about the potential for investment in his country.[32] He also met with the influential Rockefeller family, and repeatedly affirmed his commitment to an anti-communist stance, arguing that a third World War was likely on the horizon.[33] While there, the Bangkok press ramped up its criticism of the Prime Minister, and, as a cartoon in *Phim Thai* illustrated, he was presented as an individual for whom American fears about the future of Southeast Asia had become central to his personal survival.[34] Sitting around an indigenous fortune-telling system, Phibun was depicted in the cartoon sitting outside Capitol Hill, wildly predicting to the American President and Secretary of State that a 'Third World War is a certainty'. With Phibun clearly siting beneath the towering figures of President Eisenhower and John Foster Dulles, onlookers were shown observing a bizarre spectacle of international relations. The Thai leader, described underneath the cartoon as a 'Prophet', was depicted as a leader who exploited American ignorance about what was really going on in Asia, and feigned local Thai knowledge in order to convince them of his claims. Presenting the American leadership as naïve, it showed Phibun as both cunning and desperate (Figure 4.1).

Figure 4.1 Cartoon from *Phim Thai*, '*Honyai*' [The Prophet], 15 May 1954

Cultural spectacle and Thai modernity   127

In fact, behind the scenes, Phibun clearly recognised the damage that the relationship with America was having upon his own credibility, and even before the trip he had begun to re-align his position internationally. During Bandung, Thai government representative Foreign Minister Prince Wan Waithayakorn had publicly voiced a strong, pro-US, pro-SEATO message. In private, however, he had made efforts to relax tensions between the Thai and the Chinese, making contact with Prime Minister of the People's Republic of China, Chou En-lai. Then, while Phibun had been abroad, the political situation at home had become increasingly complicated. Police General Phao had made it clear to the United States that he wished to make a move against his main political rival, Sarit Thanarat. Intent upon consolidating his position, the move would also have undermined the finely balanced factionalism that was ultimately keeping Phibun in power. Only after US Ambassador John E. Peurifoy made it clear that he did not support the coup did Phao decide to abandon his plans. For Phibun, however, the event further emphasised the vulnerability of internal political structures to Thailand's deepening relationship with the United States. Despite the US rebuke to Phao, the police general's close relationship with the CIA meant that he continued to remain America's most important ally in the country.[35]

When he returned from America, Phibun therefore embarked on a public relations shift, in which he aimed to rehabilitate his political career and undermine the power that both Phao and Sarit maintained through their contacts in Washington. Arriving back in Bangkok, he claimed that Thailand would become a full democracy, with him and his ministers taking part in regular press conferences. Sanam Luang was rebranded 'Hyde Park' and opened up as a place for public speeches and debates, and he announced that he would run for election in February 1957. Employing the language of the Free World, it was nevertheless a move that allowed him to establish distance from his American allies. Toward the end of the year, as popular calls for democracy and self-determination grew, Phibun continued to search for a new public relations message that would re-enforce his position as a man who guaranteed the country's independence, and that might rejuvenate his premiership.

Phibun and the twenty-fifth Buddhist Centennial

It was in this changing political climate, driven by Phibun's determination to reclaim ideological legitimacy internally, that plans were laid for the celebrations of the twenty-fifth Buddhist Centennial. Easily identifiable as external from US influence or from the polemic politics of the Cold War, the celebration of Buddha's enlightenment 2500 years earlier provided a clear opportunity to rejuvenate state-led spectacle. With Phibun intent on regaining political control, it could also be used to claim a commonality with the other Buddhist nations of Asia. Drawing upon a clear appetite inside the country for new cultural narratives about what it meant to be Thai, the event could be rooted in nostalgia for 'traditional' customs, disillusionment with the recent past, and an ongoing

128 *Cultural spectacle and Thai modernity*

hunger for development and modernity. As a result, during the organisation of the event, attempts were made to ensure the religious occasion was associated with a projection of the country's political and economic independence under a popular, democratically elected regime.

In the two years leading up to the celebrations, Phibun sought to foster the loyalty of the population by sponsoring a religious revival. Intending to elevate his own image as the patron of Thai Buddhism, the state focused efforts on a programme to restore thousands of temples, and began a restoration of major historical sites including Ayutthaya and Phimai.[36] On provincial tours, Phibun made great efforts to portray himself as a devout Buddhist, presenting the temples he visited with donations and Buddha images. In doing so he was able to consolidate his position within the monkhood and further utilise the network of temples and Buddhist priests that had long been an important channel for the distribution of public relations material.[37]

Then, in the lead-up to the 2500th year of the Buddhist calendar, Phibun encouraged religious figures to support the government's promotion of the event. The true name of the occasion was a reference to the 'meridian point' of the Buddhist calendar, from which the faith would retreat after two-and-a-half millennia of growth. But, as Thanomjit Michin has explained, this 'would have meant that the event would have been of little benefit to the government, because it would suggest that Thai society (predominantly Buddhist) would lose its established order and enter a period of chaos'. As a result, Thanomjit has explained, 'Field Marshal Phibun Songkhram saw it as vitally important to try and change this belief, and ordered those with knowledge of Buddhism to put forward the view that the imminent decline was incorrect'.[38] Instead, the Prime Minister banned the use of the word 'meridian', insisting upon the name 'the 2500th year of the Buddhist era'.[39] In doing so, he promoted the idea that the date should be viewed as a new beginning, during which time the Buddhist faith could be sustained and Thailand could be at the centre of a revived religious life. It could also, he hoped, then be used to support his own political comeback as a popular Thai leader.

In attempting to mobilise large sections of the population, the event also drew upon nostalgia for the past, best illustrated by the re-introduction of a procession of royal barges that had been largely omitted from state spectacle since the 1932 revolution. Historically important as naval vessels, the role of the barges had become increasingly ceremonial through the late nineteenth century. However, with Thai leaders keen to project themselves as modern, the boats were often regarded as less important in displaying power than those state spectacles that happened on the city's newly built roads. This had changed from the early twentieth century when, following the death of King Chulalongkorn, the boats began to be re-introduced as part of the Royal *Kathin* ceremony, an event during which, over a number of days, the King travelled to temples across the city in order to present monks returning from a three-month retreat with new robes. In the early twentieth century, no more than 30 of the boats would be used on the final day's visit to Wat Arun, which sat on the opposite side of the

Cultural spectacle and Thai modernity 129

Chaophraya River from the Grand Palace.[40] However, in the final few months of absolute monarchy, as the old regime struggled to shore up its legitimacy, the barges had been employed twice, once to mark the opening of the newest and most modern icon of the changing city, Sapan Phut bridge, and again to commemorate the 150th year of Bangkok. The latter in particular was an explicit attempt to celebrate the city's development as a modern global space. It was also the first time in over a century that the boats were used to recreate a large lineal military like procession of over 150 boats.[41]

Then, following the revolution, the boats had stopped being used, and as a result had quickly fallen into disrepair. During the Second World War they suffered bomb damage, and by the end of the conflict only 12 of the vessels remained unscathed.[42] In discussions regarding what should be done with them, the Bureau of the Royal Household and the Fine Arts Department lamented their loss, arguing that they were 'beautiful examples of an ancient art', the transport 'of the Princes and Kings of old ... they are an ancient artefact of the nation and of Thai history'.[43] What was less clear, however, was what the appropriate role of the boats should be now that so many were damaged, and in consideration of the fact that the state lacked knowledge about how they might be restored or maintained. It was estimated that simply moving the three main boats alone would cost the Thai state 14,000 baht.[44] It also required contact to be made with an individual who had participated in the 150th anniversary of Bangkok celebrations to find out how it might be done.[45]

In March 1948, the Fine Arts Department predicted that the total cost of refurbishing the boats as objects for mere exhibition would be 44,720 baht, but it also identified the possibility that the boats might be used once again to decorate the contemporary Thai state. According to the head of the Fine Arts Department, who at this point was Phya Anuman Rajadhon, recreation of the 1932 event should probably be considered impossible, noting that the boats involved would need to number between 50 and 60 to be considered a 'large procession'. He instead suggested that of all those boats that had not been damaged beyond repair, 24 might be salvaged, boats that could then be deployed at future government events. He therefore put forward the idea that, with the Navy organising and training a new generation of oarsmen, with the Royal Household investigating and commissioning the production of traditional costumes, and with the Fine Arts Department responsible for restoration and preservation, the fleet could be brought back into full use at state ceremonies for a cost of 244,000 baht.[46]

At some point between then and the middle of the decade, the Phibun government committed itself to the plan. Under the authority of the Ministry of Culture, established in 1952 and headed by Phibun himself, the Fine Arts Department was thus assigned 1,530,000 baht to make the procession take place as part of the 1957 celebrations.[47] The decision was symptomatic of the Phibun government's desire to harness symbols of royal power in order to bolster both the bureaucratic state and the personal prestige of the Prime Minister. It was also illustrative of Phibun's increasingly open competition for

130 *Cultural spectacle and Thai modernity*

legitimacy, not only with the royalists, but also with the King himself. As Christine Gray has explained, the conversion of the National Council of Culture to a Ministry was done specifically to claim a greater degree of ownership over the rituals of state and to reduce the power of the new King. As Gray explains further, the ministry developed 'an ideology of Thai culture that was linked to Thai nationhood and to Thai kingship, but not to the Chakri dynasty'.[48]

Indeed, since the return of the King, who came to reside permanently in Thailand from 1950, the Phibun government had sought to restrict the King's movements, limiting his ability to make contact with the Thai people. As Chanida Chitbundid has explained, while the institution maintained a symbolic capital, King Bhumibol himself had very little opportunity to establish a popular constituency of his own. Restricted to the palace by a regime that continued to limit royal influence, King Bhumibol relied largely upon a weekly music concert, held at Suan Amporn gardens, to build popular support in the city.[49] While a number of musicians from the universities and other government departments gained access to the monarch through the event, it was nevertheless limited. Where King Bhumibol had been more successful was in securing his reputation as a moral leader committed to the betterment of the Thai nation and its people. By the middle of the 1950s, the crown had become a legitimate institution for receiving charitable donations from wealthy members of Bangkok society, including the Chinese community. Funds raised at private events were quickly redirected to good causes, establishing what Paul Handley has described as 'a circle of ever multiplying merit, through which all Thais were encouraged to contribute to the king to participate in his virtue', and rendering King Bhumibol 'the undisputed master of social welfare and the absolute paragon of selfless sacrifice'.[50]

This meant that for Americans interested in formulating a psychological strategy for the country, the King was seen as a vital way of exploiting the 'myth of traditional independence' in order to present Thai identity as intrinsically anti-communist. It had also come to be seen as a way of channelling distaste for the current administration into an alternative political identity that maintained the King as the principal figurehead of the nation. At the 1954 Constitution Day Fair, The King had been invited to play a crucial role in attending the American stall, and in late 1955 his image as a 'popular' figure in Thai consciousness had been re-confirmed when he had travelled with the Queen into the Thai countryside on a tour of the northeast.[51] They received a rapturous welcome from a rural public who had never seen a ruling monarch, and images of the trip soon began to filter through to the Bangkok press. Otherwise interested in the daily proceedings at Hyde Park, which had by the end of the year become a hotbed for political protest, the press juxtaposed images of chaos and ideological incoherence in Bangkok against those of a community of Thai unified behind the image of a benevolent monarch. Keen to employ the symbolic capital of the monarch for the state, Phibun's use of the royal barges, and his intention that the King would occupy a central role in the procession,

Cultural spectacle and Thai modernity   131

showed a clear desire to present this unified cultural identity under his own leadership.[52]

In the months leading up to the February elections, Phibun sought to conflate the forthcoming religious and cultural revival with his own political comeback, ramping up his merit by making trips to important temples and announcing plans for the construction of a Buddhist town on the outskirts of Bangkok, to be named Phuttamonthon. With the election set to take place only months before the occasion, it was labelled the vote that would 'decide the government of the twenty-fifth Buddhist Centenary', and in campaign posters Phibun was referred to as 'the man who built the Thai Nation'.[53] As a result, policies on the campaign trail were announced, with striking commitments to ambitious projects such as complete nationwide electricity coverage, as well as the connection of all provinces by road.[54] In doing so, Phibun re-asserted the view that lineal development remained an inherently Thai project, supported by the Thai state and indeed by his own leadership. It also rejected the claim that such modernisation programmes were dependent upon US support.

Rather, the message attached to the occasion was one that emphasised parity, at least in terms of aspiration, between the desires of the Thai and the Americans for an independent identity. Indicative of that fact were the plans for the construction of an enormous statue of the Buddha, intended to be a source of pride for all Thai. Designed by the Italian artist also responsible for the Democracy and Victory monuments, Silpa Bhirasi, the statue was initially intended to be 45 metres tall. However, time restraints meant that the set of statues cast were much smaller. Despite that, propaganda material for the event featured the Buddha statue taking on its intended meaning as 'a national wonder'.[55] Striking in its similarity to the way the Statue of Liberty towered over the American people in USIS propaganda distributed in Thailand at the time, the poster used to advertise the event depicted a towering image of the Buddha pictured over a population that stood in awe. In doing so, it suggested that the Buddha statue should assume the same importance for the Thai as the Statue of Liberty had to Americans.[56]

The poster also projected the event as a truly national one, stating that 'you are invited to come and celebrate with the government, the 25th Centennial of the Buddhist Calendar'. The message was one of cultural unity and of a benevolent state that remained concerned about the people's needs. This was further reflected in the cost of the event, nearly 65 million baht, 2 million of which was intended to provide food and drink to those who attended.[57] In line with the modernisation plans intended for completion in the event's honour, the event also sought to re-affirm the role of cultural betterment as a tool for nation building on a lineal trajectory toward full independence. Moreover, for those attending, it would have felt markedly similar to those events of the past 25 years, in particular Constitution Day. On 13 May, the procession of carnival floats down Ratchadamneon Avenue, and the competition to decide the most beautiful of the floats, would have provided clear references to the legacy of those state-led occasions. For those who attended the events in Bangkok, as

132 *Cultural spectacle and Thai modernity*

well as for those who participated in villages, listening on loudspeakers across the country, the message would have been clear: the event was the government's, and they were the guests.

During the celebration, displays on Buddhism were accompanied by stalls promoting the government's economic policies, and, as with the Constitution Day Fair, the period leading up to the Twenty-fifth Centenary provided private companies with an opportunity to cash in on the up-coming spectacle, lauding the event as ushering in a new era of consumption. The Dai Fah Department store, two days before the opening ceremony, announced that there would be a sale during the celebrations, with many reduced prices.[58] It also explained that it continued to find the best products, most modern and useful, from across the world. For foreign companies such as Philips Electronics, the event offered a great opportunity in the sale of radios, and the company invested heavily in promoting its products, placing large adverts on consecutive days just prior to the opening ceremony. Recognising the opportunity offered by the event, much of which would be broadcast on radio, they were to employ the same images of the Twenty-fifth Centenary as the government, clearly recognising the state's iconography in promoting their own products.[59]

Most important, however, was that in the context of the Cold War, the event would be used as a declaration of Thailand's new position internationally. Taking the opportunity to free political prisoners, and even sanctioning the publication of a collection of Leftist essays written by students from Thammasat University, the Prime Minister made his strongest assertion yet that the Left would be welcomed back into the political system.[60] Moreover, guests of honour at the opening ceremony were to include U Nu, who, despite maintaining relations with America, had shown a strong inclination toward establishing a neutral foreign policy.[61] Buddhist monks from Japan were invited, and during the week-long festivities, supporters of a neutral foreign policy claimed that the grandiose occasion had elevated Thailand's status in the region. Speaking during the event, one of the most outspoken of those, Thep Chotinuchit, claimed that the sheer scale of the celebrations was evidence of how the Phibun government 'has not lost to Nehru', and 'has proven that Thailand can also be neutral in the search for peace'. Pointing to the release of political prisoners as evidence of the government's new openness, he also pointed to the presence of other Asian guests, claiming that 'it is the good vision of this government to make it clear that it is now time for the government to show itself as neutral and begin to find a route toward global peace'. We should side with 'neither one side nor the other and refuse to be mastered by either Eisenhower or Bulganin'. As the Buddha had taught, he explained, so Thailand should find the middle way in the world.[62]

Representing disunity

Despite the carefully laid plans, the celebrations were not enough to halt criticism of Phibun. The February elections, far from being the forerunner to a

Cultural spectacle and Thai modernity   133

revival of fortunes for the Prime Minister, had ended in crisis when many had claimed that the ruling party, *Seri Manangkhasila*, had tampered with votes to secure victory. Under pressure, Phibun had declared a state of emergency, fuelling questions about his commitment to a democratic society. Students from Chulalongkorn University, already well established as a centre for criticism of the regime, marched through Bangkok in anger over what they believed was a falsified result, and in the following months it became clear that the government was rapidly losing its legitimacy. When the opposition, the Democrat Party, boycotted the Twenty-fifth Centenary, the event became even more pointedly associated with the regime.[63] Then, on the morning of the opening ceremony, King Bhumipol announced that he too would not be attending, after coming down with a cold. As Thak Chaloemtiarana has noted, it was as if the 'cosmic forces had turned against Phibun'.[64]

As the Twenty-fifth Centenary approached, newspapers generally opposed to Phibun struggled to find a clear line on how to report the event. Regardless of the proposed boycott, newspaper editors could be in no doubt that the celebrations would attract large crowds, and they had to recognise that their readership would want to be informed. As one of the most popular newspapers, with one of the highest readerships, *San Seri* thus provided regular updates and published schedules of the daily activities.[65] At the same time, however, it attempted to place its own meaning on the event, the most obvious of which emphasised the birth of a new era rooted in the language of peace and neutrality. In an editorial on 14 May, the Buddhist centennial was framed as an important chance for renewal, stating that we are 'about to embark on a new era of our lives, let it be a Buddhist centenary of peace'. At the same time, the newspaper asked its readers whether the new nation, rooted in the Buddhist principle of peace, should really have Phibun at its centre. In a cartoon published the day before the opening ceremony, the newspaper poked fun at the Prime Minister's performance of religious acts (Figure 4.2). Depicting the Prime Minister dressed in full military garb and marching pompously toward a temple, the newspaper presented him not only as aloof and distant from the population, but more pointedly as an ageing fascist leader. Followed by two lower-ranking officials in what looked like a goose step, each carried offerings to the temple and, with their eyes closed, was oblivious to the couple looking on. Commenting on the spectacle in front of them, the byline informed the reader that the man was encouraging his wife to follow the Prime Minister, 'Go and make merit with them', he said, 'then in the next life you'll be able to see him again!' Confused, the woman looked on at the spectacle with a question mark hanging over her head.

In an age when the country was about to enter a 'new era', the cartoon held a double meaning, with the word for 'next life' also translating as 'next nation'. The question posed, therefore, was whether readers really wanted to live in a nation where Phibun continued to govern. It also inferred that Phibun's merit making was both superficial, and failed to correlate with how others in the country felt about their religious faith. As the week's events unfolded, and as

134 *Cultural spectacle and Thai modernity*

Figure 4.2 Cartoon published in, *San Seri*, 11 May 1957

rumours about the cost of the celebrations began to surface, such narratives were used to suggest that the merit-making projects were self-serving, and had little interest in the real needs of the people. On 18 May, an editorial in *San Seri* wondered whether the estimated 64 million baht would have been better spent on projects that would have tangibly improved things for the country. The building of new schools, for example, would have been a real investment in the lives of the people, and would have left a lasting legacy for the nation.[66] In a letter published the following day, one reader reinforced the point, claiming that the building of the temples and the plans for Phuttamonthon could surely not provide the same amount of karmic merit as the construction of buildings that would be useful to the country.[67] The message was that this was a public relations exercise that ultimately served only to further the gulf between the aspirations of the government and the people.

Elsewhere, this sense of a separation between the government and the people was expressed in more explicitly cultural terms. Here, the claim was that while it was natural for the Thai people to want to mark the religious occasion, public relations objectives had corrupted what would have otherwise been a purely spiritual event. In a letter published in the section *Panha pracham wan* of the *Sayam Rat* on 22 May, a reader voiced his unease about the event, stating that he did not agree with the cost and had already decided not to attend. However, upon passing Sanam Luang, and upon seeing the vast number of monks there, he said that he suddenly felt the need to follow his Buddhist faith despite his political sensitivities. Conflicted, he had returned

Cultural spectacle and Thai modernity   135

home, only to read a column in *Sayam Rat* encouraging readers to make merit, and this had compelled him to change his mind. After eating and getting changed, he left for Sanam Luang. In the next question to Kukrit, however, he revealed that he was unable to set aside his political convictions:

> I hate those people that have tormented the country, and I myself pray and wish that they will receive much suffering in the next life, equal to the karmic debt they accumulated in this one. If we can get all of the millions of people who are angry with them to go out and make merit in order to curse them, will that achieve any results?[68]

Kukrit's response to the letter was to explain that to do such a thing would itself be a sin and that those whom he hated would have to face the karma they had accumulated on their own. Nevertheless, while critical of the emotive response, Kukrit's point remained that the Buddhist faith was not something that should, or indeed could, be employed for political purposes. While critical of his reader's outburst, Kukrit nonetheless made his own pointed criticism of the event and its organisers. With Kukrit also now openly opposed to the Phibun regime, his charge was that the event had been used to serve a political purpose, and proven the widening gulf between the priorities of government and the aspirations of the 'people'.

By the end of the following month, such a view about the Twenty-fifth Centenary remained, and was continuing to provide proof of the regime's faltering position. A magazine attached to the newspaper *Thai Mai*, part owned by the Chinese businessman Prasit Kanjanawat, *Ta Khlong Thai Mai* [*New Thai Photographer*] had rarely commented on politics. Instead, it had presented itself as a lifestyle magazine reporting 'photo news', and like other such magazines was interested primarily in reports on the cosmopolitan lives of Bangkok's citizens. However, with pressure continuing to mount on Phibun, and with his political demise seeming an ever-likely reality, the criticism that had surrounded the event remained. Published in August, the magazine's belated look at the Twenty-fifth Centenary continued to reflect the sense of dissatisfaction and cultural estrangement that had already been used to spin the event elsewhere.[69] At the heart of this critique, once again, lay the issue of cost, a fact made evident on the first page of the extended feature. Here, photos that depicted men at work in preparation for the week's activities, crafting the boats and erecting the emblematic statue of the Buddha, were accompanied by a text that sought to provoke the reader to think about the money spent. In particular, readers were encouraged to think about whether it had been worth it:

> So, in the very end, the celebration of the Buddhist twenty-fifth centennial was able to take place, even if it is impossible to know how on earth it was paid for ... For those who wish to dwell on it, fearing they might have spent the gold reserves of the nation, or that they had to organize the whole thing on credit, the ceremony has now been and

136   *Cultural spectacle and Thai modernity*

> gone, and according to the feeling of the government, it has gone off beautifully. For the people who actually paid for this event, well it would be best if they just forget about it, but not before bearing in mind what it feels like – meaning what you feel like – when you hear about that money ... Anyway, for now let's just look at the pictures.[70]

Loaded with sarcasm, the comment was in line with the rest of the report, which often seemed confused, presenting images that seemed to celebrate elements of the event, while criticising others. However, with the question of value at the forefront of the representation, the magazine went on to portray the crowds who attended as a community of Thai people who were there because of their general character rather than a political affiliation with the state. Photos that depicted mass participation were in this sense contextualised by explaining that the real reason for the crowd's attendance was their inherent commitment to Buddhism. In contrast, by mixing the religious ceremonies with its own agenda, the government was portrayed as having undermined the event's true meaning. While it made clear that the occasion did 'receive the interest of the Thai people, who are intensely Buddhist', it also asserted that 'the people did not intend to come and admire the "Way of Spending the money of the Nation in an enormous quantity"', but 'came instead to further the growth and strength of the Buddhist faith'. Juxtaposing images of government officials with the devout crowd in attendance, the magazine thus claimed to report on two very different worlds. A picture of Phibun Songkhram and his wife Laied, along with other members of the government, sitting at the front of the opening cere-mony on 13 May was thus accompanied by an explanation that these were the 'seniors, that us Thais, all 18 million of us, know so well', who had 'gathered at the event with their usual airs and graces'.[71] Elsewhere, however, images of Thai young and old presented a community uninterested in pomp and ceremony, but rather in their very real and personal concern about the importance of making merit (Figure 4.3).

The magazine was polemical and dogmatic, with a clear opinion about what the people in attendance were feeling, and making cast-iron assumptions about their moral integrity, based upon the nature of their interest in the celebration. At one point it even split the crowd into two types: those who were there to make merit, and those who were there to enjoy the shows and have fun nearby. Of the latter, it questioned whether such activities were 'dirty' or 'immoral', and in doing so clearly asked its readership how they had identified with the celebrations.[72] Securing the legitimacy of a boycott, *Ta Khlong Thai Mai* thus used the politicisation of the event as a tool to objectify the 'Thai' who had made the journey to Sanam Luang. Those who attended were cast as a spiritually inclined population who, by drawing upon an internal 'nature', exhibited an authenticity that those who enjoyed the secular activities run by the state could not.

Elsewhere in the magazine, this focus on the crowd continued to be employed to reconstruct the event in the minds of its readership. In the case

Cultural spectacle and Thai modernity 137

Figure 4.3 The crowd at the opening ceremony, *Ta Khlong Thai Mai*, August 1957

of the barge procession, pictures of the boats were placed alongside pictures of those who had attended, crammed onto the banks of the river and clearly deeply engaged in the proceedings (see Figure 4.4).[73] The caption that accompanied the picture, however, explained that the people struggled to see the boats because there was nowhere to sit.[74] Unlike the government-organised activities, where the crowds dressed in formal outfits, this picture depicted

Figure 4.4 Crowds watching the royal barges, *Ta Khlong Thai Mai*, August 1957

people in casual clothes with babies sitting on their mother's knee, and families out together. The implication was that, while the event had drawn huge crowds of 'normal' people, it had somehow left those who attended feeling ostracised from the experience due to a lack of thought by the organisers about how to include them. In another case, the lens looked from the standpoint of the crowd itself. The picture of the winning carnival float, constructed by the Department for Vocational Education, filled the frame, locating the reader firmly on the street corner as it passed. Here the caption asked the reader to 'look and help tell us what you think its meaning might be?'[75] Suggesting a lack of authenticity, it identified the confused ideological message of the event. A float competition might have been familiar to Bangkokians, but here the competition among government institutions failed to assert a clear message to the crowds in attendance. The women who sat graciously on top of the float were paying respect as if to the Buddha, but the caption questioned to what they were really paying respect.

However, there was one image that, occupying half a page in the magazine, stood out as particularly striking. Taken on the morning of 13 May at Sanam Luang, the picture was of a large crowd of people dressed in white shirts staring directly into the lens of the camera (Figure 4.5). The caption described the crowd as 'excessively large', looking on at the front of the ceremony for one reason alone, 'to come and admire the King'. However, as the caption explained, they would be left disappointed because 'the King had come down with a cold' and it was to be 'the head of the Privy Council who opened the ceremony'.[76] Flocks of people in uniformly smart clothes, surrounded by flags,

Figure 4.5 Crowds at Sanam Luang 'wait for the king', *Ta Khlong Thai Mai*, August 1957

appeared to identify a population keen to engage with the proceedings. Here, therefore, the crowd's assumed relationship to the monarch was employed to once again imply estrangement from the political order, suggesting that the only reason for the large numbers was to catch a glimpse of the King. Transforming the image from one of apparent success into abject failure, the government's lack of legitimacy was thus juxtaposed to that of a popular monarch who, it could be claimed, far better represented the aspirations of the Thai people.

Imbued with the symbolic capital of a near-forgotten past and untainted by the messy politics and economics of the post-war years, the magazine thus indicated how King Bhumibol was increasingly becoming associated with a potential moral and spiritual renewal for the Thai nation. Having spent his political career trying to limit the monarch's power, Phibun had clearly hoped that during May 1957 he too might draw on that perceived moral integrity to bolster the legitimacy of the Thai state. However, with the King not attending the event, that hope had been unfulfilled, and as Phibun's moral authority to govern drained away, it was clearly the monarch to whom much of that legitimacy flowed.

The critique offered by *Ta Khlong Thai Mai*, while seemingly focused on undermining Phibun, also questioned the ideological integrity of a whole generation of political leadership, in effect providing a critique of all those who had taken power from 1932. The assertion that Thai cultural practice was external from a participation in competition and consumption was in turn used to offer a damning analysis of the current Thai establishment, namely that they were unable to represent the Thai people, not only because the election was flawed, but more fundamentally because they did not understand the cultural practices of their own people. Thai cultural behaviour, it seemed to assert, did not need to be developed because it was already self-evident, and participation with the national state did not need to be fostered because what it meant to be Thai was rooted in the day-to-day priorities of a traditionally

140 *Cultural spectacle and Thai modernity*

inclined population. With respect to the King, it argued that traditional forms of hierarchy were already embedded within the psychology of the Thai people, and that it was Phibun's inauthenticity as a 'Thai' leader that prevented him from being able to secure that support. Neither pro-communist nor pro-American, the message was that Thailand needed a change in which the best interests of the people would be truly reflected. This, it inferred, could not be achieved through simple electoral politics, but rather through a deeper understanding about what being Thai already entailed. Phibun had failed to exploit the changing view. Nonetheless, by the end of the decade, the construction of a cultural identity that displaced existing notions of political and economic independence would become a fundamental part of Thai statecraft and its propaganda. Following the coup that would remove Phibun, a new regime under Field Marshal Sarit Thanarat would be marked by the elevation of the monarch's role in society and would exploit such cultural narratives to undermine notions of universal citizenship and to legitimise authoritarian rule.

Notes

1 The royal barges were obviously moved from time to time, and there was a rare outing for one barge in 1950, during the funeral of King Ananda (Rama VIII), but the statement refers to the use of a large number of barges in a public spectacle. By the 1950s, Bangkok's younger population would have never had the opportunity to see such a procession.

2 After the revolution, a number of royal ceremonies were discontinued, including the *Tod kathin* which had previously included use of the boats. Also, the Ploughing ceremony was discontinued in 1936. See Christine Gray, 'Thailand – the soteriological state in the 1970s', PhD thesis, University of Chicago, 1986, p. 197.

3 Kobukua Suwannathat-pian has argued that the twenty-fifth centenary was used to distance Phibun from the 'coup group', meaning the various military and police officials upon which much of his power rested. See Kobukua Suwannathat-pian, *Thailand's Durable Premier, Phibun Through Three Decades, 1932–1957*, Oxford, Singapore and New York: Oxford University Press, 1995, pp. 141–142.

4 Having been cancelled in 1955, Constitution Day did return in 1956, but bore little relationship to the original event in both scale and design.

5 Pacharalada Juliapechr, *Naeo khit rueang kueng phutthakan nai sangkhom thai phutthasakkarat: 2475–2500* [The concept of 'Buddhist Meridian' in Thai society, 1932–1957], MA thesis, Thammasat University, Bangkok, 2005, p. 11.

6 *Kamnot kan ngan phutthaphayuhayatya lae phuttha prathip bucha nai kan chalong phutthasatawat, Anuson ngan phutthaphayahayatra than chonlamak nai kan cha-long 25 phutthasatawat* [Brochure to accompany the Buddhist Barge Ceremony for the celebrations for the 25 Buddhist centenary], 14 May 1957.

7 NA ST 0701.29/10 [3] '*Prakat chak chuan suan ratchakan lae prachachon chat krabuan nae na ngan chalong wan chat*' [Announcement to invite the bureaucracy and the people concerning the organisation of Nation Day Celebrations], p. 23.

8 Chatri Prakittanonthakan, *Khanarat chalong ratthathmmanun*, p. 134.

9 NA ST 0701.23.2/32 *Pathakatha kitchakan khong sinlapakon nai nganchalong rap thammanun* [About the proceedings of the Fine Arts Department at Constitution Day Fair], 13 December 1939, in Chatri Patiknonthakan, *Khanarat chalong ratthathmmanun*, p. 139.

10 Ibid., p. 134.

Cultural spectacle and Thai modernity 141

11 US NA Decimal File F 50–54, Box 2560, 892.191-BA/4-554. Graham S. Quate, Acting Economic Counsellor, US Embassy, Bangkok to Department of State, Washington, DC, 24 December 1953, 'Soviet Exhibit at the Constitution Day Fair, Bangkok, Thailand during December, 1953'.

12 Kenneth Osgood, *Total Cold War*, p. 221.

13 'Propaganda triumph at Thai Fair', *Business Week*, 25 December 1954, p. 21; 'America triumphs at Bangkok Fair', *Life*, 1 January 1955, p. 47.

14 US NA Decimal File 50–54, SA 250, Box 5628, 892.191-BA/10-454. American Embassy, Bangkok to Department of State, Washington, DC, 7 December 1954, 'Constitution Fair'.

15 *Business Week*, 25 December 1954, p. 21.

16 *Life*, 1 January 1955, p. 47.

17 NA (Newspaper Archive) M.13 '*Ran American nai ngan chalong ratthathammanun*' [The American Stall at the Constitution Day Fair], *Khao Phanit*, 12 December 1954.

18 NA (Newspaper Archive) M.13 *Ratthathammanun pi thi 22* [The Constitution Day Fair, Year 22], *Khao*, 12 December 1954.

19 US NA Decimal File 50–54, Box 5628, 892.191-BA/12-854, Ambassador Peurifoy to President of Cinerama Inc., 8 December 1954.

20 This is the argument made by Daniel Fineman in *A Special Relationship*.

21 Sopha Chanamool, *Chat Thai*, pp. 112–123. Also see Kasien Tejapira, *Commodifying Marxism*, p. 120.

22 US NA, Decimal File 50–54, Box 5632, 511.92/11-552. US Embassy to State Department, 5 November 1952, 'Revised Draft of the USIS country plan for Thailand'.

23 Ibid.

24 Ibid.

25 Ibid.

26 Ibid.

27 Ibid.

28 Ibid.

29 White House Office, National Security Council Staff Paper, 1948–1961/NSC Registry Series, 1947–62, Box 15 A82-18. Psychological Strategy Board (PSB), Washington, DC, 'U.S. Psychological Strategy with Respect to the Thai Peoples of Southeast Asia', 2 July 1953, p. 16. Thanks to Nattupoll Chaiching for providing me with this document.

30 Chris Baker and Pasuk Phongpaichit, *A History of Thailand*, New York: Cambridge University Press, 2005, pp. 146–147.

31 Phibun had taken it upon himself to bypass the normal diplomatic channels and invite himself to the United States in order to 'acquaint himself with current conditions'. Secretary of State John Foster Dulles, upon hearing about the intended visit, said that 'it is not clear to me that the merits of this visit were weighed against other possible requests for similar invitations'. But in response, it was explained that Phibun had made up his mind and had informed the Ambassador not just of the visit, but of the precise days he intended to travel. To try and convince John Foster Dulles, the Ambassador explained that Thailand was central to US psychological operations regionally, remaining 'the sole secure base for United States counter action against communism of the mainland of Asia'. It was also explained that 'with the changed communist tactics it will become even more important that Thailand remain a friendly Asian voice in Asian councils, and a pioneer of anti-communist Asian unity'. Finally, the Secretary of State agreed. US NA, Decimal File 1955–1959, Box 208 033.9211/1-1255 CS/W, Secretary of State John Foster Dulles to Mr Murphy, 12 January 1955.

142 *Cultural spectacle and Thai modernity*

32 Speaking at the Far East American Council of Commerce and Industry at the Waldorf Astoria, Phibun confirmed that Thailand would stand by America in the war against Communism, but that in order to do so, he would need to focus on more than just military spending; as he explained, 'while defence is supreme, good living in the home is no less important'. He thus encouraged direct American investment in the economy. See 'Premier Phibul invites US capital to Thailand', *Bangkok Post*, 13 May 1955, p. 7.

33 On 1 May, three days after his arrival in New York, Phibun and his wife were guests a private dinner attended by the Rockefellers, as reported by AP, 2 May 1955. See 'Phibul for US capital today', *Bangkok Post*, 2 May 1955, p. 3.

34 *Honyai* [The Prophet], *Phim Thai*, 15 May 1954, p. 3.

35 Daniel Fineman, *A Special Relationship*, p. 212.

36 Chris Baker and Pasuk Phongpaichit, *A History of Thailand*, p. 147.

37 In US documents about psychological warfare in Thailand, the monkhood and the system of village temples was regarded as an important channel for government propaganda. Psychological Strategy Board (PSB), 'U.S. Psychological Strategy with Respect to the Thai Peoples of Southeast Asia'.

38 Thanomjit Michin, '*Chomphon Po Phibun Songkhram kap ngan chalong 25 phuttasatawat 2495–2500*' [Phibun Songkhram and the 25th centennial celebrations of the Buddhist calendar, 1952–1957], MA thesis, Thammasat University, Bangkok, 1988, pp. 6–7.

39 NA MT 0201.2.1.18/45,1, Phraya Chindarak, Acting Sectretary to National Culture Institute Committee, *Kan chai thoi kham bang kham* [Clarifying the meaning of certain words].

40 The estimation that 'no more' than 30 boats were used is made in H.G. Quaritch Wales, *Siamese State Ceremonies: Their History and Function*, London: Bernard Quaritch, 1931.

41 Institute for Thai Studies, Thammasat Univerity, '*Krabuan phayuhayatra chonlamak*', *chat phim nueng nai okat phraratchaphithi mahamongkon chaloem phrachonmaphansa 6 rop*', Bangkok, 5 December 1999, p. 11. According to this document, it is the 'large' nature of the event, meaning the number of boats involved, that makes the 150th Centennial event so special. Footage of the procession is available at www.youtube.com/watch?v=mtCAEb_nu6g&feature=player_embedded [accessed 22 December 2014].

42 Royal Household to the Fine Arts Department, '*Ruea phraratchawong*' [The Royal Barges], 28 February 1947, in Phonrueatri Somphop Phirom, *Ruea phraratchaphithi phayuhayatra chonlamak*, Bangkok: Samnak phim Amarin Printing and Publishing, 1996, p. 116.

43 Ibid.

44 Fine Arts Department to Cabinet Secretary, '*Kan kep raksa ruea phraratchaphithi tang tang*' [The storage and maintenance of the ceremonial barges], 4 September 1947, in Phonrueatri Somphop Phirom, *Ruea phraratchaphithi phayuhayatra chonlamak*, p. 118.

45 Ibid.

46 Fine Arts Department to the Cabinet Secretary, 1 March 1948, in Phonrueatri Somphop Phirom, '*Ruea phraratchaphithi phayuhayatra chonlamak*', p. 120.

47 NA ST 0701.10/26, 2, Pho. Sriyanon, President of the Committee to organise the celebratrions for the 25th Buddhist Centenary to the Cabinet Secretary (administrative section), 13 December 1956, '*Ngop praman kan chat ngan chalong 25 phutthasatawat*'.

48 Christine Gray, 'Thailand – the soteriological state in the 1970s', PhD thesis, Chicago, IL, 1986, p. 219.

49 Chanida Chitbundid, *Kronggkan an nueang ma chak phraratchadamri: kansathapana phraratcha-amnat nam nai Phrabat Somdet Phrachao Yu Hua* [The Royally

Cultural spectacle and Thai modernity 143

Initiated Projects: The Making of King Bhumibol's Royal Hegemony], Bangkok: Foundation for the Promotion of Social Sciences and Humanities Textbooks Project, 2007, p. 77.

50 Paul Handley, *The King Never Smiles, A Biography of King Bhumibol Adulyadej*, New Haven, CT: Yale University Press, 2006, p. 131.

51 For specific analysis of the Royal Tours, and their relationship to the Phibun's struggle for political survival, see Prakan Klinfong, '*Kansadet phraratchadamnoen thongthi tangchangwat khong Phrabat Somdet Phrachao Yu Hua Bhumibol Adulyadej phutthasakkarat 2483–2530*', [His Majesty King Bhumipol Adulyadej's Visits to Provincial Areas, 1950–1987], MA thesis, Chulalongkorn University, Bangkok, 2008, pp. 84–134.

52 Kobukua Suwannathat-pian argues that the inclusion of the King in the Twenty-fifth Centenary was an attempt to pacify royalty 'in the hope of joining hands with the palace in an endeavour to reduce the unhealthy power of the Coup Group'. See Kobukua Suwannathat-pian, *Thailand's Durable Premier*, p. 142.

53 As a letter published in *Sayam rat* in 1956 revealed, campaign posters carried the tagline '*Phu sang chat thai*'. See letter entitled, '*Takrut*', published in *Sayam Rat*, 23 December 1956, in Kukrit Pramoj, *Panha pracham wan chut mai mai,* Bangkok: *Samnak phim kaona*, 1964, pp. 721–722.

54 Thanomjit Michin, '*Chomphon Po Phibun Songkhram kap ngan chalong 25 phuttasatawat 2495–2500*', p. 2.

55 In an initial memo about what the government wanted to achieve, it was explained that the statue should be considered a national wonder, set within a park that people could visit. This, it was made clear, should pay particular attention to impressing international visitors and providing Thais with a monument of which they could be truly proud. See NA ST 0701.10/5, '*Kan chat ngan chalong 25 satawat*', 30 July 1954, p. 2.

56 Poster promoting the Twenty-fifth Buddhist Centenary, NA SR 0201.63.1/5, '*Ngan chalong 25 phutthasatawat*'.

57 NA ST 0701.10/26, Pho. Sriyanon, President of the Committee to organise the celebratrions for the 25th Buddhist Centenary to the Cabinet Secretary (administrative section), '*Ngop praman kan chat ngan chalong 25 phutthasatawat*', 13 December 1956, p. 3.

58 '*Hang Tai Fa Co, Ltd. Ngan chalong khroprop 25 pi nai phutthasatawat thi 25*' San Seri, 11 May 1957, p. 9.

59 'Philips', *Sayam Nikon*, 10 May 1957, p. 6.

60 The collection was written as the celebration of a coming new era, and included Leftist essays by radical intellectuals including Jit Pumisak's important contribution to Leftist literature, 'The face of Thai feudalism today'. While the book was produced independently of the Phibun government, the inclusion of the Prime Minister's photograph in the inside cover indicated that it had been 'sanctioned' by the administration. See *Nitisat rap satawat mai* [Law in the new millennium], Bangkok, 1957. Thanks to Nattupoll Chaiching for photocopying this book for me.

61 Matthew Foley, *Cold War and National Assertion in Southeast Asia*.

62 '*Chak natang sayam nikon phoeng cha du di ni hlae*', *Sayam Nikon*, 18 May 1957, p. 3.

63 Suthachai Yimprasert, *Phaen ching chat thai, wa duai rat lae kantotan ratthasamai Chompon Po Phibun Songkhram khrang thi song (phutthasakkarat 2491–2500)* [Planning the Thai Nation: The State and the state's opposition in the era of Phibun Songkhram during the second term], Bangkok: *Samnak phim 6 tularamluek*, 2007, p. 379.

64 Thak Chaloemtiarana, *Thailand: The Politics of Despotic Paternalism*, p. 73.

65 Regular timetables were included in the newspaper providing details about what was going to happen over the following day.

144 *Cultural spectacle and Thai modernity*

66 '*Kan khlueanwai khong yaowachon*' [The Youth Movement], *San Seri*, Bangkok, 18 May 1957, p. 3.

67 '*Songkhram Yen*' [The Cold War], *San Seri*, Bangkok, 18 May 1957, p. 7.

68 Anonymous letter published in *Sayam Rat*, 22 May 1957, in *Kukrit Pramoj kap panha khong thai samai lueak tang mai riaproi*, Bangkok: Kasem bannakit, 1969, p. 372.

69 *Ta khlong thai mai*, Bangkok, August 1957.

70 '*Kan triam ngan chalong 25 phutthasatawat*' [Preparing for the 25th Centenary], ibid., p. 6.

71 The tagline in Thai reads '*Than phuyai sueng kon thai Thai kwa 18 lan ruchak khao di yu laeo pai ruam ngan yang tem yot*', ibid., p. 8.

72 Ibid., p. 10.

73 Ibid., p. 13.

74 Ibid.

75 Ibid., p. 10.

76 Ibid., p. 9.

5   The Tourist Organisation of Thailand and Cold War propaganda

The removal of Phibun Songkhram in a coup in 1957 was a pivotal moment in the post-war transfer of power from a small clique of government bureaucrats and military officers to a wider set of local and global interest groups. While, for a year after the coup, the exact development path of the Thai state was far from obvious, with Leftists looking best placed for political advancement, the 'revolution' of October 1958 laid out a very clear set of new objectives for the nation. Any inclination toward neutrality on the world stage was rejected as the new political elite sought to transform the country into a client of the United States, both politically as an ally in the Cold War, and as an economic partner in the expansion of US-led Capitalism. Sarit's invitation to advisors from the World Bank to take an active role in the country's future development was a message to the country and the world that the new regime was willing to accept direct foreign involvement in the Thai economy.[1] In further support for the 'internationalisation' of the Thai state, the new government provided the Chinese merchant class with the freedom it needed to work with international and Thai partners, consolidating their dominance of the country's import and export markets.[2] In the years that followed, new infrastructure and improved access to resources, as well as large amounts of US investment, aid and loans, led to rapid growth and a rise in living standards for many urban Thais. While in-favour military officials and civilian bureaucrats continued to gain from the growing wealth of the nation, the revolutionary era opened economic doors to many.

However, while Thailand's status as a client of an American-centred global order might have paved the way for new avenues in wealth production, it was also to usher in a period of authoritarian leadership.[3] From the moment when the Sarit regime came to power, state-initiated violence escalated steeply as the country entered a 'state of emergency'.[4] Moreover, the violence committed by the state was highly publicised. As with Phibun's first term in office, ideological production was recognised as fundamental to the success of the regime, and Sarit enjoyed the almost total support of the country's mainstream media. In the media, Thailand was presented as a country whose people were under almost constant threat from violent forces. Sometimes named as Communist, sometimes not, such forces were presented as an existential threat to the peaceful

146 *The Tourist Organization and propaganda*

life of the nation, and thus used to legitimise the regime as the country's ultimate protector.

With a language of violence employed as a principal tool to frame the daily life of the country's citizens, notions of culture were also transformed during the Sarit years. In particular, the new regime placed great emphasis on staging events that identified a stable and timeless identity and presented the regime as presiding over a Thai cultural renaissance. Events such as the royal barge ceremony and the *Tod Kathin*, the Surin elephant round-up, or the *Loi Kratong* festival were thus promoted in the local media as spectacles within which the authentic nation could be viewed, and held in juxtaposition to external forces that were, for better or worse, driving the nation's future. As a result, such narratives provided the basis for modelling an 'authentic' Thai way of life that could be presented as being under threat. Moreover, in the context of the Cold War, such a cultural life, free from the complex political and economic identity concerns attached to being a nation subservient to global systems of governance, was the solitary space from which to assert the 'fact' of an independent Thai nation.

What is particularly significant about how Thai cultural narratives emerged during the Sarit era, however, was the way in which they continued to be constructed principally for consumption by an elite urban readership. Throughout Phibun's first and second terms in office, cultural narratives had been concerned with establishing a largely urban-centred way of life that could easily be conformed to, as greater numbers were drawn into an enlarged national community. Now the subject of such cultural narratives shifted to establish symbolic characters that represented the majority population: de-centralised, standardised and localised personalities who could be brought into the centre in order to be admired and consumed. This, in turn, freed urban notions of what it meant to be Thai from declarations of universality, but also from the responsibility associated with attaching the nation to individual aspiration and lived experience. Rather, in line with the opening up of Bangkok as a political and economic centre for a global class of elite consumers, these new ideas about what it meant to be Thai lent themselves to the conformation of a new 'high-society' urban identity.

When engaging with the global stage, determined principally by the ideological constraints of the Cold War, urban Thais were thus encouraged to think of themselves as cultural actors who should participate in the preservation, celebration and spread of knowledge about Thai culture in order to foster the dream of a harmonious free world alliance. They were encouraged to present a stable vision of cultural unity and national integrity based upon a historic sense of freedom. Cultural exhibits were no longer to be found principally in museums, but in the realm of an anthropological way of life, rooted in traditional practices and behaviours. Rural populations, or the poor communities who lived on the banks of canals, were in turn established as the principal community of the nation, the gatekeepers of Thai identity, who held the keys from the past and the answers to the future.[5] In doing so, such ideological

The Tourist Organization and propaganda   147

production provided the tools with which urban Thailand was able to present itself as a 'safe' location for a 'new world aristocracy', to establish a local outpost of the free world.[6]

Thainess thus emerged during the period as an internationally recognisable commodity associated with a modern way of life that confirmed the integration of urban Thailand into the American, Cold War, order. Reinforcing the personal experience of modern life, it also offered avenues for the performance of modern citizenship within the international system. A paradoxical experience of Thai authenticity, achieved through participation in a commercial activity, this 'commodified authentic' was a complex phenomenon. As Elizabeth Outka has explained, it did 'not imply a search for authenticity per se but rather a search for a sustained contradiction that might allow consumers to be at once connected to a range of values roughly aligned with authenticity and yet also to be fully modern'.[7] It was an exclusive identity, in which the authentic nation was experienced as participation in US consumer culture with all of its ideological assertions about the supremacy of American power.

This chapter isolates one of the principal institutions that, established by the Sarit regime, was to drive this change, the Tourist Organisation of Thailand.[8] Established in the aftermath of the revolution, from its outset the organisation was interested in promoting the country not only to foreign visitors, largely American, but also to an urban-based Thai community. Its Thai-language publication *Anusan Osotho* [*Osotho Magazine*] was produced in a regular monthly edition available to purchase throughout Bangkok. Adopting a style not dissimilar to *Life*, and strikingly similar to the US propaganda magazine *Seriphap* [*Freedom*], *Anusan Osotho* provided a unique space for those interested in establishing themselves as global citizens to become consumers of new cultural products. Through this publication, through the organisation's new modern building on Rachadamnern Avenue, and through new cultural spectacles, the Tourist Organisation sought to secure an elite urban interest in participating in an international project to experience 'local' culture as part of the free world order. It also contributed to the formation of a cultural industry interested primarily in the reproduction of US Cold War ideology.[9]

The ideological location of Thai culture and the Sarit revolution

The political instability that rocked Thailand in the months following the elections of February 1957 had focused attempts by those now openly vying for power to draw from the popular sentiments being voiced throughout Bangkok. The city's students and intellectuals, whom Daniel Fineman describes as 'the most politically active segments of the population at this critical time', voiced the belief that the Americans had helped the Phibun regime to rig the election.[10] At the same time, the more Left-leaning newspapers continued to call for neutrality, claiming that tying the country so firmly to the fate of the USA risked endangering the population. While the Twenty-fifth Centenary had for Phibun been an attempt to formalise a shift away from the American alliance

148 *The Tourist Organization and propaganda*

(see chapter 4), most of his critics rejected its validity. Moreover, by this time Police Chief Phao Siriyond had become a figure of hate, portrayed in the press as a gangster, whose access to American funds continued to bolster his position.

It was Field Marshal Sarit Thanarat who was best placed to make the most of the political crisis. He was regarded as 'the most distant, unpredictable, and ostensibly anti-American' of the three most powerful men in the country.[11] He gained important support both from the student community and, increasingly, from the newspapers, over which he had significant influence. In June, Sarit began to move actively against the Phibun regime, setting up the Sahaphum Party and attracting many new allies opposed to the existing regime. The Party soon developed an anti-American line and gave further credence to the idea that Thailand should 'be friends with all countries' but exclusively allied to none. Most striking, according to Daniel Fineman, was that by July, the anti-American sentiment started focusing on the CIA, with Sarit himself joining an anti-CIA campaign. By repeatedly alluding to the clandestine operations of the US government, this was to feed popular feeling that, while Phibun talked about independence, the Thai government continued to act upon the whim of US demands.

As a result, when Sarit launched his coup against the Phibun government on 16 September 1957, it was directed as much against the underground CIA operation Sea Supply as against the existing regime.[12] Sarit and his troops, supported by a large crowd of supporters, marched on its offices and came face-to-face with the CIA station chief John Hart. A stand-off ensued that soon came perilously close to a full occupation. Fineman describes it as 'the single most frightening clash between Americans and Thais in the history of relations between the two countries'.[13] It also showed the extent to which the Phibun regime and American interests had grown together in the minds of the Bangkok public. Thus, when Sarit came to power following the coup, it was clear that if he was going to continue receiving the vast amounts of US aid that kept both the military and the country afloat, he needed to make a clean break from the past.

Initially, he struggled to do this. In the aftermath of the coup, Sarit continued to assert the view that he was a clean and principled politician, distinctly different from the exiled regime of Phibun and Phao. He respected the democratic reforms that Phibun had brought in during the two-year period of democratisation, and elections in December 1957 had led to a rise in Leftists elected into parliament. Moreover, with the press now almost entirely free, anti-American rhetoric continued. At the same time, however, relations between US officials and Sarit improved rapidly, with American policy makers recognising that in Sarit they had someone who could far better serve the interests of the United States. While the new government, it was understood, needed to show its independence from the USA, what Sarit actually sought was a far clearer and more stable relationship with his foreign patron.[14]

Importantly, following the coup of 1957, Sarit had not taken office himself. Before the election in December he had chosen Pote Sarasin to run the

The Tourist Organization and propaganda 149

government, and following the vote he installed Thanom Kittikachorn, largely because of his own ill health. Sarit was suffering from cirrhosis of the liver, and was forced to leave Thailand in January for treatment in the United States. With democratic government continuing in Bangkok, Sarit began to foster plans while in America for a formal end to the constitutional period. Upon his return, he quickly informed those close to him of his plans, and on 20 October 1958 he led a revolution against his own government. Seeking to replace the old regime entirely, Sarit's new government was immediately different in both character and style, and was to quickly prove the 'most repressive and authoritarian in Thai history'. It 'abrogated the constitution, dissolved Parliament, and vested all power in his newly formed Revolutionary Party', while at the same time banning all political parties and imposing strict press censorship.[15] Within two months, Sarit had ordered the execution of five ethnic Chinese on the charge of being Communist, and had arrested a string of influential Leftist intellectuals. The State Department, while it might have been cautious in articulating public support, nevertheless offered clear and unequivocal endorsement for the transformation of the Thai political system into a full blown, extra-constitutional, military dictatorship. The skill of the Sarit regime, and of the alliance struck with America, however, was the way in which it was able to present itself as independent at the same time as it established US interests at the cornerstone of its policy commitments.

In particular, the internal legitimisation of the revolution and the authoritarian regime that followed was rooted in the idea that the state was forced into a state of emergency, where the normal rules of democracy and constitutionalism had to be discontinued. In his speech to mark the fourth anniversary of the revolution, Field Marshal Sarit Thanarat explained it as follows:

> On the day before the revolution, that took place on 20 October 1958, our nation was about to fall into a great danger that if compared to a person, might be described as a bad fever ... the threat of Communism had revealed itself as a danger so great that those who worried about the safety of the nation came together to voice their common concern about the future survival of the nation. It was in this context that I made a revolution. And the authority of the revolution, which follows in accordance to the laws that we have passed have meant that our attempts to suppress Communism have left it crushed, so that, for the people and the nation, it has been almost entirely eliminated.[16]

Prefacing the temporary end of democracy with a need to protect the country from Communism, the regime strongly asserted its alliance with the United States, and the bi-polar version of the world constructed through Cold War ideology. It also, however, promoted the idea that the difference between his regime and the preceding one was that now the country had seen a revival in both its economic fortunes and its cultural identity. These, it was made clear, were mutually dependent, for as the speech went on to identify, the maintenance of

150 *The Tourist Organization and propaganda*

peace was a prerequisite for economic growth. By protecting the country from Communism, and by maintaining a harmonious and unified Thai society, Sarit explained, the government had, in co-operation with the World Bank, been able to achieve a rapid development of the country's economy.[17]

Newspapers, all of which offered unflinching support for the regime, reinforced this view, endlessly asserting the threat of violence.[18] Presenting Thailand itself as disconnected from such violence, they also enforced the totalitarian ideology, in which any threat to Thai daily life could be viewed as Communist, and where Thai cultural life needed to be protected by a strong state supported by American allies. Separate from the difficult business of contemporary global politics, Thai daily life was thus sentimentalised and viewed in juxtaposition to the conflicts determining life throughout the region. Articles that explained the newly invigorated cultural calendar in detail were presented as ideologically neutral, located on newspaper pages littered with messy international conflicts. Heavily censored and largely free from satirical content, the newspapers therefore supported the idea that the threat of violence was the principal obstruction to a peaceful society.

Crucial to Sarit's political success, therefore, was the performance not only of an authoritarian state that could act as protector, but also of one interested in protecting an everyday Thai way of life. While the revolution ended any talk of establishing an egalitarian national community, it did so by replacing it with a new narrative about Thai citizenship, based upon what was presented as the 'real' character of the Thai people. Describing the new political system to the foreign-language press, government spokesman Thanat Khoman explained that 'the fundamental cause of our political instability in the past lies in the sudden transplantation of alien institutions onto our soil without careful preparation and more particularly, without proper regard to the circumstances that prevail in our homeland, the nature and characteristics of our own people'. 'If we look at our national history', he went on to explain, 'we can see very well, that this country works better and prospers under an authority – not a tyrannical authority, but a unifying authority, around which, all unifying elements of the nation can rally.'[19] According to Thak Chaloemtiarana, therefore, the Sarit regime 'can be said to be revolutionary in the sense that it tried to overthrow a whole political system inherited from 1932, and to create one that could be described as more "Thai" in nature'.[20]

In truth, however, the ideological basis for the Sarit regime was rooted not in an anthropological understanding of Thai cultural character, but rather in a global consumer culture emanating from the United States that was concerned principally with the logic of the Cold War. For over a decade, US representations of Thailand had depicted it in such a way, as an *Oasis on a Troubled Continent*. Home to a pristine cultural community, uninhibited by the baggage of colonialism and in need of protection from the threat of Communist aggression, Thailand's status as a peaceful haven remained intact and, despite the anti-American sentiment that had dominated the country's foreign relations over the previous years, Thailand remained a friend and an

The Tourist Organization and propaganda   151

ally. Maintaining the relationship with the USA would therefore require the Sarit regime to find its own way of replicating the constructions that dominated American visions of Thai society. That was the task with which the newly established Tourist Organisation of Thailand was principally charged.

The Tourist Organisation of Thailand and Cold War ideology

Established less than a year following the Sarit revolution, from the beginning the Tourist Organisation was under little illusion that the success of a tourist industry would depend on the ability to capture American hearts and minds. Charged with establishing a tourist industry that would contribute to the economic growth of the country, the initial investigations of the authority confirmed that Americans were by far the most important group. In Inter-continental Hotels' promotional material sent to the Thai government in 1960, it was pointed out that American tourism was the 'biggest single item of all dollar earnings for the United Kingdom, France and Italy', arguing that the same could increasingly be possible for countries of the 'Far East'.[21] Two years later, and arrival statistics showed that American visitors provided the largest number of arrivals. In the same year, the Pacific Area Travel Association (PATA) supported the view that America should be considered the most important tourist market.[22] While Europe was the second most promising area, the report claimed that 'indications are that only about 20 per cent of the American total will become available from all European countries in over the next five years'.[23] Responsible for both conducting research into what tourists wanted, and then channelling such research into compelling advertising campaigns, the authority thus became fixed on convincing visitors that Thailand would provide them with the experience they desired. In doing so, it would have to present Thailand in a way that was attractive to a US population for whom tourism had already become a way of extending American influence and channelling the power of American consumer culture as a means to change the world.

As Christopher Endy has explained, since the end of the Second World War the US media and the US state had supported the view that tourism could act as a powerful tool in dispelling negative sentiment toward America fostered first by Nazi and now by Soviet propaganda. First by *Travel* and then by the *Readers Digest* in 1949, US tourists were encouraged to think of themselves as 'ambassadors of good will', who when abroad should 'speak humbly but confidently about the virtues of American foreign policy'.[24] Fuelled by the prosperity of post-war American society and infused with strong views about the integrity of American power, tourism had thus emerged as a supremely ideological activity. In a climate of increased prosperity, where the belief in American moral authority in the world was axiomatic, writers such as James Michener channelled enormous energy into informing American society about Asia, and into encouraging the private American citizen to adopt the responsi-bility of their state in their interactions abroad. Functioning as a 'cultural

152 *The Tourist Organization and propaganda*

space' through which Americans could imagine their relationship with the world through a set of benevolent and mutually beneficial interactions, the US tourist emerged during the Cold War as an 'emblem of America's benign, non-imperial internationalism'.[25]

Central to the promotion of Thailand to US tourists, therefore, was confirmation of the idea that it was a friend and an ally, and therefore a safe place for them to travel. In a press release issued by the Tourist Organisation in 1962, Americans were informed that Thailand was 'an eastern outpost of the Free World', and that a 'visit to Thailand is a unique experience: it represents the Orient at its best'. Importantly, it also sought to emphasise the fact that the country posed no threat of violence toward the visitor:

> Bangkok – and all of Thailand – is at PEACE. Peace is the essence of Thailand. The alarms of Far-eastern events in recent months will not disturb you. No evidence presents itself, in the form of military personnel or preparations, to disturb your PEACEFUL visit. Please come: traditional Thai hospitality and courtesy will make your visit to Thailand an event which will not dim in memory.[26]

Apparently untouched by the Cold War, Thailand was sold as a place where Americans could dissociate themselves from the frequent reports in newspapers and magazines, and on television screens, of the conflicts that riddled Asia. A common theme of US portrayals of the country since the end of the Second World War, Thailand was portrayed as a country largely unaffected by the Communist-inspired conflicts that raged on its borders, and therefore as a country where Americans could enjoy getting to know a different culture without risk to their safety. As such, Thailand's status as a country unaffected by decolonisation and self-determination was used to reassure visitors they would receive a warm welcome. As an article in *The New York Times* explained in 1957, the fear of the American tourist in Asia was that he regularly had to confront the threat of violence from a local population that viewed the 'white man' with 'neurotic suspicions', 'fears', 'long-suppressed resentments and hatreds'.[27] In Thailand, however, the message was that 'hospitality and courtesy await!'.[28]

Secure in the knowledge that they would not be confronted by a hostile Thai population, Americans were instead invited to witness a display of cultural activity put on for their benefit. Daily performances were regularly staged for tourists at convenient sites across the city, such as Thai folk dancing at the Sonprasong School, and the Kodak show, which gave visitors the opportunity to capture the perfect shot of classical Thai dancing.[29] Also, a string of 'traditional' cultural spectacles was organised by the authority throughout the year. In May 1962 it was reported that special facilities had been arranged, free of charge, outside the Grand Palace so that 120 tourists would be able to 'obtain a close-up view of the ancient ploughing ceremony', an event that His Majesty the King would be personally attending.[30]

The Tourist Organization and propaganda   153

In promotional material produced by the organisation, visitors would be informed of this privileged access to the events and images that had featured for over a decade on screen and in print back in the United States. A Tourist Organisation supplement in the English language, *Bangkok World Sunday Magazine*, provided tourists with weekly updates as to what the week ahead promised; and in the authority's main English-language publication *Holiday Time in Thailand*, adverts sought to entice audiences to the most lavish displays of Thai culture.[31] Supported by assurances that the events were rooted in a centuries-long tradition, events such as the royal barge ceremony, which was performed on a near-annual basis throughout the 1960s, were explained in their 'authentic' cultural context. *Holiday Time in Thailand* in August 1961, three months prior to the ceremony, promoted it as a unique encounter with the 'real' Thailand, which until now foreigners had witnessed only on the big screen. It did so by noting that 'His Majesty the King will play a predominant part' in an 'important ceremony' that 'mirrors the pomp and circumstance of Ancient Thailand; rare, singular and gorgeously decorated, the Royal Barges pass in procession down the Chao Phya River', 'an event unequalled in Pacificana'.[32]

Reinforcing the view that Thailand was rooted in an age-old tradition, *Holiday Time in Thailand* also presented the country as a place now engaged in a process of rapid modernisation. 'Once upon a time', one such article explained, 'there lived a people called the Siamese', where 'the men went around wearing funny little hats and looking inscrutable', where 'young ladies spent their time curling and uncurling their fingers and doing exotic dances', and where 'Every so often an English governess would turn up to try and civilise them'.[33] Now, however, largely as a consequence of this peaceful way of life, change was coming to the country in the form of foreign intervention in the economy.

> In a southern suburb of Bangkok in the middle of paddy fields new factories are springing up. Foreign investors, taking advantage of the stability and rapid development of the economy, are flocking to Thailand in great numbers. Among the big names are International Pharmaceuticals, Colgate, Firestone, Merck, Sharpe and Dohme, Anglo Thai (Ford) and Toyota.[34]

Echoing strongly the principal themes of American depictions of the relationship between Thailand and the USA, visitors were thus encouraged to think of Thailand as a place where development was happening as a result of foreign investment and in harmony with traditional cultural practices. This, in turn, presented Thailand as a site of victory for the peaceful alliance between the USA and one of its Asian allies. A cultural industry, which sought access to an American market, the Tourist Organisation produced material that served as the facilitator of cultural diplomacy between the two countries. In doing so, it sought to reinforce what Christina Klein has described as 'the universalizing assumptions of modernization theory by offering proof that, in spite of their differences, Americans and people in developing nations could learn to understand each other'.[35]

154 *The Tourist Organization and propaganda*

The Tourist Organisation sought to convince Americans that Thailand offered an opportunity to 'get to know' an Asian nation as part of a larger US imperial project. As an editorial in *Holiday Time in Thailand* in 1962 explained, 'we stand on the threshold of a vital awakening among peoples and nations', which comes from the 'conscientious desire, individually and collectively, to understand each other – culturally or otherwise', and which might lead to 'peace and good-will'.[36] Drawing from an international language about tourism, promoted through organisations such as the PATA, the magazine adopted the American-held vision that travel should contribute to the formation of political and economic alliances built upon friendship and understanding between different cultures. Displacing any notion of a competing modernity, Thailand's 'character' was nonetheless constantly reinforced as one governed not by a freedom based upon modern democratic citizenship, but by one dependent on the maintenance of deeply held customs and traditions.

This presumption, that Thai culture existed outside of the trappings of modern life, was further reinforced in the more elaborate and headline-driven activities organised by the organisation. In the same year as the Sarit revolution, rumours of anger toward Americans, particularly in Southeast Asia, had been used to strengthen the argument that Americans needed to engage more with local communities when they travelled. William Lederer and Eugene Burdick's 1958 novel *The Ugly American* portrayed a fictional country in Southeast Asia where the battle for the hearts and minds of the local population was being lost due to a lack of American interest in the 'real' needs of the local population. Christine Skwiot has explained how the authors 'condemned a US diplomatic corps and other emissaries of the nation for preferring to lead globe-trotting, country-clubbing, party-going lives in capital cities over working with the people to develop new aspiring nations and their economies'.[37] Working to provide the antidote to a failure of 'people-to-people' diplomacy, American tourists were, according to Skwiot, encouraged to work 'against the grain of luxury-loving bureaucrats, or at least, to supporting their peoples' aspirations for self-determination'.[38]

Trips out into the countryside, far away from the luxury and convenience of the modern city, were therefore used by the Tourist Organisation of Thailand to provide tourists with experiences that helped them to feel like they were experiencing a more authentic version of the country. One of the most obvious examples was the institutionalisation of the Surin elephant round-up as an annual event.[39] The first was held in November 1960, when the province's governor had invited the Tourist Organisation to participate in an event that he had organised independently. Agreeing to support it, the Tourist Organisation had also made it clear to the governor that it could not be responsible for organising an event so far from Bangkok. Instead, it committed to publicising the event to potentially interested foreign visitors.[40] A year later, however, and the Organisation began to take a more active role in the spectacle, both in its organisation and its promotion. On Friday 17 November 1961, therefore, staff from the organisation, including its President, General Chalermchai, accompanied

The Tourist Organization and propaganda   155

Thais and foreigners on a specially organised overnight train from the capital, to make the 420 km journey to the north-eastern province.[41] When they arrived at the station they were ushered into cars to complete the journey, another 42 gruelling kilometres along dusty roads to the *amphur* of Tha Tum, home of the provincial airfield. After breakfast, at 9 00 am the spectacle began with the re-enactment of a local custom in which *mahouts* performed the ritual of making offerings to the spirits to ask for a successful elephant round-up. Then, during the round-up itself, about 100 animals were successfully herded together before the crowd, and following that a ceremonial dance called the *Den sak* was performed by the young women of the village, who led a procession of the elephants. Finally, the more light-hearted part of the day was marked by an elephant race and then elephant rides for the foreign tourists.[42]

Demand for tickets to the 1961 event outnumbered places, and General Chalermchai, at the December meeting, noted the success of the trip.[43] Upon returning from a meeting of the PATA in Hong Kong (in March) he went further, reporting that the PATA Chairman himself had singled out the elephant round-up, saying that the Tourist Organisation should elevate it to an annual event of national importance.[44] As a result, General Chalermchai confirmed that plans to do just that were now well under way. However, he also recognised that, in order to make that possible, the Tourist Organisation would have to take the lead in making the arrangements. In particular, he made it clear that the facilities had to be made suitable for guests, and thus announced that the organisation would be investing 100,000 baht in the construction of a thousand-seat grandstand. Another obvious problem was the transport arrangements, and he therefore made it clear that he would be working closely with the Ministry of Transport to encourage it to lay concrete on the road from the *amphur* to the provincial capital. He would also ensure that the bridges along the route were passable. Finally, by working with the Railway Department, he would develop the public amenities at the station to a standard suitable to look after guests.[45] Recognising the spectacle as one that held a particularly strong, and in many ways surprising interest for foreigners, General Chalermchai concluded that 'the success of the event is clear', providing an 'exotic experience for the foreigner'.[46] In July 1962, a PATA press release confirmed the sentiment, inaugurating the event as the 'annual elephant show', 'the only one of its kind anywhere, and exciting!'[47]

The popularity of the Surin elephant round-up, just as with the other activities organised by the organisation, lay in the fact that it offered a vision of the authentic Thai nation as one determined through cultural sovereignty that displaced concerns about economic and political independence. In line with modernisation theory, Thailand was presented to Americans as a country where modern life remained limited to the exclusive spaces associated with cosmopolitan social practices and lifestyles presumed to have emanated from the West. Thainess, on the other hand, was presented as an identity governed by the rhythm of the annual cultural calendar. Living in a constant tension with the modern world, the change that was coming to Thailand, in the form

156 *The Tourist Organization and propaganda*

of roads and infrastructure, was to be tempered by protection of 'pure' cultural traditions. By applying value to those cultural traditions, Americans were sanctioned to think of tourism as an activity that supported that endeavour. The buying of handicrafts, just as with Jim Thompson's Thai silk, allowed for the maintenance of traditional lifestyles that might otherwise be undermined by modernity. Moreover, by laying on trips that allowed Americans to escape the comfort of the hotel, the Tourist Organisation provided visitors with experiences that provided access to a 'real' version of the country, which was presumed to exist beyond the hotel's walls. In doing so, it also confirmed the idea that the authentic nation existed outside modern time-keeping, elevating the American visitor onto a different temporal plain and serving to reinforce the distance that existed between guest and host.

Tourism and global culture

However, while the primary function of the Tourist Organisation was to promote Thailand to foreigners, it would also recognise the interest of urban Thai populations in a tourist culture that since the middle of the nineteenth century had developed as an important social activity marking an individual's participation in a 'civilised' global culture.[48] Attached to the networks of trade and commerce emanating from Europe, hotels in particular had emerged following the country's opening up to European interests in the middle of the century, and had quickly come to provide space for the cultivation of an elite-oriented imperial culture within the country. Hotels such as the Oriental had acted as a space within which a privileged Thai community could seek access to the European-centred world, to learn about imperial social practices and develop networks with colonial representatives.[49] Over time, the desire to project Thailand as a modern and civilised community, and to foster deeper relations with those powers, led to the building of a number of Thai-owned hotels, the most famous of which was at Hua Hin.[50] It also inspired wealthy Thais to take up the European interest in travel. Aided by the building of the railways from the beginning of the twentieth century, such internal travel to a small number of locations was by 1932 regarded as a powerful marker of civilised behaviour.[51]

Under the constitutional regime, and in particular under Phibun Songkhram, the policy to nationalise such practices led to a greater emphasis on internal tourist promotion as a marker of Thai identity. Moreover, seeking to provide the Thai bureaucracy with its own privileged space within which to cultivate both networks and culture, the government commissioned the building of a new hotel at the bottom of Rachadamnern Avenue, opened in 1942. The Rattanakosin Hotel was in many ways designed to be the flagship of the Prime Minister's national construction programme, and was built with the intention that it might rival the other great modernist hotels of Europe and America. Nestled at the bottom of the new commercial centre, the hotel would offer visiting bureaucrats the opportunity to stay at a Thai-owned establishment designed to provide an 'example of a Thai Hotel that displays the elegance of the Thai people'. It would, as such, offer Thais the opportunity to 'eat well, and live well', within a space of privilege where Thai communities were located at the top.[52]

However, as one of the last wartime additions to the Bangkok skyline, it had immediately struggled to live up to expectations. With Thailand under Japanese occupation, travel both to and around the city was difficult and dangerous, and despite attempts to encourage the bureaucracy to hold events there, the status of the hotel as a source of pride for Thai communities had faltered. This was compounded at the end of the war when, as American and British troops flooded into the city, the Rattanakosin was often viewed in a derisory fashion. As Alexander MacDonald described it, the hotel was seen as 'a government building enterprise which assembled into one structure all the worst sins of modern architecture'.[53] Recognising its failure to live up to the expectations of international guests, a modernisation programme was implemented, including the provision of a 24-hour water supply and lifts.[54] By the middle of the 1950s, with visitors continuing to prefer foreign-owned establishments, the ambition of a Thai-owned hotel that could act as a symbol of pride for the Thai nation remained unfulfilled, and in 1954 the Prime Minister concluded that, with the numbers of foreign visitors continuing to increase, there was an urgent need to build an 'even more modern' hotel.[55]

The construction of the Erawan Hotel, finished in 1956, was intended to overcome this problem, and in many ways proved an instant success among foreign visitors. However, the apparent achievement of the regime to successfully provide a 'first-class' experience had already lost its ideological authority within the country. Upon opening in January 1957, the hotel immediately achieved full occupancy. But the addition of the hotel to the city was largely ignored by the press, who had grown suspicious of visitors from the USA and who viewed the government's economic policies as fundamentally opposed to the interests of the population. Situated on the other side of town, away from the buildings constructed to serve a Thai community, the building did little to counter the sentiment. Instead of a place for a Thai 'victory' on the world stage, the Erawan was rather a site for elite interaction and relationship building, and as a result failed to capture the imagination of an urban Bangkok population that continued to view the Thai–American partnership as opaque and corrupt.[56]

At the same time, internal tourist promotion, having formed a mainstay of government propaganda during the Second World War, occupied a far less prominent position in the following decade. While it had continued, the reduction in Thai living standards, and the growing gulf between American and Thai consumer cultures, were reflected in a highly fragmented tourist literature. Magazines produced for Thai readers continued to display tourism as an elite activity. However, removed from the Ministry of Commerce and placed under the authority of the Public Relations Department, the then named Tourist Bureau had been under-resourced during much of the 1950s,

158 *The Tourist Organization and propaganda*

manned by only six members of staff.[57] Moreover, tourist promotion, while continuing to promote travel as an important feature of a civilised lifestyle, avoided the aspirational messages that had governed tourist literature previously.[58] Failing to account for the divergence in Thai living standards from those in America, tourist literature offered little reassurance of a more leisurely future for the citizens of Bangkok.

Literature intended for foreign readers, on the other hand, continued to see tourist promotion as a way of informing important visitors of Thailand's independent status as a modern, civilised country. Particularly toward the middle of the 1950s, as the country prepared for elections, the Tourist Bureau sought to promote the country as a nation that sought parity with the West. Published in 1956, to commemorate the New Year, a magazine produced by the Bureau, titled *Democratic Thailand*, presented the country as a place where 'the supreme power rests with the people' and a place that 'has kept pace with the advancement of the world in all fields'. 'Education, culture, commerce, industry and fine arts', it explained, 'have been developed to a degree comparable with other advanced countries'.[59] It also expressed the government's emphasis on culture, claiming that 'all nations are now aware that culture is the one and only factor making for lasting national prosperity, that a high cultural standard is indispensable for international understanding and is the only effective weapon for fighting evil ideologies'.[60] Its front cover, far from displaying iconic scenes replicating the desires of potential guests, displayed an image of the Parliament, Democracy Monument (built to celebrate the constitution), and Victory Monument (to celebrate the victory against the French).

From the birth of the Tourist Organisation of Thailand, however, it was made clear that the organisation would operate in an entirely different manner. With the bureaucracy having become regarded as an aloof community that was out of touch with the aspirations of the people, the Tourist Organisation sought to embed itself in urban Thai life. Acting somewhere between a government department and a private authority, it was made clear from the outset that it would work on a more informal basis.[61] Importantly, it also maintained two names. While to foreigners it would be known as the Tourist Organisation of Thailand (latter referred to as the Tourist Authority of Thailand), to Thais it would maintain its initial name, The Organisation for the Development of a Tourist Industry. Tied once again to a lineal developmental trajectory, tourist literature produced for Thai communities thus regained the aspirational tone it had taken during the 1930s, fusing the message of economic prosperity with an equally powerful message about Thai cultural identity. As Sarit Thanarat explained at a ceremony to mark the opening of the organisation, later reprinted in its Thai language mouthpiece, *Anusan Osotho*:

> The benefits that the state can gain from a tourist industry are not in the direct income received by the government, but in an income that can't be seen. Moreover, what is most important is that it allows us to display the culture and virtue of the Thai people for the world to see.[62]

The Tourist Organization and propaganda   159

Promoting tourism as a way of removing the gulf between how Thailand was viewed internationally and how Thais thought of themselves, *Anusan Osotho* provided its readers with insights into what visitors appreciated about the country, in order to foster a new sense of national pride over characteristics that had been lost in the post-war years. As an accompanying article in the first edition claimed, 'Thailand has an exquisite natural beauty, a generous and hospitable native population, extraordinary art and culture and a rich tradition, all qualities that will attract foreigners in large numbers', but at the moment, 'the value of these things are not clear to us, for they have been buried deep in the mud'.[63] Using foreign interest in Thai culture as proof of its virtue, the statement exploited anxieties about the failure to represent the nation to the world, in order to claim the need for a re-investigation of where the value of being Thai really lay.

At the same time, the Tourist Organisation made efforts to re-establish the arenas of privilege within which urban Thai communities could successfully integrate into the elite world of what was now an American imperial culture. Seeking to transform the representation of the alliance with the USA from one that indicated competition into one based upon the mutual celebration of difference, such spaces served to mark Thailand's participation in global culture flows by referencing Thai culture as an adornment to American-led modernisation. The Erawan Hotel, while continuing to promote itself as one of the most civilised and international spaces in the city, nevertheless was to conform to the expectations of tourists arriving largely from America by, 'for the sake of the tourist trade', ensuring that it provided 'a Thai atmosphere'.[64] Held in December 1960 to announce changes to the hotel, a press conference provided what the *Bangkok Post* described as a 'Thai treat for tourists'.[65] Attending journalists were served a meal in which the usual Western and Chinese cuisine now also featured Thai dishes, and they were also shown examples of what *San Seri* described as a 'revolution back to the costumes of the past'.[66] The maids, it was explained to journalists, would now be dressed in 'Chiengmai styles' made with Thai silk, and the waiters would be dressed like palace pages. Only the concessionaire would continue to wear the international 'admiral's uniform'.[67] In a similar way to how Thai fabrics were used in *House & Garden* to psychologically reference the centrality of American modernity, so the modern hotel was decked out in reassuring markers of a culturally unique location to reassure guests of the harmony between the forces of Thai tradition and American-led development. For Thai audiences, however, while the changes might have enforced a certain hierarchy, they also provided evidence of the country's relevance to that American order.

Indeed, once re-vamped, the Erawan became a centre for the cultivation of cosmopolitan culture, and was presented in *Anusan Osotho* as an international hub. Cultural representatives from around the world, including film stars, musicians and beauty queens, stayed at the Erawan, and in doing so brought the other free world nations into the Thai-owned site. Allowing the Thai state to associate itself with the messages being projected internationally,

160 *The Tourist Organization and propaganda*

activities at the Erawan became iconic reminders of how internal ideological assertions fitted with its status internationally. As was reported to the Bangkok public in 1963, three beauty queens who were travelling the world promoting the Miss World Contest were guests of the Tourist Organisation and therefore were staying at the Erawan Hotel. The image of Thai government employees mixing freely with modern women of the free world was proof that Thais were now able to participate, and that the state was able to facilitate that participation.

Apart from the Erawan Hotel, the Tourist Organisation also opened a number of buildings that were to become central locations for Thais to mingle with foreign visitors, and within which Thailand's revitalised cultural life could be displayed. At the shopping centre on Sri Ayutthaha Road, shoppers could purchase Thai handicrafts, and from April 1962 a new, modern headquarters on Rachadamnern Avenue was opened that included a display and sales centre. Moreover, in *Anusan Osotho*, the open and informal nature of the Tourist Organisation was repeatedly emphasised, and images of visitors to the centre were regularly accompanied with text telling readers the number both of foreign and Thai guests. In one example, therefore, it was explained that in July 1961 a total of 1044 people visited *Osotho*, 682 of whom were foreign and 373 were Thai, while below, General Chalermchai was pictured in conversation with foreign delegates from the New York World Fair, engaged in what was described as an 'exchange of opinions'.[68] In the national press, adverts were placed which invited members of urban high society, including 'students, cultured people and journalists', to attend important events such as the opening ceremonies of the Seventeenth General Assembly of the International Union of Official Travel Organisations (IUOTO) on 6 November 1962.[69]

Projecting an image of authority and knowledge about the wants and desires of visitors, the Tourist Organisation thus presented itself as an important player in the state's attempts, following the Sarit revolution, to integrate the country into a US-centred community of nations. It was also able to promote itself as a principal actor in negotiations with international representatives as to how Thailand should be portrayed on the world stage. However, by establishing an equally strong public relations message to Thai citizens, and by making great efforts to open up privileged international spaces to urban Thais, it worked hard to make the city's engaged population feel included in the process. In doing so, the organisation was able to present the new cultural narratives about what it meant to be Thai as a way of establishing communication with the international community.

Free world citizenship and cultural representation

The role of the Tourist Organisation in promoting a renaissance in Thai cultural identity through its association with the free world was facilitated by *Anusan Osotho* in the form of regular letters to the editor. As had long been a feature of publications that sought a popular following, letter writing was used to cement the organisation in the minds of its readership as an open and engaged

The Tourist Organization and propaganda 161

institution, actively involved in an organic conversation with the general public about what should and should not be an appropriate representation of the nation. The letter pages were presented as a space where confusion, or even dissatisfaction, about the organisation's activities could be voiced openly and then dealt with in a public forum. With political censorship and freedom of speech heavily restricted by state-led media, the tourist magazine was therefore one of the few government-sponsored publications that took on a democratic tone, where – free from political or economic debate – the very meaning of what it meant to be Thai could be discussed freely. As one letter, from Thonburi resident Chalermchai Thalalakson, declared in 1961, 'I love *Anusan Osotho*. It is informative about all sorts of things. But I also consider it to be my magazine as much as anyone else's. I have a right to criticize, praise and express my opinion.'[70]

Almost exclusively from Bangkok, the letters published in the magazine engaged seriously with the Tourist Organisation's projection of a national culture and, at this early stage in its development, with the way it should represent this culture in its conceptual form, through photography and print in both its Thai- and English-language material. As Chalermchai's letter explained, despite appreciating the magazine, he questioned the extent to which the authority was failing to take this responsibly seriously, stating that 'the front cover should be of a view of natural beauty'. As for the organisation's English-language publication *Holiday Time in Thailand*, he complained that 'the pictures here shouldn't be ones that are not beautiful to look at, especially when they are to be displayed to foreigners, like pictures of an old and decrepit house, or a dwelling on the river with a shirt and trousers hung up, staring out at the viewer'.[71]

Yet, in response to Chalermchai's letter, the Tourist Organisation took on an authoritative tone, explaining that his assumptions about what were appropriate photos in promoting Thailand were not necessarily correct. It assured him that when it came to the Thai-language publication, the majority of pictures would always remain the ubiquitous waterfall, lake or paddy field, that when it came to foreigners, the organisation had to think about what it was they actually wanted to experience. The editors thus explained that, according to their research, 'in the aftermath of the Second World War the majority of tourists travelled to different countries in order to mix with local native populations, to places that were exotic and new'. It also explained that American-made films, in particular *Walt Disney's Siam* (1954) and *Around the World in 80 Days* (1956), had framed Thailand in a certain way, and that, in reference to the reader's criticism of a *klong*-side dwelling (a house beside a canal), life on the water had emerged as a central theme. It explained that these images could not be removed from the mind of the foreigner, and that the organisation thus had no choice but to embrace and, more importantly, exploit them. It also encouraged the reader to understand the psychology of the foreign visitor, to recognise that this development need not necessarily be cause for alarm:

162 *The Tourist Organization and propaganda*

If you were to hear what foreigners say when they meet those Thai who live on the side of the *klongs*, I am sure you would actually be very pleased. They say that these people have radiant and smiley faces, they are warm and welcoming, open and friendly; they say that they are the best ambassadors of the nation in the project to develop peace and understanding across the peoples of the world, much more successful than a bureaucrat could ever be ... The fact is that a modern Western looking building would have no value to a tourist who has come to look at houses which are unique to our country, because there is nothing exotic or enticing about it to them. Such a picture belongs only in a document dealing with the development of the country.[72]

Published in July 1961, another letter emphasised the fact that foreigners had very specific ideas about what they wanted to see when they came to Thailand, and that very often they sat uncomfortably with urban Thai sensibilities. Claiming to have 'many *farang* friends', the writer said that they would 'often request for him to take them on a trip into the countryside'.[73] Yet this, he made clear, was difficult, because there was no suitable place to go: 'if I was to take them they would not be satisfied with what they would find, the native population are just not ready to receive such guests, and even if they are willing, they are just not pure enough for us to show them to foreigners with pride'.[74] To rectify the problem, he suggested that the organisation should 'set up a show village that is close to Bangkok which continues to look after the authentic order and culture of the Thai people in order to display to foreigners'. These villagers, he went on, should 'be dressed in the typical dress of the countryside, they should be living the typical life of the countryside and they should show the typical music and dance of the countryside'.[75] Drawing from existing mantras about a civilisational lag between Thai communities and international ones, this letter argued for a 'purification' of rural culture to a yet-unachieved authentic state. Recognising this state to be manufactured for the sake of tourism, it was nonetheless representative of a 'typical' way of life rooted in the cultural traditions of rural communities. In other words, he argued that the 'real' Thai culture could be liberated, or uncovered and polished, through an embrace of the tourist trade. Both letters, however, serve as examples of how the Tourist Organisation facilitated a conversation about Thailand based upon what foreigners wanted to experience, and which in turn contributed to the view that there needed to be an active reconstruction of the nation's iconography specifically in response to those needs.

Encouraging young and aspirational social groups to join such a discussion was further achieved through an engagement with the country's artistic talent. Long engaged with the latest trends in art, and for nearly two decades employed by the state in various guises to secure civilisational narratives of a Thai artistic parity with the civilised nations of the world, the Tourist Organisation played an important role in driving forward a change in style and purpose in artistic expression among the urban population. As with the letters, it did so in order

The Tourist Organization and propaganda 163

to focus artistic minds on what form Thai culture should take, so that it might service a growing tourist industry. On 23 September 1961, therefore, the Tourist Organisation combined forces with the Shell Oil Company and Thai International Airlines in announcing an art competition, the aim of which was 'to induce both Thais and foreigners to admire what is beautiful about the country'.[76] The subject matter, it was stipulated, 'should contain beautiful landscapes, architecture, customs, and culture of Thailand', and those who entered should paint an image that would display a clear value in the promotion of tourism.[77] They should, it was stipulated, identify 'Thailand's fascinating tourist attractions, through artistic expression', in order to provide 'encouragement to Thai artists'.[78]

For the winners, the rewards would be great. First, the competition provided students of the fine arts with the opportunity to have their work judged by Thailand's most prestigious artists. The judges included Professor Silpa Bhirasari, the famed Italian artist labelled the father of modern art in Thailand, Ajarn Fua Haripitak of Silapakron University, and Ajarn Hem Vejakorn, described as 'one of Thailand's outstanding artists'.[79] Others judging the competition included Ray C. Downs of the Bangkok Christian Centre, Ester Samuel of Shell Thailand, and Christian Hunderup of Thai International Airways. Prizes on offer were 4000 baht plus an air ticket to Hong Kong for first place, 2000 baht for second, 1000 baht for third, and 500 baht for an honourable mention, of which there were three. With two categories, oil and water colour, a total of nine prizes were handed out.[80] Two hundred and nineteen people entered the competition.[81]

On the night of the contest results, the Prime Minister presided over events. In his speech, Sarit stated that he was pleased so many had entered, claiming it to be evidence of the 'progressive trends' amongst Thailand's youth, especially when considering the 'character and types of media selected for the competition'.[82] He went on to say that the nature of the entries proved that the youth were helping 'to develop and express our national heritage and culture', that they spent their leisure time in 'useful occupations', and that he was therefore 'confident of the enhancement of our national culture'.[83] He also re-asserted the importance of the initial stipulation that the entrants should think about those images that would have a value in promoting tourism. It is unsurprising therefore that those who were chosen as winners displayed clear awareness of the debates over representation that had taken place in *Anusan Osotho* over the previous year. The winner of the oil paintings, Taval Dajanee, depicted an old farmhouse, half falling down, that was strikingly similar to the image commented on in the letters. Depicting a life far away from the city, the site was one where modernity remained unreferenced, and while no person was featured in the picture, it was clear that the house was occupied, with a piece of cloth hanging over a window and signs both inside and outside of activities associated with rural life. The villager who lived there had no particular character, other than that of a rural home-owner, and the relatively unkempt nature of the dwelling suggested that they were unaware that their

164 *The Tourist Organization and propaganda*

house was being observed. Instead, it was the responsibility of the artist, residing in Bangkok and with access to the tourist market, to translate the image to its international audience and, in doing so, exploit its value.

This theme was replicated in the image that won first prize in the water colour competition, where the artist again depicted the everyday practices of a Thai people unaware of their importance to the international community, this time at the floating market. In the picture submitted by Sawasdi Tantisuk, the image depicted a busy scene of men and women busily engaged in an economic life on the water. Painting from an elevated position, either from a bridge or from the veranda looking over life on the water, the picture clearly indicated to its audience, however, that the activity held a hidden value that had only been realised in the painting itself. Bearing a striking resemblance to the representation of Thailand being widely disseminated in American narratives of the country, Sawasdi's victory clearly illustrated the extent to which the image of the floating market was emerging as one of the most enduring portrayals of the nation.[84]

The paintings, and the images they portrayed, became a central element in the Tourist Organisation's drive to make urban Thailand think about the location from which foreigners viewed the country. By forming a strong bond with the elite community of Thai artists, it was also able to bring such communities into a space where they could contribute to an internationalised commentary on Thainess in the context of an emerging tourist industry. By the winter months, the two winners of the competition were producing some of the country's most sought-after work. Having completed their trip to Hong Kong, and following an extended trip to Japan in the case of Sawasdi, the Tourist Organisation hosted a display of the work it had completed abroad, a high-profile event attended by the American Ambassador and his wife.[85] During the same months, other exhibitions opened, one at the Bangkapi gallery on Soi Asok, and another at the Student Christian Centre, which opened a display of Thai sculpture.[86] These were spaces where foreigners and Thais could reflect together on what was beautiful about the nation. They were also spaces where young Thai artists could profit directly from such conversations, as they realised the opportunities that were opening up as a result of the increasingly large number of tourists passing through.

The fact that it was images of *klong*-side life that featured so strongly in the winning entries was unsurprising. Recognising the demand for that image among visitors to the city, Bangkok's art galleries had soon started selling such work in ever larger numbers. As resident art critic at the *Bangkok World*, Finnegan Swake, exclaimed in 1964, 'the floating market must represent less than 1% of canal life in this country, and yet, exhibition after exhibition, up it comes again'.[87] By November 1964, another article raved at the fact that the new galleries, which were almost exclusively designed to entice foreign visitors, were selling pictures alongside other products popular with tourists: places such as the 'Gifts Gallery', which opened on Petchburi Road in late 1964 and indulged in the sale of 'tourist tat' alongside its pictures, such as 'Bangkok Dolls, Thai

The Tourist Organization and propaganda 165

cotton, wood carvings and other souvenirs'.[88] Illustrative of the extent to which the country's artists had developed their talent in order to cater for a cultural industry attached to tourism, such articles also reinforced how the art market was providing many in Bangkok with access, however limited, to a consumer culture located in the USA.

Trips into Thainess

From the early 1960s, *Anusan Osotho* began encouraging Thai readers not only to think about how foreign visitors viewed Thailand, but also to participate in the same tourist culture. Relaying the tourist experience through an encounter with an everyday Thai culture, the organisation reinforced the essential premises of modernisation theory, and fostered closeness between Thai and American actors by informing Thai readers what it was that American visitors valued within the country. Told from the privileged arena of a global consumer society, the magazine thus provided new narratives from which the urban consumer could once again explore, with pride, a Thai identity that the outside world seemed to prize so highly. It also opened doors, as Thais once again could recognise the presence of an international, cosmopolitan space at the heart of their city, in turn opening up channels for new relationships to be forged with American-dominated networks of international finance and development. Importantly, this new elite was no longer dependent upon its commitment to an ethnically Thai nation premised upon economic and political independence. Rather, it was built upon a common elite interest in US consumer culture and a familiarity with the ideological premises of the alliance with the USA.

One of the first events promoted to both foreigners and Thais was the Surin elephant round-up, which featured in the Thai press throughout the decade as an occasion through which Thais and foreigners were able to catch a glimpse of a rare spectacle, and which for *Anusan Osotho* provided the opportunity to re-orient Thai readers toward the new cultural vision of the country. In November, the magazine reported on the approaching event both as a new experience and as one that drew attention to a traditional Thai culture rooted in the everyday life of the population. The magazine's front cover diverted attention from the usual interest in ancient temple structures or natural views, instead featuring the capture of wild elephants by a rural population in a distant province (Figure 5.1). It invited the prospective Thai tourist to participate in the gaze of the foreigner, observing what appeared to be the cultural spectacle of an unspoiled everyday life, apparently disconnected from urban and therefore modern social practices.

This was further reinforced inside the magazine, where readers were asked to think about the people of Surin, and particular of Tha Tum, as engaged with elephant herding as a way of life, 'the people here take the elephants from the forest in order to train them to work harvesting teak, and sometimes they might sell a baby elephant abroad, for which they can make good money'.[89] The story was of a people whom urban Bangkok was unlikely to have heard

Figure 5.1 Front page, *Anusan Osotho*, 2, 4 (1961)

about, but who were the custodians of an intriguing set of customs that foreigners recognised as fascinating. It therefore promoted the event as part of a cultural renaissance following a generation of ignorance, revitalised by tourism. Following the event, *San Seri* described the trip as a chance for 'city dwellers' and 'foreigners' to see something that was 'hard to find anywhere in the world'.[90] Here, images of the event were interspersed with pictures of a packed grandstand brimming with urban Thais and foreigners, appreciating the spectacle together. The message was clear, that a cosmopolitan tourist

The Tourist Organization and propaganda 167

culture was available to all who had the means, and indeed the desire, to re-learn what it meant to be Thai.

These themes were further reinforced in an article covering the Royal Barge Ceremony in 1962.[91] Written not by a staff member, but by a Thai who had taken two foreign friends to the occasion, it was an account in praise of those who had organised it, explaining that the event had been put together by the 'Tourist Organisation and the Navy (who had) worked together to organize it in order to welcome foreign tourists who wanted to come and watch the troop of barges'.[92] His account of the experience, from beginning to end, was one in which those responsible had worked out, to the finest detail, what foreigners would appreciate. It explained how, upon arrival at the back of Wat Arun, he and his passengers found a Navy officer who smiled at them, and politely directed them to the car park, which he found packed with cars and tourist buses. Having parked his vehicle, he then described walking toward the enclosure, demarcated by a piece of rope, where he found the entrance manned by a member of the Tourist Organisation, busy directing people to their seats in the grandstand. From there, the day's event was described as spectacular from beginning to end, crammed full of photo opportunities and moments of total awe, an experience of unrivalled entertainment:

> As for the many hours then spent in the grandstand, staring at the Chaophraya river flowing past, well, you might expect it to be a period of isolation and boredom. But on that day it was the complete opposite. It was fun from beginning to end, and I did not feel bored, isolated or sleepy for one moment because opposite to the grandstand, there was a stage which had been put up by the Navy in which the tourist authority had organized entertainment of the highest quality ... these elaborate dancing and theatrical displays meant that some used up their camera film before the barge ceremony had already begun, but the Tourist Organisation had thought about that too, because they had organized a stall selling the film.[93]

What was particularly noticeable about his account was that he clearly identified the Barge Ceremony as an activity organised for an elite community of foreign visitors and the Thai urbanites who accompanied them. He noted, for example, how throughout the afternoon there was a floating bar, which had been set up to sell snacks such as hot dogs and fizzy drinks for the visitors. He also found the toilet situation particularly impressive, noting that this was one of the hardest things to organise, but that they were of such a high standard that they 'made me feel shy, because they were better even than the toilets in my house'.[94] He noted how the grandstand was of a very high quality and how it had been erected at a perfect angle to the river to give the spectators an ideal view of the event as it unfolded, 'meaning the sun didn't get into the eyes, and you could take the most beautiful pictures'.[95]

However, it was his explanation of the later stages of the afternoon that were most revealing, the moments before the event reached its climax. At 3:00

168 *The Tourist Organization and propaganda*

those sitting in the grandstand started to alert each other that there was something happening on the opposite side of the river, on the dock outside the Royal Palace. Clamouring to see, and getting out their optical zoom cameras to view the activities, the crowd got excited as they realised that the King, the Queen and the Crown Prince were getting into the white royal motorboat in order to leave for the start of the ceremony up-river. After an hour of further entertainment, the tension moved up a notch. Members of the Tourist Organisation staff started to gather in the space between the grandstand and the river, and a loudspeaker announced that everybody was to go back to their seat because the procession was coming around the bend in the river and would shortly be coming into view. The author then explained how the procession, from being just a dot far in the distance, moved slowly closer, until finally the full procession could be seen, 'the rhythmic sound of the oars entering in and out of the water, pulling the boats along, arranged together in a perfect line'.[96] The article continued to assert the experience as one of global participation; a cultural exchange of unity over and across national boundaries; but what was most noticeable was the agreement about what a commitment to that common ground entailed:

> It was put together beautifully, and would be even more beautiful if there weren't modern new buildings being built around it ... it wasn't just me who thought this, everybody there commented on how the new buildings ruined this beautiful vista of the past, and that the situation would only continue and that we should quickly work together to protect it.[97]

Interpreting the event as an experience of integration into the American imperial order, it also reinforced the standard ideological assertions that located a traditional Thai culture external from the process of modernity. More than that, it argued that, despite any hunger for change, the city's skyline must be protected in order to acknowledge the importance of local cultural traditions. In this sense, therefore, a celebration of Thai culture as the marker of an identity, which made sense to the nation's free world status, also held the implication that Thai communities remained necessarily subservient to a modernity imagined as emanating out of America. While elsewhere in the magazine, the state's commitment to development was clearly referenced as fundamental to the current state of the country, with examples on occasion even appearing on the front cover, the primary agenda remained the promotion of Thai culture as a means to secure the economic transformation of the country. While the front cover of *Osotho* magazine would commonly include new images of a specifically Thai way of life, the edition in Figure 5.2 shows evidence of a previous partnership between a foreign entrepreneur and the Thai state. In 1905, a blurb on the inside cover explained, Edward T. Miles had invested in a bucket dredge which he had brought to Siam and used to start the tin-mining industry on the island of Phuket, which now brought the island more than 100 million baht in revenue.

Figure 5.2 Front Page, *Anusan Osotho*, 3.12, July 1963

Such an idea, that modern life was distinct and separate from Thai cultural life, was further emphasised in an article looking at the floating market, which was introduced with the question 'why do so many foreigners choose to travel all those thousands of thousands of miles in order to see a Thai floating market?'.[98] To find the answer, the Thai author had attempted to enter into the world of the tourist. He had dressed up as a 'typical tourist', and had gone down to the pier at the base of the Oriental Hotel, from where the majority of trips departed in the morning. Arriving at the crack of dawn, he

170 *The Tourist Organization and propaganda*

had joined a trip with the intention 'to observe and listen' to the guide and the tourists, in order to understand what was so special about the experience. Before he started, he admitted to being an 'utter fool' to have not understood before how wonderful *klong*-side life actually was. He also proposed a hypothesis as to why foreigners saw the floating market as so important, pointing out that Thai communities as far back as the kingdom of Ayuttaya had lived alongside the water, making this a way of life rooted in the nation's past. Moreover, he identified how travel to Thailand carried the desire to escape from the trials of modern life,

> The majority of tourists who come on holiday to Thailand come from either America or Europe, and where in their cities are they going to find rivers and *klongs* like in Thailand? Their cities are crammed full of tall buildings, some 100 floors high, and the reality of everyday life is of a clamorous, chaotic, existence. They might be well developed, but that development has killed what is the natural heart of their land. And so, for them to have the opportunity to flee from those tall buildings, and their busy everyday life in their cities, how could they not fall in love with a trip in a little river taxi? To sail swiftly up the Chaophraya river, enter into a little *klong*, and move into a world that is truly natural, to stare directly into a picture of everyday Thai life, unlike anything they have ever seen before.[99]

As 30 boats waited to leave the pier, the author explained how groups of foreign tourists, particularly the women, were dressed in high-end fashion that overwhelmed and intimidated him. He went on to describe how, as they left the dock and travelled up the Chaophraya, the guide pointed out another boat carrying banana leaves, which he explained would be used as the wrapping for Thai deserts, and then pointed out some trees on the bank that he said were very expensive. In response, the author noted how one of the women, whom he described as an American 'mem', exclaimed, 'uncle, uncle, that's the wood that the table in my room in America is made from'. Then, entering a small *klong* for the first time, he explained how foreigners had the first chance 'to see a real image of Thai life taking place on either side, totally filling their vision'. He reported that the daily life of the 'villagers' living on the banks of the *klong* was just getting under way, some people were washing clothes and children were splashing happily in the water, smiling and waving at the boat when they saw it pass. This he described as an 'authentic image' that he found 'particularly refreshing', 'the best representatives of the nation, better than any diplomat could ever be'. The foreigners waved back, and took pictures of the boys and girls before the boat moved on.[100]

However, as he went on to explain, while this image was in many ways the polished gem that General Chalermchai had sought, it was also one which Thais themselves had to work hard to achieve. Removing himself from the world of the foreigner, he then chose instead to enter the world of the Thai responsible for mediating the experience. Talking with the guide, he explained

The Tourist Organization and propaganda   171

that he must now begin to speak in Thai, presumably to reassure the reader that the foreigners would not be able to understand. The guide explained that his job is harder than it may seem, and that the idyllic life on the *klong* had to be manufactured so that foreigners might witness the 'correct' image. He said that every day there were rarely fewer than two or three dog corpses floating in the *klong*, and that when he saw one, he would 'quickly try and deviate their attention by pointing somewhere else', but that this didn't always work. The other issue the guide was keen to highlight was the way in which children living on the *klong* would very often excrete directly into the water. He begged the author to contemplate 'what this will make the foreigners think?', and that 'the *klong* is a place they think of as peaceful and beautiful', and that when they see things like this, 'they will soon become prejudiced and disgusted'. He thus concluded that 'all Thais should work together to iron out these character flaws', and that when on a tour he often castigated the villagers living on the *klong* for doing such things.[101]

Having tried a variety of local foods, and having visited a temple, the final stop was at a shop where tourists could stock up on Thai silk, umbrellas and various other products. The author described a sign hanging over the shop, welcoming people to the 'floating market industry'. However, revealing his increasingly sophisticated understanding of what the foreigner wanted and the role the Thai must take in providing that experience, the author felt that the sign made the shop look too modern, and that it would be better to keep the market looking as natural as possible. The sign, he felt, should be taken down so that foreigners didn't realise the shop was there only for their benefit. It was 'things like this', meaning the value of a shop that just looked like a normal house on a *klong*, he explained, 'that we have to recognize have more value than a sign welcoming them'.[102]

Finally, the author took on the role of the Thai tourist, occupying a liminal space somewhere between a member of the global elite, the tour guide, and his own identity as an elite member of urban Thai society with a memory of the recent past. Entering 'deeper into the *klong*', and as coconut trees rose up over their heads, he explained that the boat travelled into the heart of a 'magical land'. Explaining that what the tourist really wanted was to see an image of a young woman, wearing a piece of cloth like a sarong, covering her breasts, bathing in the water, 'because it is something they have never seen before', he also introduced urban Bangkok to the spectacle, noting that 'since the government had restricted the wearing of such garments ... people living in the city are unlikely to have seen anyone dressing in such a way', 'but that on the *klong*, people still wear these things, making it an authentically Thai activity that is rooted in the past'.[103] 'When I see it', he explained, 'it made me feel weak at the knees, it was an image that was far better than a woman in a bikini, because a bikini is too revealing, but these clothes ... phew ... I don't have the words. The foreigners, they love to take photos of the girl in this outfit, not because they have perverted thoughts, but because it is something they find strange and exotic.'[104]

172   *The Tourist Organization and propaganda*

An uneasy development

While the Sarit revolution was framed on the premise that it would bring modernity and progress to Thailand, from the very beginning it was a style of development far removed from the ideology of the 1932 revolution. Encouraging the free inflow of US capital, and ensuring the convertibility of US profits through the removal of protection for Thai interests, it was a definitive moment in the internationalisation of the Thai state. It had also helped to bolster Sarit's position in the country. Opening new doors to private enterprise had helped to undermine Sarit's political opponents, providing a more tangible break with the past 25 years of Thai political history. Moreover, by reducing the ability of government bureaucrats to enrich themselves though beneficial contracts and monopolies, Sarit was able to court a much wider catchment of urban society, including the Sino-Thai community whose capital was highly valued by the regime. Then, from 1962, the Industrial Investment Promotion Act began the formal process of endorsing private industries that were regarded as nationally important, of which over half would be joint ventures with foreign capital. Overall, this meant that in addition to the 28.2 billion baht of World Bank loans made to Thailand over the course of the plan, military aid and investment from abroad led to an enormous volume of foreign capital flowing into the country. Steep economic growth, averaging 7.3 per cent during the first six-year plan, rewarded investors heavily and quickly led to the emergence of a newly confident and diverse community of Thai consumers, increasingly able to indulge in cosmopolitan lifestyles.[105]

Set in the context of these rapidly changing socio-economic conditions, tourism was designed to provide Bangkok with a cultural industry that served several agendas. On one hand, it offered very real opportunities for wealth creation. Handicrafts, associated with traditional industries, had already become prized in US minds, and in particular Thai silk was to provide Thai and foreign investors with access to the American market. Also, for those who had money to invest, rising tourist numbers provided clear opportunities for restaurateurs, hoteliers and tour providers. On the other hand, tourism supported a psychological engagement with the ideological framework of Thailand's integration into the American-centred world order. Promoting the idea that Thailand was a nation imbued with a unique cultural tradition and iconography, tourism helped to secure the country's position as a member of the free world, and provided those who resided in Bangkok with the appropriate language to engage with that new world aristocracy.

While it has long been argued that the Sarit revolution represented a return to traditional cultural practices, or more recently the abuse of those traditions for the sake of Sarit's own political legitimacy, it is important to recognise the role that Cold War ideology played in the construction of that cultural universe. Prior to the 1958 revolution, cultural policy had been seen largely as a tool through which the state might cultivate forms of universal practice and behaviour that were regarded as a prerequisite for global citizenship. Now,

The Tourist Organization and propaganda 173

however, the state sought to explain to urban Thailand that the government would be able to secure global relevance for urban consumers without having to reform the entire society. Instead, it would merely have to recognise the forms in which Thai culture was viewed on the international stage. Whether passive, submissive, peaceful, hard-working, happy, in touch with nature, or merely rooted in traditional customs and behaviours, these framings were ones that many urban Thais struggled to recognise, and therefore had to learn.

Cultural policy under Sarit was thus geared toward a new kind of diplomacy, in which the mutual celebration of difference could be used to foster the fusion of US imperial culture with the self-awareness of an urban Thai, high-society identity. Littered with references to a Thai culture external from the forces of modernity, it nonetheless was used to foster pride among concerned Thais that their presumed cultural heritage did have some universal value, somewhat paradoxically, in its uniqueness. At the same time, however, these narratives, which were manufactured, performed and gradually assumed by urban Thailand as their own, continued to exploit the sense of anxiety that Thais could never consider themselves fully equal. Far from the claims of the 1932 revolution to the universal nature of citizenship in a global community of nations, the Tourist Organisation paid reverence to American consumer culture as something that could only ever be aspired to, achieved only for a limited period of time through the participation of Thai actors in cultural spectacles that had a global resonance. As with the trip to the floating market, the Thai flirtation with American modernity was often retold in ways that emphasised not only excitement, but also distance; a sense that, however hard the Thai actor tried, he could never really be fully included, and that once he returned home, he would retain a sense of inadequacy. Thus by the end of the trip, having taught the American beauty about the oddities of *somtam* and Chinese spaghetti, and having enjoyed his own sentimentalisation of Thai culture that he admitted knowing very little about, the author described how his acceptance into the world of the 'mem' was the prize he really sought, a goal deep down, he knew he could never really hope to achieve:

> At about 11.00 am the river taxi was ready to take the tourists back to the Oriental Hotel pier. I shook hands with the beautiful 'mem' and her kind father at Ratchawaradit Pier before getting out. The beautiful 'mem' said that she would write to me, and told me to write to her as well. My mouth dropped open and I nodded to accept her request. Just after I left however, I realized I hadn't given her my address, nor did I have hers. If I sent her a letter, even in 10 years, it would not arrive.[106]

Notes

1 The World Bank had provided loans to Thailand prior to the 1958 revolution, but importantly, all major decisions regarding the country's development were taken internally by the Ministry of Finance. The World Bank visiting mission

174 *The Tourist Organization and propaganda*

that took place between 1957 and 1958 had recommended a central agency for economic planning, and it was this recommendation that was taken on by the Sarit regime. The Board of Investment, the Budget Bureau and the Office of Fiscal Policy were all headed by Western-trained technocrats and were designed to restructure the Thai economy. While, prior to the revolution, American agencies had to work largely outside the central state, they were now formally brought into government. See Chris Dixon, *The Thai Economy: Uneven Development and Internationalisation*, London and New York: Routledge, 1999, p. 79.

2 A key characteristic of the Sarit government was a commitment to curtail the interventionist approach to the economy taken by regimes since the 1932 revolution in order to privilege the Thai. This change opened up opportunities for Sino-Thai who had remained central to economic activity throughout the constitutional period, but were now given enhanced freedoms to develop business models and participate in joint ventures with foreign investors. See Suehiro Akira, *Capital Accumulation in Thailand 1855–1985*, Chiang Mai: Silkworm Books, 1996, pp. 178–199.

3 Thailand's status as a client state following the Sarit Revolution is well established. For a particularly comprehensive analysis, see the Thai-language study by Kullada Kesboonchoo Mead, '*Kanmueang Thai yuk Sarit-Thanom phaitai krhongsang amnat lok*' [Thai politics from Sarit to Thanom under the world power structure], Bangkok: unpublished study, Chulalongkorn University, 2007. The other study, already referred to in this thesis, is Jim Glassman, *Thailand at the Margins*.

4 'State of emergency' here refers to Giorgio Agamben's terminology (also described as a 'state of exception') describing how, as the result of a perceived threat to the fundamental basis of Thai citizenship, citizenship itself had to be temporarily discontinued and replaced by a regime for whom the rule of law was suspended, and state violence would be used in an arbitrary sense. See Giorgio Agamben, *State of Exception*, Chicago, IL: University of Chicago Press, 2005; and *Homo Sacer: Sovereign Power and Bare Life*, Stanford, CA: Stanford University Press, 1998.

5 In other words, that the articulation of a Thai 'now', meaning the urban elite sense of living in a modern moment, is experienced through their active engagement with American culture, prefaced by the experience of 'commodified authentic' expressions of Thai culture. The selling of 'authenticity' and 'tradition' as experiences of modernity is well covered in a number of publications. In particular see Elizabeth Outka, *Consuming Traditions, Modernity, Modernism and the Commodified Authentic*, New York: Oxford University Press, 2009. For a book that deals with similar themes see Graham Huggan, *The Post Colonial Exotic: Marketing at the Margins*, London: Routledge, 2001.

6 I use the phrase 'new world aristocracy' to refer in particular to a class of American high society who regarded themselves as free from the trappings of an old world elite, who nonetheless sought experiences that confirmed their inheritance of an elite cultural world, but at the same time felt the need to display their moral superiority to it. It is a flexible term, but one that is well suited to a depiction of the American visitor during the period. I also regard the Thai elite, who integrated themselves into American imperial culture, as participating in, and in some cases joining, this 'set'. For a more detailed analysis of how Americans abroad viewed themselves, see Christine Skwiot, *The Purposes of Paradise: U.S. Tourism and Empire in Cuba and Hawaii*, Philadelphia, PA: University of Pennsylvania Press, 2010.

7 Elizabeth Outka, *Consuming Traditions*, p. 4.

8 Throughout this chapter I refer to the Tourist Organisation of Thailand as an umbrella term to cover all the various institutions that worked under its authority. This is in line with how it was referred to in most official literature at the

The Tourist Organization and propaganda 175

time. But, as explained below, the organisation had different official names for different parts of its operation.

9 Christina Klein has described how American cultural output and propaganda was able to provide its allies with the symbolic and ideological capital needed to form such 'cultural industries'. Christina Klein, *Cold War Orientalism*.

10 Daniel Fineman, *A Special Relationship*, p. 235.

11 Ibid., p. 234.

12 Sea Supply was a clandestine CIA operation used by Willis Bird to channel aid, particularly to Police General Phao Siriyond. Arming the police with modern weaponry, this aid served to bolster its position in the country, allowing it to compete directly with the army.

13 Daniel Fineman, *A Special Relationship*, p. 242.

14 Ibid., p. 250.

15 Ibid., p. 254.

16 '*Nayok prasai khroprop 4 pi patiwat*' [The Prime Minister marks the fourth anniversary of the revolution], *San Seri*, 21 October 1962, p. 3.

17 Ibid.

18 Benedict Anderson has noted how violence was used during the Sarit regime as a tool to service the state's propaganda agenda. One of the first acts of the revolution, the public execution of men accused of being behind a Communist plot, is thus viewed by Anderson as an event that took place 'in the spirit of public relations, mass-media-style'. See Benedict Anderson, *Spectre of Comparisons: Nationalism, Southeast Asia and the World*, London and New York: Verso, 2002, Ch. 7.

19 Quoted in Thak Chaloemtiarana, *Thailand: The Politics of Despotic Paternalism*, p. 92.

20 Ibid.

21 NA (2) KD 1.1/60, '*Krongkan sang rongraem thi sanoe kho hai ratthaban hai khwam sanapsanun*', Intercontinental Hotels to Thanat Khoman, Foreign Minister, January 28 1960, '15 Reasons why you can't go wrong when you select an Intercontinental Hotel'.

22 Travel statistics for 1960 indicated 21,570 US nationals visiting Thailand, compared with 11,211 from the United Kingdom, the second largest figure. By 196, the number of US arrivals had soared to 47,780, while the number of visitors from other nations remained relatively stagnant. See NA ST 0701.9.10.9/6, 'Foreign Visitors by Nationalities 1960–1961'. For the recommendations of PATA, see NA ST 0701.9.10.9/4, Marvin Plake, Executive Director of the Pacific Area Travel Association to the Tourist Organisation of Thailand, 'Three Years plan for T.O.T's overseas offices', 18 October 1963.

23 Ibid.

24 Christopher Endy, *Cold War Holidays*, p. 1.

25 Christina Klein, *Cold War Orientalism*, p. 109.

26 NA ST 0701.9.10.9/3, '*Khao san chak Osotho*' [*News from Osotho*], Bangkok, July 1962, p. 121.

27 Peggy Durdin, 'The potent lure of Asia', *The New York Times*, 7 November 1957.

28 NA ST 0701.9.10.9/3, '*Khao san chak Osotho*' [*News from Osotho*], Bangkok, July 1962, p. 121.

29 Advertised regularly in the Tourist Organisation Magazine, *Holiday Time in Thailand*, the Kodak Show of Thai classical dancing, was held every Wednesday and Saturday from 9 am between November and May. It was sponsored both by the Tourist Organisation of Thailand and by Kodak Products Division, The Borneo Company Ltd.

30 'Plowing ceremony held tomorrow', *Bangkok World Sunday Magazine*, 6 May 1960, p. A1.

176　*The Tourist Organization and propaganda*

31　*Holiday Time in Thailand* was an irregular publication, often postponed or reorganised to ensure quality. As a result, referencing is inconsistent in order to provide the specific information needed to identify the issue.

32　'Fact Sheet Number 4, Usually on floating market: the Royal Barges', *Holiday Time in Thailand*, 2.8(August 1961): 65.

33　'Thailand old and new', *Holiday Time in Thailand*, 4.3(1963): 34.

34　Ibid.

35　Christina Klein, *Cold War Orientalism*, p. 200.

36　*Holiday Time in Thailand*, 3.2(1962): 2.

37　Christine Skwiot, *The Purposes of Paradise*, p. 170.

38　Ibid.

39　For an anthropological study of the elephant tourism and its impact on the largely Khmer population of Surin, see Alexander Denes, 'Recovering Khmer ethnic identity from the Thai national past: an ethnography of the localism movement in Surin Province', PhD thesis, Cornell University, 2006.

40　Ibid., p. 25.

41　'*Farang thueng kan khlong nai Thai*' [White foreigners admire elephant herding in Thailand], *San Seri*, 20 November 1961, pp. 1, 5.

42　'*Kansadaeng kiaokap chang thi Surin*' [The Surin Elephant Show], *Osotho Magazine*, 2(4) (November 1961): 24.

43　NA ST 0701.9.10.9/3, p.10. *Banthuek rai ngan kan prachum khanakammakan osotho krangthi* 9/1961 [O.So.Tho minutes, 9/1961].

44　NA ST 0701.9.10.9/3, p.18. *Banthuek rai ngan kan prachum khanakammakan osotho krangthi* 2/1962 [O.So.Tho minutes, 2/1962].

45　Ibid.

46　Ibid.

47　NA ST 0701.9.10.9/3, p. 121, Jack Gabriel, 'Thailand's coming up fast for tourists', *Pacific News*, 11 July 1962.

48　Saranmit Prachansit, '*Kitchakan hotel nai Prathet Thai phutthasakkarat 2406–2478*' [Hotel business in Thailand 1853–1935], MA thesis, Chulalongkorn University, 2000, pp. 31–52.

49　Visitors to hotels such as the Oriental saw the buildings as grand expressions of the majesty of imperial modernity, and often described them as places within which to perform civilisation and modernity to a local audience. One such an example was Professor Maxwell Somerville, who visited the Oriental in 1897 and described it as illustrative of the genius of 'a European colonist' whose building meant that 'all classes of Siamese opened their eyes with wonder'. See Andreas Augustine and Andrew Williamson, *The Oriental, Bangkok*, 2000, p. 37.

50　Sorasan Phaengsapha, *Ratri pradap thi Hua Hin Bangkok*, Bangkok: Samnak phim sa san di, 2002, pp. 47–69.

51　Saranmit Prachansit, '*Kitchakan hotel nai Prathet Thai phutthasakkarat 2406–2478*', p. 67.

52　NA (2) SR 0201.72/1, Director of the Crown Property Bureau to the Cabinet Secretary, 7 July 1943, '*Kho khwam ruam mue sanapsanun kitchakan khong rongraem*' [Request for support for activities concerning hotels].

53　Alexander MacDonald, *Bangkok Editor*, p. 21.

54　NA (2) SR 0201.72/1, 19. Cabinet Secretary to The Prime Minister, 20 July 1950, *Kho khwam ruam mue chak nuai ratchakan tang tang nai kan samrong hongphak wai khaek chao tangprathet na Rongraem Rattanakosin* [The Crown Property Bureau requests the support of various government ministries to prepare rooms at the Rattanakosin Hotel so they are suitable for foreigners].

55　In a meeting on 13 October 1954, the Prime minister said that Thailand could expect increasing numbers of foreign visitors, largely international representatives arriving in Thailand for various meetings. Only months before SEATO's

The Tourist Organization and propaganda 177

headquarters was inaugurated in Bangkok: this was presumably part of the planning, but also a response to Bangkok's emerging profile as a regional hub. As a result, it was claimed that a new modern hotel needed to be built. See NA SR (3) 0201.50/2 Deputy to the Cabinet Secretary to the Minister of Finance, '*Rongraem*' [Hotel], p. 1.

56 A survey of the newspapers during the early months of the Erawan reveals very little interest in the new hotel. In the midst of election campaigning, it is easy to see how it could have been overlooked. But it is also important to recognise that, with much of the press taking an anti-government line, the Erawan project might have been a difficult story to cover, evidence of something the government was doing well. Also, it is worth noting the significant role that Police Chief Phao Siriyond played in the early hotel industry. Even before the end of the Second World War, Phao's name appears regularly in relation to the construction of various hotels. Further research into this role is needed, but would surely be worthwhile, to better understand both the role of tourism in Thailand, and the emergence of Phao and his contributions to Thai state building. Nevertheless, for the sake of the current study, it is important to recognise how Phibun had struggled to distance himself from Phao during the years preceding the coup, meaning that both Phibun and Phao were viewed with almost equal distrust. Phao's involvement in the Erawan would not have helped the cause of the hotel.

57 '*70 pi Krom pracha samphan*' [70 years of the Public Relations Department], Bangkok: 2004, p. 185.

58 Tourist magazines produced by the Tourist Bureau tended to be irregular and of lower quality than the glossy *Thongtiao Sapda*, which had been produced by the Ministry of Commerce during the late 1930s and early 1940s. See Chapter 2.

59 *Democratic Thailand*, Government Tourist Bureau, Department of Public Relations, 1957.

60 Ibid.

61 In early planning for the setting up of the tourist industry, it was argued that it should have the characteristic of a 'free agent' [*Nuai ngan isara*], and employees should be taken on a more informal [*Lukchang*] basis. See NA ST.0701.9.10.9/1, '*Khao khrong samrap kan chat tang ongkan rue samnakngan thatsanachon*' [Plans concerning the setting up of a Organisation or Office of Tourism], p. 3.

62 Chalmerchai Charuastra, '*Kan damnoen ngan khong Osotho*' [The operations of the Tourist Organisation of Thailand], *Anusan Osotho* 1.1(1960): 9.

63 Ibid., p. 10.

64 'Erawan Hotel a "Thai treat" for tourists expanding', *Bangkok Post*, 20 December 1960, p. 6.

65 Ibid.

66 '*Erawan hai phanakngan taeng chutmaithai roem patiwat khrueang baep chut kao phuea duedut chai chao tangprathet*' [The Erawan makes its workers dress in Thai silk suits, for a revolution back to old style dresses in order to invite foreigners], *San Seri*, 15 December 1960, p. 5.

67 *Bangkok Post*, 20 December 1960, p. 6.

68 '*Phu ma yuean*' [Visitors], *Anusan Osotho*, March 1961, p. 56.

69 *San Seri*, 3 November 1962.

70 Chalermchai Thalalakson, '*Yak cha khian sarakadi thongtiao*', *Anusan Osotho*, 1(11) (1961): 68.

71 Ibid.

72 Ibid.

73 *Anusan Osotho*, 1(12) (1961): 63.

74 Ibid.

75 Ibid., p. 64.

178 *The Tourist Organization and propaganda*

76 NA ST 0701.9.10.9/3, '*Prakat rueng kanprakuat phap khian khong ongkan song-soem kan thongthiao Prathet Thai*' [Announcement concerning the painting competition of the Tourist Organisation of Thailand].

77 'TOT, Shell Thai, Painting Competition', *Holiday Time in Thailand*, 3(2) (1962): 31.

78 Ibid., p. 31.

79 Ibid., p. 41.

80 Ibid., p. 31.

81 Ibid., p. 31.

82 Ibid., p. 42.

83 Ibid., pp. 42–43.

84 See Chapter 1.

85 'This week in Pictures, An Art Exhibition', *Bangkok World Sunday Magazine*, 4 November 1962, p. A4.

86 'TOT and Bangkapi: two art shows start art season', *Bangkok World Sunday Magazine*, 4 November 1962, p. 6.

87 Finnegan Swake, 'Subjects in art', *Bangkok World Sunday Magazine*, 19 April 1964, p. 5.

88 Finnegan Swake, 'Art round up', *Bangkok World Sunday Magazine*, 22 November 1964, p. 6.

89 '*Kansadaeng kiaokap chang thi Surin*' [The Surin Elephant Show], *Anusan Osotho*, 2(4) (1961): 25.

90 '*Farang thueng kan khlong nai Thai*' [White foreigners admire elephant herding in Thailand], *San Seri*, 20 November 1961, p. 5.

91 '*Pai du krabuan phayuhayatra kap Osotho*' [Going to watch the Barge Procession with Osotho], *Anusan Osotho*, 2(5) (1961): 12.

92 Ibid., p. 13.

93 Ibid., pp. 13–14.

94 Ibid., p. 14.

95 Ibid., p. 14.

96 Ibid., p. 15.

97 Ibid., p. 57.

98 '*Talat Nam Wat Sai*', *Anusan Osotho*, 3(4) (1962): 23.

99 Ibid., p. 24.

100 Ibid., p. 46.

101 Ibid., p. 47.

102 Ibid., p. 58.

103 Ibid., p. 47.

104 Ibid., p. 47.

105 Suehiro Akira, *Capital Accumulation in Thailand*, p. 181.

106 *Anusan Osotho*, 3(4) (1962): 59.

6 *It's a small world after all*
Thailand's integration into free world culture

> I can't believe it, can't possibly believe it
> What will my people think? Surely this must be a dream.
> Apasra Hongsakula, Winner of Miss Universe 1965, acceptance speech[1]

On 24 July 1965 an 18-year-old Thai girl named Apasra Hongsakula was crowned the most beautiful woman in the universe at Miami Beach, Florida. Awarded over 500,000 baht in prize money, she was subsequently thrust into a busy social circuit as an international celebrity.[2] Just over two weeks later, she was treated to a first-class cabin on board a Scandinavian Airlines/Thai Airways flight back to Bangkok. Touching down at Don Mueang airport at 11:00 am on 10 August, she was met by a crowd reported to be over a million strong, keen to catch a glimpse of their new national hero on her victory procession.[3] The owner of the *Thai Rat* newspaper sent a 200,000 baht Chevrolet Impala to ferry her along the heavily lined streets from the airport to the city. On TV sets, news reports claimed that approximately 90 per cent of the population, 28 million people, watched the spectacle.[4] It was an incredible outpouring of emotion and national pride that gave a clear indication of how removed the country now was from the middle of the 1950s. It was also an illustration of the extent to which anxiety and anger over the relationship with the United States had been transformed into a successful alliance under the rubric of Cold War ideology.

International beauty pageants had long been central to the articulation of the American-centred world order, and the 1965 Miss Universe competition had been no different. A chance for international 'delegates' from over 50 countries to meet each other and form lasting friendships, it also provided American society with powerful assertions of a harmonised 'free world' community. The parade of friendship, for example, saw floats carrying the 'celestial beauties' around Miami, donning the latest fashions from the world's top designers. Icons of modernity, the representatives came with gifts from their respective countries, presents that best reflected the life of the populations they represented and the economic practices they were engaged in. Participants also had to come prepared with their own national costume so that they might walk in the parade of nations, in which they would be awarded for the best native

180 *Thailand's integration into free world culture*

dress. This feature in particular meant that the Miss Universe competition, as Jan Bardsley has explained, 'much like the Olympics, championed uniqueness through national costume events and peace through international competition'.[5] It was also a real-life event that replicated the message of the PepsiCo display at the 1964 World Fair, *It's a Small World*, made up of 350 dolls that 'winked, blinked and sang of world peace'.[6] A spectacle with international relevance, the Miss Universe pageant provided tangible proof of the expansion of a benevolent American power and its ability to bring the people of the world together.

In Thailand, the victory of Apasra in America was viewed as a defining moment for the Thai nation, with the day of her return cast as a truly historic event.[7] Already, news of her activities and behaviour in Miami had been reported with particular attention to her selfless commitment to the Thai nation, and her flawless ability to help the international community better understand her home country. The Thai language newspaper *Prachathippatai* [*Democracy*] commented on 28 July that, in all her interviews with the press, she consistently refused to claim a superior status over the rest of her people. Instead, the paper emphasised how she was hoping to 'represent all Thai women'.[8] The paper marvelled at her impeccable manners and posture, and argued that her success was something all Thai women should be proud of. Exiting the plane, wearing a Thai costume made of Thai silk, Apasra was thus welcomed back as a symbol of Thailand's elevated status in the world, an accepted member of a civilised global society.[9] Sponsored by the Tourist Organisation of Thailand, upon her return she was treated like a Hollywood VIP, gifted the most expensive and luxurious room at the Erawan Hotel for four nights, and elevated to a status of near royalty.

While the pride expressed in the Thai press was profound, it was nevertheless only the most recent in a series of Thai 'victories' on the world stage. In a media environment that remained tightly controlled, the period from Sarit's 1958 revolution through to the middle of the 1960s was narrated in a variety of ways that promoted the current regime as the protector of the Thai nation and of its international standing. The alliance with America, far removed from the way it was portrayed prior to 1958, was now discussed in almost exclusively positive terms, and the ideological rationale of the Cold War from an American perspective dominated internal discussions about the nation's internal priorities. Development economics combined with the maintenance of internal security was repeatedly emphasised as the principal reason for military control of the state, and words such as freedom and peace became almost entirely associated with the American struggle globally.

Yet, despite the continued integration of Thailand into the US sphere of influence, there remained a forceful assertion in editorials and columns of an independent Thai cultural life that made Thailand a unique and special country. Victories on the world stage such as that of Apasra were, in a similar way to the cultural spectacles that now littered the social calendar back in Bangkok, used to bolster claims that Thailand had now become an esteemed member of the 'free' world of nations. Emphasising many of the civilisational notions of the Phibun era, including that there existed a global hierarchy of nations, these victories were commonly used to narrate the idea that Thailand was now finally being recognised appropriately within the international community. From an American perspective, these activities also helped to indigenise the policy objectives of the US government, creating what appeared to be a strong, stable and independent ally that was nonetheless committed to serving the needs of the country's American patrons.

Marking integration: the world tour of King Bhumibol and Queen Sirikit

If there was one event that most clearly marked Thailand's fuller integration into the American sphere of influence following the revolution of Sarit Thanarat, it was the arrival of King Bhumibol and Queen Sirikit in the United States in 1960. Landing first in Hawaii on 14 June, where they met with Elvis Presley on the set of *G.I. Blues*, they then travelled to California on 18 June. While there, they took time to visit a number of Hollywood studios and chat with film stars and other celebrities. This was an important preface to the main part of the trip, which began in Washington on 28 June when a crowd of 75,000 were reported to have welcomed the King and Queen to the east coast.[10] The following day, the King gave a speech to the US Congress in which he spelt out the desire for even closer relations, assuring his guests that 'we are one in purpose and conviction'.[11] Then the royal couple travelled to New York, where they were treated to a ticker-tape parade through Manhattan. In the remaining weeks, they journeyed to, among other destinations, Cambridge, Massachusetts, the birthplace of the Thai monarch. Over the next six months they would receive official welcomes across Western Europe, from the United Kingdom to France and Spain, before returning to Thailand in January the following year.

Unlike the trip made by Phibun in 1955, this trip was portrayed back at home in purely positive terms. Newspaper editors and columnists billed the visits as an important and proud moment for the Thai nation. With Kukrit Pramoj in charge of the publicity for the trip, regular updates from the other side of the world were published daily, along with photos taken over the previous days that were intended to update Thai readers with the exciting and unfolding news. Less than a month into the trip, *Sayam Nikon* began to publicise a series of special editions of its photo magazine, focused exclusively on reporting the various places and people the young couple had visited. Readers were, for example, invited to enjoy looking at pictures of the King and Queen visiting major US cultural sites, as well as taking time out of their busy schedule to visit the Disneyland theme park with their young family. Overall, the message to the Thai audience was that Thailand was experiencing a warm embrace by both the United States government and the American public, and that this should be source of great pride.

182   *Thailand's integration into free world culture*

In an editorial published in *San Seri* in early July, entitled 'A warm welcome', it was claimed that since the King and Queen had arrived in Hawaii the welcome had been remarkable.[12] The ticker-tape parade, which the newspaper stated that over 700,000 New Yorkers had come to watch, was described as a privilege offered to only the most esteemed guests and, according to the King, had felt 'like he was in a film'. At the same time, the editorial made clear, wherever the King and Queen went, they were offered access to America's most powerful people. In particular, the editorial highlighted the King's invitation to speak at the US Congress, a first not only for a Thai monarch, but for any monarch of the Far East. This in particular was singled out as historic, and an event that would inspire an extraordinary sense of self-importance in all Thais. Reporting the words of Kukrit Pramoj, the article confirmed that the trip had done immeasurable good. While 'we are grateful for all the economic support we have received from the US over the past 10 years', Kukrit explained, 'none of it can compare in the minds of the Thai people with the warmth of the welcome you have given to our King and Queen'.[13]

As well as celebrating the kindness offered by their American hosts, articles and opinions in the international media were also liberally shared with the Thai public, with particular insight offered into the way the King and Queen had ingratiated themselves with the American public. In these depictions, the King was routinely pictured as a simple and humble man who was able to speak truthfully and honestly to his American guests. As a *Newsweek* article reported during the trip, the King made a great effort while attending the numerous functions to insist that 'we like simplicity', and when asked by President Eisenhower what his favourite Thai food was, had claimed it was a simple bowl of noodle soup. Re-printed in both English and Thai in the Thai-language newspaper *San Seri*, the article went on to juxtapose the King's humble appearance to his 'beautiful, trim-figured (19-inch waist) wife', who would repeatedly break out in 'dazzling Balmain gowns and suits selected from her travelling wardrobe of 200 outfits (packed into 84 pieces of luggage, against three trunks and two suitcases for the King)'.[14] Elsewhere in the American media, the extraordinary wardrobe of the Queen dominated coverage. As *The New York Times* described on 27 June, in an article entitled '130 costumes by Balmain set for visit', the Queen was depicted 'as unreal a princess of "The Thousand and One Nights" ... the most beautiful queen of the Orient', who had brought with her to America, 'a huge and wonderful wardrobe, of fairy-tale dimensions and a collection of jewels few could rival'.[15]

In a clear indication of the extent to which American and Thai coverage reinforced each other during the trip, Thai newspapers revelled in the attention given to the Queen's wardrobe. However, unlike the coverage in the American media, which tended to take the 'Thai' character of the dresses for granted, in Thailand the costumes were explained as harmonised versions of old and new. In an article published just before the trip began, on 12 June, *Sayam Nikon* announced that the Queen would be celebrating the 'Thai style' during her trip, and that she would be taking over 40 'real Thai' outfits.[16]

Figure 6.1 King Bhumibol and Queen Sirikit with President Eisenhower and First Lady Mamie Eisenhower, The White House, June 1960

However, while the article also explained that the outfits were the product of much work, and had been created in order to reflect the 'authentic history and culture of Thai women', there was also a clear assertion that they were modern adaptations. In particular, the article pointed to the fact that the traditional use of a sash across the front and a long dress parted down the middle had been 'a style since the times of the Sukhothai Kingdom but that over time the dress of Thai women has changed in order to keep up with the times, right up to the current day'. The Queen, 'nevertheless feels', the article continued 'that Thai women should return to dressing in a Thai style' on 'some occasions', because it is 'beautiful' and 'would help develop an appreciation of the country's past'. The newly created 'Thai style' must also, however, be 'adapted' so that it was acceptable to a modern way of life.[17]

The frankness about the invented nature of her wardrobe was repeated in newspaper articles following the trip.[18] The same was true for the Queen's own reflections of the trip, published in both Thai and English in 1968. There she noted how, prior to the world tour, there was 'no typical national dress code like our neighbouring countries, whose native costumes have become well known world-wide, for example, the Indians with their saris, the Chinese with their silk gowns, and the Japanese with their Kimonos'.[19] To prepare for the world tour she had therefore ordered for a 'search to be made in royal palaces, or noble homes for photographs and portraits of former queens', so she could study their dress practices, particularly when they were accompanying the King on official visits. But they had found that during the colonial era, queens would generally mix the Western styles with Thai ones, or in

184 *Thailand's integration into free world culture*

some cases would wear Western dress. For her, she explained, this 'would not be appropriate, and the Western news media would criticize the strange look of our half-Western, half-Thai national dress'.[20] Consequently, after a careful study of pre-colonial dress styles, a new set of costumes were created which could be considered uniquely Thai.

The prominence given to the issue of dress, before, during and after the trip, is illuminating because it sets out the primary narrative of the visit to America in the Thai media: that of two countries 'getting to know' each other in order to develop a closer and more rewarding relationship. As Kukrit Pramoj explained to the Thai people, the trip was an opportunity to show America 'the authentic face of the country', in order that America might better understand the identity of the Thai people.[21] Dress was important, not only because the Queen was able to assert the fact that she was Thai in the eyes of her guests, but because she was equally responsible for establishing that she came from a country with a long, proud history, independent from that of Thailand's new international patron. However, by establishing clearly that the dresses worn were modern inventions, she also helped to reassert new ideas, present in tourist literature and other such media, that Thai culture in this new American-led era needed to be re-packaged through a disciplined and committed effort by all interested Thai parties. What was 'Thai' certainly needed to be easily recognisable and verifiable through a loose academic analysis. But it also had to adopt many of the civilisational global norms that were so embedded into Thai urban consciousness. An utterly modern understanding of modesty, for example, would continue to dominate any newly created 'Thai style', despite its clear roots in Thailand's earlier integration into European imperial culture.

While the Thai outfits were in fact worn only selectively, mainly for official gatherings and functions, they were nonetheless by far the most dominant theme of reports about the Queen during the trip. They were also used to highlight the status of Thailand within the Thai–American relationship. On 9 July it was reported in *Sayam Nikon* that the Queen had been attending a formal gathering at the Bergdorf Goodman department store in New York.[22] When she arrived, it went on, she was delighted to see that, separately from the private party she was attending, a fashion show was in progress displaying the 'latest modern hats'. It was reported that the Queen was fascinated and had diverted from her group to have a look. Yet her entrance was to transform proceedings as the gathering became focused on *her* and *her* Thai outfit. They marvelled at its beauty, and in particular the colour combinations of white, pink and apple green. The Queen then presented two hairpieces that she happened to have on her person, made of Thai silk and diamonds. These were then included in the show before being returned to her later in the day. Taking the primacy of American modern styles as the premise of the story, the event was also able to illustrate American enthusiasm for the Queen's distinctly Thai style. As a result, Thailand was, in this example, able to participate in the fashion show on the world's most modern stage. In truth, the assertion made in the article was fundamentally prescriptive, in that the adopted Thai styles had only been developed so that they would be explicitly of interest to Americans. Yet, at the same time, the American interest in a Thai hairpiece was used to elevate the status of the Queen and reinforce the view not only that she was an excellent representative of the Thai people, but that she reflected their interest in developing a modern, globally relevant identity.

Overall, the idea that the King and Queen acted as cultural representatives of the Thai people while abroad was adopted before the family's departure. This was part of a broader effort that, regardless of the authoritarian nature of the Thai state at the time, sought to secure the legitimacy of the monarchy through a language of democracy. In a set of speeches given on the eve of the trip, Prime Minister Sarit explained that the world tour was an important return to the King's traditional duties, reminding Thais that historically the country's kings and queens had always travelled abroad to secure international friendships, and that he was pleased to be facilitating the trip on behalf of the Thai people. Adopting a distinctly democratic language, the King then went on to thank the people for understanding and supporting the trip, which was for him 'the most important thing, for if the people didn't agree, then I (the King) could not go'.[23] 'The reason I am going', he continued, 'is for the sake of the nation':

> I am going as your leader and I carry with me the feelings of the Thai people in order to show the foreigners that we are friends and that we seek friendship and to ask them to work with us. On this trip that I am making therefore, we are going as representatives of the Thai people.[24]

Rather than a forceful assertion of the national interest against a more powerful foreign superpower, the trip was thus cast as the start of a better relationship built upon a friendly exchange that would ultimately benefit the whole of Thai society. Recognition of Thailand's distinctive identity retold repeatedly through the dress of the Queen was a major part of this, but so was the implicit understanding that close relations with America demanded literacy in modern American culture and an ability to absorb the 'best' America had to offer. Throughout the trip, episodes such as the Queen's interest in American hat styles were mirrored by the actions of the young King, who was repeatedly portrayed as fascinated by what he witnessed. Pictures of King Bhumibol enthusiastically taking photos out of his car window, or avidly asking questions about the activities he viewed, clearly established him in the Thai press as a figure keen to absorb as much as he could from American society. Further images of the King taking part in an impromptu jazz session helped to emphasise the fact that he was already naturally literate in this new American culture, and as a result was the ideal figure to mediate the relationship between the two countries.

According to Christine Gray, throughout the post-war period pilgrimage was an important method for Thailand's prospective leaders to secure victory in a race for virtue that would ultimately settle who had the right to rule. Set within the context of the post-war political and economic crisis, Gray argues that throughout the 1950s pilgrimages provided an opportunity to display interest in

186   *Thailand's integration into free world culture*

a 'search for methods' that might solve the country's problems. Despite the distinctly modern nature of such problems, Gray sees the frequent pilgrimages made during the period as rooted in historical narratives concerned with restoring order. 'Thai pilgrims, monks and laity', she explains, 'generally experience a "disturbed heart" about existing moral conditions before embarking on their journeys', and, 'like the protagonists of mythic tales, they observe new sights, meditate on their moral significance, and achieve new levels of awareness on their journeys.'[25] Under such a model, the trip to America by the King and the Queen was the definitive visit of a generation. Made to the centre of what was now the country's principal foreign patron, the trip served to formally introduce American knowledge and power as the principal force governing the country's future. However, by asserting the royal couple as uniquely able to mediate that relationship, the trip was also to establish the King and Queen as the modern, democratic champions of the nation.

Indeed, upon the arrival of the royal family back in Bangkok in the middle of January, *San Seri* ran a special edition of the newspaper, filling page after page with a lavish celebration of the trip's achievements.[26] King Bhumibol, the editor proudly exclaimed, was the first leader in this 'age of democracy' able to 'establish a new level of recognition, so that the civilised countries of the world now know us better, both in terms of our Arts, Culture and Traditions!'.[27] Re-telling the arrival of the King, Queen and children back into the country, and their subsequent procession from Don Mueang airport, the paper told how 'what must have been a million people' stood cheering the words '*Chaiyo!*' and '*Trong phra charoen!*' They were there, the paper explained, to show 'their admiration for the success of the royals in establishing recognition for the Thai nation'. As a result, it concluded, the shouts of joy were deemed to have come from a 'genuine place' that reflected the 'authentic' sentiments of the people.[28]

Recounting the many successes of the trip, the paper focused less on diplomatic events than on the special moments that had identified the unique ability of the couple to represent the country effectively. Particular attention was paid to the King's hobbies, including his interest in sports such as badminton, golf and water-skiing, as well as his jazz performances, which the paper claimed had helped to humanise him to his guests and had secured his reputation as the modern monarch of a traditional nation. At the same time, the paper devoted much space to the Queen alone, who it claimed had dazzled the international community wherever she had travelled. Returning to the endless foreign newspaper articles that had focused on her beauty, the newspaper claimed that if there was a contest to settle who was the most beautiful royal in the world, she would surely be crowned the 'queen of queens'. Moreover, despite her beauty she had also been able to show humility to her guests and, in doing so, to overcome historical misunderstandings. As the newspaper explained in a separate article, one of the greatest of these was how the Chakri monarchs had been represented in *The King and I*, a clear potential stumbling block for Thai–American relations. However, upon viewing a screening of the film, the Queen had said that for her it was really just fun, and should be viewed as entertainment. Moreover, while what was depicted in the film 'might not match exactly with the historical sources', it nevertheless 'offered Thais an ideal public relations opportunity'.[29]

Thai cosmopolitanism and the free world

The Queen's statement about *The King and I* was indicative of how far removed Thai nationalist ideology now was from what had been promoted by the Phibun-led government both before and after the Second World War. It was also an indication of how much closer Thailand now was to a full integration into the cultural narratives that underpinned the film's message. Indeed, from *The King and I's* global release in 1956, the Thai government had made it clear that it rejected the film's portrayal of the country. The depiction by Yul Brynner of King Mongkut (1851–68) was deemed to be in contradiction to the very basic premise of Thai history. In particular, the film undermined the reverence that had been fostered by Thai nationalists both before and after the 1932 revolution for the reforming Chakri monarchs who had secured Thai independence from European colonialism (before the sixth and seventh reigns). Regardless of the ties that bound Thai officials to American foreign policy, the Thai government objected strongly to the film, stating in official documents that it was a 'musical comedy, but a comedy for people of very low level'.[30] The idea that an English governess had been responsible for transforming the Thai monarchy from an outpost of despotic feudalism into a reforming state able to confront the external forces of modernity was unacceptable.

However, despite support for the decision to ban the film, newspapers and lifestyle magazines in Bangkok also questioned whether or not the Thai public could afford to ignore a stage show and film about their country that was clearly so important to Americans.[31] The statement by the Queen thus re-cast the film from a production that identified the problematic assumptions that underpinned Thai–American relations into a source of potential cultural interaction. On one hand, she asked Thais to loosen up their view of Thai history, emphasising the idea that, as a piece of entertainment, Thais should not take it too seriously. On the other, she made it clear that, regardless of the unfavourable depiction of a Chakri monarch, Thais should not let the public relations opportunity created by American interest in the film pass them by.

Overall, the royal couple's journey through America and Europe had therefore helped to secure a new narrative about how Thais should respond to their international situation. During the trip, the Thai media presented the King and Queen as an idealised middle-class couple who were able to expertly navigate the complex interaction between Thai cultural norms and the international community. However, while these interactions were often cast as simple expressions of cultural exchange, they were also depicted as successful due to the ability of both to harness American modernity appropriately. As such, the trip conformed directly to activities of the government back in Thailand, which was seeking to capture urban Thai imaginations by overseeing a cultural

188   *Thailand's integration into free world culture*

renaissance facilitated by high-end tourism and the consumption of 'traditional' Thailand. Moreover, while tourism might have made the nation newly accessible to Thai consumers, the world tour reaffirmed the view that Thailand was now explicitly tied to a free world culture based in the United States. It helped to reassure Thai readers that American friendship could be assured, not simply because of commitments from the US government, but because those commitments were embedded in more basic sentimental channels that were guaranteed by American knowledge of, and affection for, Thailand's culture and tradition. Finally, the introduction of the King and Queen as cosmopolitan members of a free world community of nations provided explicit examples and practices for urban Thai communities to follow, if they sought to participate in that integration. One of the most obvious of these was the need for Thai consumers to mark their cosmopolitan identity through the purchase of appropriate goods and services. Increasingly, fashions that had been made popular during the world tour, and which most notably incorporated Thai silk, emerged as a principal such commodity.

For many in Bangkok, Thai silk in the early 1960s remained a product associated largely with international tourists. Especially for the more high-end dressmakers in Bangkok, Thai silk remained the material of choice for American visitors to take home with them. As Miss Lily Liang, who owned a shop on Suriwong Road, made clear in 1962, about 50 per cent of all her business was done in Thai silk, and of that 'most of the business is done in a flurry of activity just before a woman leaves Bangkok for home'. In Bangkok, she made clear, 'Thai silk is used mostly in fancy dress or evening wear'.[32] However, that was also changing, with more and more Thais seeking ways to incorporate the material into their everyday wardrobes. This was certainly a challenge, not least because the designs that used Thai silk tended to be more appropriate for cooler climates. To solve the problem, dressmakers such as Miss Liang were adapting the designs so that they came unlined and were therefore cooler. As a result, they were becoming more popular. In the aftermath of the world tour, growing interest in the material was rooted in a desire to emulate the Queen, whose wardrobe had been so celebrated in America, and who had been repeatedly described as one of the most beautiful women in the world. Throughout the decade, pride in the beauty of the Queen was thus instrumental in establishing an urban identity connected directly to the country's integration into an American imperial centre.[33]

In August 1964, when an assistant of Pierre Balmain visited Thailand for a five-day trip, it was widely reported that she was a guest of Wiri Phasnawid, the head of a local tailoring school that was hosting the trip to better understand the latest fashions from America.[34] By that time, Wiri was already a well known figure in Bangkok, regularly appearing on TV to inform Thai viewers about how to develop a sophisticated wardrobe. In a programme that had aired on Channel 4 on 29 November 1962, for example, Wiri had taken her audience through a demonstration of modern fashion. Describing the Queen as the quintessential icon for all Thai woman, the programme also

Thailand's integration into free world culture   189

emphasised silk production as a 'Thai industry' that should be promoted in the creation of a modern wardrobe.[35] With the TV now a principal outlet for display of the latest trends, gaining knowledge of American fashions remained paramount. But, as Wiri had made clear, it was also increasingly taken for granted that a dress made of Thai silk and which incorporated a 'Thai style' was equally as important. On 11 December 1964, another display of the latest 'Thai fashions' modelled by stars of 'Thai TV and film' included a range of specifically Thai-inspired designs. In an article covering the forthcoming display toward the end of October, it was stated that Thai silk was not only a favourite of American visitors, but was now 'becoming popular with the English'.[36]

Thai silk therefore continued to be tied explicitly to Thailand's international reputation, and throughout the 1960s this was continually reinforced by displays of Thai-style dress on the world stage. Toward the end of 1962, for example, Thai silk suits were incorporated into an international tour made by Pan American Airways of 'haute couture' fashion from around the world,[37] and in July 1964 a group of Thai girls, labelled 'Thailand's first professional fashion mannequins', embarked on a three-week tour of Singapore and Hong Kong to model dresses made with local materials, including silk.[38] At the same time, concerns were raised that rising popularity of the material amongst Thai consumers threatened the material's reputation as a high-end, luxury product. In this regard, the fact that the material was popular with foreigners was regularly noted as a reason to ensure that the standard of silk needed to be high. In July 1965, *Prachathippatai* reported that the President of the Department for the Development of Industry was seeking to enforce a minimum standard for the production of Thai silk, in order to maintain its international reputation as a luxury product.[39] Speaking to a seminar on tourism and tourists in March 1966, Jim Thompson reinforced the point, offering his personal advice on the role Thai silk played as a uniquely 'Thai' commodity. In doing so, he emphasised the need to ensure that Thai silk remained a trusted product. Production, he made clear, should adhere to high standards, not only to protect Thai silk as a brand, but also to protect the reputation of all Thai products. He further warned that there were current cases of shops selling sub-standard silk to unknowing buyers, a practice that should be viewed as a 'dangerous' development which could potentially undermine the image of the nation.[40]

Nevertheless, over the course of a few short years, Thai silk emerged as one of the primary commodities through which urban Thais could participate with a cosmopolitan version of Thainess. Celebrated as uniquely Thai, silk served to unify internal consumption practices with those of the international community. In July 1963, a regular column in *Bangkok World Sunday Magazine* entitled 'News for Nang Sao' thus noted how in recent years there had been a great increase in the popularity of Thai silk, 'both in and out' of the country.[41] It also explained how, still 'a rather exclusive product outside of Thailand', Thai silk nevertheless remained a must-buy for tourists who would

190 *Thailand's integration into free world culture*

invariably 'put a visit to one of the large silk shops high on their lists of things they want to do'. However, while those large establishments might be the obvious choice for temporary visitors, 'residents' of Bangkok had the opportunity to invest more time in finding a shop that suited their particular desires. They had time 'to shop around for the best prices' and 'to find the shops that offer special services such as making a small amount of custom-patterned silk, and in having the chance to see the actual making of the silk'. The article then went on to describe a trip to one such example, a shop that provided the chance to see silk made in a 'genuine home-industry manner complete with a "primitive" setting'. S. Theb's Silk Factory, located just 200 yards from the Grand Hotel, offered a unique experience for shoppers to witness the production process, for, as the article explained, 'honeycombed in what the owner of Theb's, Mr Theb Sobsamai, jokingly refers to as a "big slum" are the rooms and houses of Thai silk production'.[42]

Taking the buyer on a trip over bridges, *klongs* and 'some evil looking water', in search of a purchasing experience that was now associated explicitly with the act of buying Thai silk, the article was careful not to describe the buyer. As was common in the column, the 'resident' who had access to the experience was in this article designated not by whether they were Thai or American, but by whether they were engaged in the consumption habits deemed part of modern life in the capital. While knowledge of the geography of Bangkok's downtown shopping district was taken for granted, and the ability and desire to purchase fashions and accessories were discussed as a matter of course, mention of who the resident consumer might be was seen as irrelevant. As a result, the article fit neatly into the usual agenda of the column, which would frequently portray Thailand's urban consumer society as enlivened by the country's integration into a trans-pacific arrangement of power. To be sure, 'News for Nang Sao' was generally written with a principally American audience in mind, but it was also used to celebrate the participation of international expatriates and local Thai consumers in a common shopping experience.

Moreover, the column invariably marked newness, narrating the experience of 'modern life' in the city through the presumed commitment of its readers to high-end consumption practices. The opening of new high-end shops, which came to dominate the Thai shopping experience in the early 1960s, invariably focused on bringing modernity in to the city, while at the same time preserving and promoting the integrity of Thai cultural products. For example, 'Design Thai' opened in 1962 and sought to 'prove that in the decorative field the Thais have been great in the past and appear to have been lost in the surge of western imitation'. Selling a range of products that incorporated designs produced originally for her New York boutique, Jaqueline Ayer now sought to sell products distinguished by a modern American look with a traditional Thai flavour.[43] Later in the year, Design Thai opened a new interior-decorating shop selling an extensive range of well selected Thai handicrafts and teak furniture to discerning urban consumers,[44] while toward the end of 1963, Narayana Phand, a huge showroom full of Thai handicrafts, was opened

Thailand's integration into free world culture 191

on Larn Luang Road.[45] By the middle of the decade, Bangkok was littered with a variety of shops built not simply for tourists to buy gifts to take home, but for urban consumers to decorate their own homes in Thai-style products.

Victory on the world stage

While the world tour had established many of the narratives that prefaced Thailand's integration into an American-centred order, it was the victory of Apasra Hongsakula at Miss Universe that helped reinforce the idea Thailand had 'won' the recognition it deserved. Since 1954, the Miss Thailand competition had no longer been a feature of the Thai cultural calendar. From then, the Constitution Day Fair had lost much of its existing meaning, and since the 1958 revolution had been permanently removed as the country descended into an extra-constitutional arrangement of power. Instead, the principal beauty pageant of the year took place at the Vajiravudh Fair, a high-society Bangkok-centric event that, despite taking place in December, was far removed from the nationally relevant Constitution Day celebrations. In 1964, the first Miss Thailand competition in a decade was decided at the Fair. As well as the gold cup and velvet gown, Apasra was also awarded 40,000 baht in prize money and two return tickets on Thai Airways to Japan. Starting with an interview on Channel 4 the following night, she was also placed immediately onto a busy social circuit, during which time the Thai public closely tracked her journey toward the Miss Universe competition.[46]

Apasra's training for the trip to the Miss Universe contest emphasised the need to learn how to harmoniously fuse modern Western styles with traditional Thai costumes and performances. Throughout the months leading up to Apasra's departure, newspapers in Bangkok were littered with details of her wardrobe, with frequent images showing her in discussion about the best material to use for her many costumes. Thai cottons and silks were relied upon heavily, with silk always privileged when on stage. At the international fashion show, it was decided that 'a subdued "national costume" – silk pasin and blouse' would be used to best project the nation, while at the Miss Universe finals, Apasra would wear a full evening gown of white Thai silk embroidered with pale pink sequins.[47]

Overall, the story told by the journey of Apasra was one of an idealised female Thai consumer engaged in a process of integration into a new international aristocracy. In the months prior to the trip, by incorporating the same narratives of self-betterment and civility that had been so prevalent for generations, she transformed herself before the watchful eyes of the Bangkok reading public. Meeting with her coach and chaperone, M.L. Kamala Sukhum, the two would reportedly work on Apasra's English and etiquette till noon, before spending the afternoon travelling to hairdressers and dress shops, followed finally by Thai dance lessons in the evening. The etiquette lessons in particular were designed to prepare Apasra for her arrival in Miami. There she would be trained to use the utensils of a Western dinner service, as well as

192   *Thailand's integration into free world culture*

engage in role plays in which Apasra would play the position of a young Thai lady who, for example, might hope one day to be a secretary in a foreign business concern. Ultimately, the purpose of the process, as explained by M.L. Kamala, was the cultivation of taste defined as the two-way incorporation of 'both Thai and Western ideas of what a well-brought up girl should be'. Underlining the process, however, was once again the clear and unequivocal declaration of thanks to the American people. As an article in the *Bangkok World* explained:

> Among the things stressed in Apasra's English lessons were greetings and, as outlined by M.L. Kamala in a progress report to the organizers; "short sentences showing appreciation of the kindnesses bestowed on her by the American people, and inviting them to visit Thailand, thus giving her a chance to return their wonderful hospitality, etc." Apasra also had to learn a song, which she will sing in chorus with the other girls the first time they make a joint appearance on the stage. Ironically, the song is "Getting to Know You", from "The King and I".[48]

The victory of Apasra in America generated an enormous amount of press coverage in Thailand. In the immediate aftermath, editors presented the event as an unprecedented opportunity to draw international attention toward Thailand, and to celebrate victory on the world stage. On 27 July *Prachathippatai* covered the decision to hold a victory procession for the returning beauty queen. Reporting on a press conference by the Bangkok authorities, who were responsible for putting on the event, the newspaper reported that for them this was an invaluable chance to show the nation's pride in what she had achieved, which had helped to promote Thailand by 'receiving an honour, the likes of which we have never experienced before'.[49] Talking about the procession, the organisers explained that they had to think carefully, and would study what other nations normally do on such an occasion to make sure it met an international standard, while keeping with Thai tradition. They also went on to explain that these moments were to be prized, and that these people were invaluable.

Apasra's journey from ordinary Thai citizen to international celebrity elevated her to the status of a national hero. In the year that followed she travelled the world, spreading messages specially tailored to the internationalist rhetoric to which the Miss Universe competition was committed. In Thailand, her victory would be remembered for much longer, as one of the defining moments of a generation and a rallying point to project a united nation. However, coming from a middle-class Thai family, whose father was a member of the Royal Thai Air force, Apasra's claim to represent all Thai people was far removed from the universalist notions it appeared to espouse. Having left her studies at a convent in Penang to participate in the Miss Thailand competition at the Vajiravudh Fair, her emergence as one of the country's most important people was from the start dependent upon her

Thailand's integration into free world culture 193

family's connections with both Thai and American figures back in Bangkok.[50] Moreover, her victory in America was embedded in an enforced set of political and economic realities that, however good they felt, were ultimately dependent upon the view that the Thai nation existed on a unique temporality from the rest of the modern world. While Apasra's victory might have promised the prospect of participation with an American-led modernity, her story also asserted the idea that Thailand was a society fundamentally split, between a class of urban consumers and a country that existed 'at large'. Perhaps most important, however, was that her victory asserted that her version of cosmopolitanism, a Thai version, depended upon conforming to that myth.

The ghost of the 'good' American

While the precise nature of Jim Thompson's disappearance remains unknown, it is clear that the politics of the event were complex. As noted above, in the two decades when Thompson had resided in Bangkok, he had not only made Thai silk known to Americans, but Thais too had adopted the material as an important commodity. However, by the 1960s, as Thai high society became increasingly self-aware of its collective, market-driven identity, it was not Thompson who made Thai culture known to them, but figures such as Queen Sirikit and Apasra. Replicating Thompson's own 'myths' about what con-stituted the 'authentic' Thai nation, these figures also framed Thainess as a fetishised identity, built upon the urban relationship to a cultural world external from, but relevant to, the expression of Thai modernity. Moreover, just as Thompson had constructed a world from his veranda, through which a subservient Thai workforce could be sentimentalised, so Thai institutions now did the same, but with the country at large. Because the indigenisa-tion of trans-pacific narratives about what it meant to be Thai depended on the continued construction of difference, Jim Thompson's role not only became ambiguous, but in fact served to betray the image of cultural independence that was now so fundamental to Thai nationalism.

To Americans also, by the mid-1960s Jim Thompson was rapidly losing his relevance. The nature of the conflict in Southeast Asia had changed, with the dream of a peaceful development turning into all-out military conflict, and the idealism that had fed American foreign policy since the Second World War now viewed with increased cynicism. At the same time, with a generation of Americans growing up with Cold War ideology as part of their everyday life, Thailand was far better 'known' than in 1945. The high-profile visit of the King and Queen to America in 1960, and Apasra's victory in 1965, had contributed to a wealth of literature and film that had familiarised Americans with Thailand, or Siam. With new institutions such as the Tourist Organisation of Thailand focused upon mediating Thai culture to US society (the organi-sation opened a bureau in New York in 1965), the increasingly indigenised culture industry made Jim Thompson largely redundant in 'explaining' Thailand to America. To make matters worse, *Vogue*, which had been such a champion

Figure 6.2 Queen Sirikit viewing Thai silk at Jim Thompson's shop in Bangkok

of the ideological value of Thai silk, finally wrote Thompson out of the narrative. In a lavish colour feature, far greater than Thompson had ever achieved in the American media, in February 1965 *Vogue* instead identified Queen Sirikit as the country's leading cultural icon, featuring both her and her outfits in a colourful spread of the Thai court.[51]

Thus, rather than helping to secure the ideological integrity of the Thai nation under this new regime of authenticity, Jim Thompson's presence in Bangkok had become an uncomfortable one, exacerbated by his unfavourable views about the Thai political classes. Unlike American policy makers, since Phibun's return Thompson had viewed Thai politics as a messy and unforgiving business, where friendships were only skin deep, and where idealism came second to self-interest. Moreover, he was not convinced by Sarit's revolution, and continued to see himself as the true protector of the country's 'real' identity.[52] A sign of the country's new found confidence, many in Bangkok came to resent Thompson and his claims to know Thailand better than the Thais themselves. His house on the *klong*, brimming with Thai cultural artefacts, was viewed by Thompson as a mecca of Thai cultural history, set within the proper surroundings. But, as Joshua Kurlantzick has explained, 'to many Thais, including perhaps influential people like the senior generals and their spouses', it seemed like an affront, suggesting that the growing awareness of Thais about their own culture remained mediocre when compared with Thompson's supreme knowledge and 'love' of the country.[53]

The indigenisation of a transpacific form of Thainess following the 1958 revolution thus made Thompson an obstacle to state building, and his continued presence in Bangkok became a betrayal of the ideological integrity of

Thailand's integration into free world culture 195

the project. Unsurprisingly, therefore, when he disappeared few in Bangkok mourned the loss, with none of his Thai friends joining the search to find him. Rather, as the Malaysian police engaged in a massive search, long-standing friend General Ed Black, commander of US services in Bangkok, was one of only a handful of officials who insisted on joining. Yet he also found little appetite to help, noting later that even the American embassies 'showed a singular lack of interest in doing anything remotely active', and that they were 'completely unhelpful' in efforts to work out what had happened. It was not long, therefore, before the man who had for a generation been the best known American living in Bangkok was consigned to the past.

However, Jim Thompson and the idealism of American society during the 1950s continued to haunt Bangkok. Acting as an ongoing reminder of the instrumental role that US consumer culture and the ideological logic of the Cold War had played in the formation of Thainess, his memory continued to provide a tension with official narratives that came to govern the historicisation of Thai identity from the 1958 revolution. While the memory of Jim Thompson persisted, Thai silk and the narratives it espoused would remain tied to the dreams of a consumer society located within the privileged spaces of New York or Hollywood. Also, the patronage offered his workers would remain rooted as much in the American desire to build a benevolent world order as in any parallel Thai ones, and while by the 1960s the American-led project had become a largely Thai-owned representation of development, the memory of Jim Thompson continued to identify the ideology's roots in a US-centred consumer culture.

Most worryingly, however, was the fact that, because Thainess following 1958 existed inside a US imperial order, it was not only the country's political and economic status that became tied to the whims and fortunes of their trans-pacific partner, but also the identity of the nation itself. The de-escalation of the Cold War in Asia that followed Nixon's trip to China, and then the curtailing of the Vietnam War in the mid-1970s, helped to reignite Thai anxieties about the country's alliance to America. During nearly a decade of student protest, and in the end a protracted guerrilla war fought largely by a young urban population, debates about political, economic and cultural representation re-emerged. Yet once again these debates failed to decouple themselves from the fundamental premises of modernisation theory. Many who considered themselves Marxists nevertheless remained committed to a paternal attitude to rural culture and to the assertion that an authentic Thai culture needed to be isolated from the modern lifestyles to which most would return in the end.

Urban Thailand therefore maintained its unity through the belief that it existed on a different temporality to rural Thailand, where the international world of commerce and the lifestyles attached to it were a privileged right, and where narratives about Thainess confirmed access. For decades, products that supported these narratives were used to adorn the homes and bodies of Thai consumers, and internal tourism continued to concern itself as much with learning about traditional ways of life as with visiting waterfalls or going to

196 *Thailand's integration into free world culture*

the beach. Fundamentally tied to a continued economic development, it was only in 1997 that the collapse in ideological legitimacy began to take place, and the end of the Cold War really began to be felt in Thailand. Since then, new political movements have flirted with a renewed commitment to US political and economic power, but have also looked elsewhere for alternatives in a multi-polar world. Moreover, disaffected Thai communities have continued to voice a desire to not be represented as infantilised 'natives', but rather as politically and economically active citizens who are as dependent on the international community as the rest of Thai society.

Notes

1 www.youtube.com/watch?v=gLqzCga2AWA [accessed 19 September 2014].
2 The full amount included the initial reward of $10,000 and an original wardrobe worth over $10,000. The rest was made up of largely of social engagements and contracts that came as part of the Miss Universe title. The 500,000 baht figure is the predicted total prize money received by Apasra before she returned to Thailand. This figure is taken from an article '*Apasra cha tong sia phasi ngoen dai?*' [How much tax will Apasra pay?], *Sayam Nikon*, 23 August 1965, p. 6.
3 '*Chak Don Mueang thueng Erawan*' [From Don Mueang to the Erawan], *Sayam Nikon*, 8 August 1965, p. 1.
4 Prayun Phitsanakha, *Apasra Hongsakul nang ngam chakkawan chak Prathet Thai* [Apasra Hongsakula, Miss Universe from Thailand], Bangkok: Rongphim Fueang Akson, 1965, pp. 1–4.
5 Jan Beardsley, 'Girl royalty: the 1959 coronation of Japan's first Miss Universe', *Asian Studies Review*, 32(2008): 375–391. Exploring many of the themes as this chapter, this article views Japan's first Miss Universe as a landmark in Japanese–US relations and in Japanese post-war identity.
6 'It's a Small World' featured 350 doll-sized animatronic figures that 'winked, blinked, and sang of world peace'. It was later installed at the Disney World theme park when it was built in 1971. See Lawrence R. Samuel, *The End of Innocence: The 1964–1965 New York World's Fair*, New York: Syracuse University Press, 2010, p. 110.
7 Sayam Nikon reported on the large crowds who met her at the airport, noting that '*Pen prawattikan*' [It was historic]. See '*Apasra "poet ok" yin di dai klap Thai*', *Sayam Nikon*, 11 August 1965.
8 '*Kiat khong ying thai dang kong lok phro khwam di*', *Prachathippatai*, 28 July 1965, p. 4.
9 William Callahan sees the Miss Thailand competition following 1965 primarily as a part of the country's foreign policy. In her MA thesis on the Miss Thailand competition, Suphatra Kopitsukkhasakun also considers the competition as embedded in the country's relationship with the international community. See William Callahan, *Cultural Governance and Resistance in Pacific Asia*, New York: Routledge, 2006, p. 61; Suphatra Kopitsukkhasakun, '*Kan prakuat nang sao Thai phutthasakkarat 2477–2530*' [The Miss Thailand Competition, 1935–1987], Master's thesis, Thammasat University, 1988, pp. 127–197.
10 This figure was the one quoted widely in both the Thai and US press. See 'President and 75,000 in streets greet Thailand King and Queen', *The Washington Post and Times-Herald*, 29 June 1960.
11 Speech given to the United States Congress, King Bumiphol, 29 June 1960.
12 This column ran over two days. '*Kan ton rap thi ob oun*' [A warm welcome], *San Seri*, 7 and 8 July 1960, p. 3.

13 Ibid.

14 'Newsmakers', *San Seri*, 12 July 1960, p. 5.

15 '130 costumes by Balmain set for visit', *The New York Times*, 27 June 1960, p. 3.

16 '*Rachani chalong-ong baep thai*' [The Queen to celebrate the Thai style], *Sayam Nikon*, 12 July 1960, p. 1.

17 Ibid.

18 An example of such an article is '*Song fuen fu kan daeng kai ying thai boran*', *Thai Rat*, 11 August 1962.

19 Her Majesty Queen Sirikit, *In Memory of the State Visits of His Majesty the King*, 2nd edn, 2004 [first edition 1968], p. 84.

20 Ibid., p. 86.

21 *San Seri*, 8 July 1960.

22 '*Somdet Phra Boromrachini son phrathai fashion muak*' [The Queen shows an interest in hats], *San Seri*, 9 July 1960.

23 '*Hai thamngan thi chop thi khuan temti yu nai khwam sa-ngop phuea prathet*' [Try your best to fulfill their responsibilities and remain calm for the peace of the country], *Sayam Nikon*, 15 June 1960.

24 Ibid.

25 Christine Gray, 'Thailand – The Soteriological state in the 1970s', p. 212.

26 *San Seri*, 19 January 1961.

27 Ibid.

28 Ibid.

29 Ibid.

30 This is a reference to *The King and I* made by the Royal Thai Embassy in Delhi after calls for the film to banned there. Yet it is clear from the correspondence that this reflects a general attitude to the film amongst Thai officials.

31 Articles in the Bangkok press would, in the middle of the decade, regularly seek to report on Thailand 'from the perspective of Americans', and *The King and I* was mentioned on occasion. For an example, see *Thai nai sai ta American* [Thailand in American eyes], *Sayam Nikon*, 6 October 1956, p. 6. An earlier such article, published in *Sayam Samai* in 1951, pointed out that the story remained enormously popular with Americans and therefore was a play that Thais could not afford to ignore: *Sayam Samai*, November 1951, p. 1.

32 News for Nang and Nang Sao, *Bangkok World Sunday Magazine*, 18 August 1962, pp. 10–11.

33 Thanks to Andrew MacGregor Marshall for providing supporting information on the extent to which this 'pride' in the beauty of the Queen underpinned Thai–American relations during the period.

34 '*Phu chuai chang chalong Praong ma yuean Thai*' [Assistant to the Queen's tailor to visit Thailand], *Thai Rat*, 12 August 1964, p. 9.

35 '*Wiri chang suea mi chue cha nae taengkai satri duai chut maithai nam samai thue lak prayat thang thiwi*', [Famous tailor to give advice on how to dress with the times on TV], *San Seri*, 27 November 1962, p. 6.

36 '*Chao Engkrit niom pha mai thai chop si som kap si chompu mak sut*' [Thai silk becoming popular with the English; they like orange and pink the best], *Thai Rat*, 31 October 1964.

37 'Thai silk suits to be shown in PanAm fashion show', *Bangkok World Sunday Magazine*, 26 October 1962.

38 'News for Nang and Nang Sao', *Bangkok World Sunday Magazine*, 26 July 1964, p. 10.

39 '*Kho rong hai rongngan to mai thai raksa khunaphap hai nak wai*' [Demand for Thai silk factories to maintain the quality of their product], *Prachathippatai*, 17 July 1965.

40 NA ST 0701,9.10.9/8, Second Seminar on Travel and Tourism, 23–25 March 1966. *Salub sala kan samanar* [Conclusions from the seminar], p. 143.

198 *Thailand's integration into free world culture*

41 'News for Nang Sao', *Bangkok World Sunday Magazine*, 21 July 1963, p. 11.
42 Ibid.
43 'From West to East: a renaissance in Thai design', *Bangkok World Sunday Magazine*, 11 March 1962, p. 6.
44 'Design Thai opens new shop', *Bangkok World Sunday Magazine*, 21 October 1962, p. A3.
45 'Shop in Bangkok under one roof', *Bangkok World Sunday Magazine*, 22 July 1963, p. 6.
46 'Miss Thailand chosen', *Bangkok Post*, 5 December 1964, p. 3.
47 'Training for the title: Apasra prepares for the Miss Universe Pageant', *Bangkok World Sunday Magazine*, July 1962, p. 2.
48 Ibid.
49 *Prachathippatai*, 27 July 1965, p. 1.
50 For details of Apasra's background, see Prayun Phitsanakha, *Apasra Hongsakul nang ngam chakkawan chak Prathet Thai* [Apasra Hongsakula, Miss Universe from Thailand], Bangkok: Rongphim Fueang Akson, 1965.
51 'Golden Court of Thailand, H.M. King Bumipol Adulyadej and H.M. Queen Sirikit. Ten pages photographed by Henry Clarke', *Vogue*, February 15 1965, p. 112.
52 Joshua Kurlantzick, *The Ideal Man: The Tragedy of Jim Thompson and the American Way of War*, Hoboken, NJ: Wiley, 2011, p. 138.
53 Ibid., p. 154.

Conclusion

Over the course of 20 years, between 1945 and 1965, Thailand increasingly came to occupy a role in the American imagination as an ally and friend in the context of the Cold War. As the first generation of Americans travelled the world within the ideological framework of an 'American century', they did so with highly prescribed ideas about the places to which they travelled. Inheriting many of the orientalist interpretations of global order from European imperialists, they also sought to secure a new moral authority, driven by American media and cultural production in the United States. In such light, Thailand was cast not merely as a typical Asian society, but as a country that needed protection from Communism, and support to develop successfully. Fused with a spattering of rudimentary historical assertions, Thailand was viewed as a unique entity, based upon its geographical location in relation to the Cold War and upon a 'myth' of independence. Emerging through American eyes as an *Oasis on a Troubled Continent*, throughout the 1950s the country was viewed as home to a hospitable and generous population, who sat comfortably with assertions of a 'free world', largely because they were themselves unburdened by the connotations. Acting paternally toward an infantilised society, Americans were encouraged to see themselves as the protectors of a naïve and unspoilt people who little understood the Cold War.

Conspicuously absent from American assertions about what constituted the Thai people, however, were those members of Thai society who drove forward nationalist ideology. The Thai political classes, and in particular the generation of leaders that emerged following the 1932 revolution, had driven changes within the country that had strongly asserted the idea of nation as a fundamental part of daily life. By opening up the bureaucracy to a wider catchment, they had also bolstered the position of an increasingly confident Thai class of consumers who vied for a stake in the economic and political development of the country. Reinforced through government propaganda, the People's Party had emphasised the need to open up the Thai economy, to diversify industry, and to aspire to cultural parity with the 'great nations' of the world. Providing new references of self-identification for the individual in an expansive Thai community, the nation-building project sought to capture hearts and minds in order to further foster notions of citizenship.

200 *Conclusion*

It was a legacy that was fundamentally at odds with the over-simplified and sentimentalised assertions of American cultural producers and ideologues. Throughout the late 1940s and well into the 1950s, while the Thai state became politically allied to America, it also continued to view cultural activity as explicitly tied to issues of sovereignty and independence. State spectacle and publicity material, while less prolific than during the era of nation building, continued to depict the cultural life of the people as inseparable from the status of the country internationally. It also continued to draw upon aspirations of Thai parity with international lifestyle standards. Privately run magazines and newspapers, now free from the state control imposed following 1932, reflected such aspirations, and reported on Thailand as a nation in the ascendancy following a brief interruption to its development during the Second World War. Set firmly within global culture flows, such magazines marvelled at America, while harbouring a commitment to the future integration of Thailand into that world.

Ultimately, therefore, the process through which Thailand was integrated into an American-centred world order could only really be a Thai endeavour, embedded in the internal aspirations for global citizenship that had governed ideas of Thainess during the following decades. Throughout the 1930s, being Thai was constructed not through an assertion of separation from Europe and America, but through a view that Thailand belonged within global narratives of civilisation. Rather than talking about 'the West', state propaganda asserted that Thais deserved to be considered 'people of the world', and in so doing tied the winning of economic and political freedoms from imperial domination as essential to the self-identification of being Thai inside the country. Cultural policies that stemmed from this ideology were not intended to simply force Thais to wear Western fashions, but were developed in order to expand the already strong interest in consumer-driven lifestyles to the nation at large, diversify the economy, and fuel the global ascendency of the Thai nation. Significantly undermined by the Second World War and the political and economic crisis that followed, such aspirations nevertheless continued into the post-war era and remained essential in the production of effective ideological material.

As post-war merged into Cold War, the Thai state struggled to maintain ownership of such ideological assertions as many of the latent anxieties that formed the basis of Thai nationalism came to the fore. As Pinai Sirikiatkul has argued, the success of Thai state ideology during the height of Phibun's power depended not only on assertions of Thai 'greatness', but also on the worry that came from being subservient to global economic pressures, and the fear that Thailand could never become truly independent.[1] The assertion that the individual citizen must aspire to full global citizenship also held within it the claim that he or she had not yet achieved such a status. Reinforcing the idea of developmental time, upon which the Thai state was guiding the country to a general betterment, it also left open the possibility that Thailand could enter a period of decline. In the complex conditions of post-war

Conclusion 201

Thailand, fears that this was exactly what had happened were exploited in order to reject the constitutional arrangement that had been inherited from the 1932 revolution. Fed partially by Marxist assertions of a potential alternative nation, and partially by conservative forces that also sought to undermine the Phibun government, new culturist notions of Thai citizenship emerged. They cast the regime as unable to represent the Thai people due to its 'aping' of the West, and moreover cast American involvement in the country as in support of an ideologically bankrupt state. Claims of hypocrisy, inadequacy and corruption only served to fuel Thai anxieties that the country was faltering, sovereignties were being lost, and an alternative needed to be found.

In response, both Thai and US state propaganda sought to emphasise distance from the other and, drawing upon the general sense of disaffection, ended up exploiting cultural narratives embedded in nostalgia and in ways of life that could be viewed as distinctly Thai. Seeking to re-ignite optimism for the future, they also directed their ideological legitimacy into the potential for a new era of development. However, because under Phibun the Thai state continued to defend a cultural policy that was independent from the USA, the overall image presented remained fragmented. With Bangkok serving as the headquarters of the Southeast Asia Treaty Organization (SEATO), and with the Thai state remaining a recipient of large quantities of US aid, it was impossible to argue that Thailand was not under US influence.

Yet, at the same time as Thais were questioning the role of the United States in sustaining the Thai political system, they nonetheless continued to marvel at American 'civilisation'. Proud that Thailand was the first country to experience a Cinerama screen, the desire to be accepted as a part of that world remained strong. But this only served to fuel anxiety further, driven by the fact that, despite the US commitment to support the Thai state, Thailand was only ever likely to be a peripheral player in the Cold War. Phibun, the Prime Minister who had once declared war on the USA, was tolerated by the Americans due to his anti-communist stance, and while further economic involvement might have been preferred, as long as Thailand continued to flood the world with inexpensive rice, US interest would always remain relatively low. While US personnel in Bangkok sought to convince Washington of the need to foster support in Thailand, they struggled to explain why the country should be given priority when events elsewhere remained a preoccupation.[2] In fact, in many ways the lack of US interest in Thailand came largely because it was such a stable ally.

However, as has been shown, limited American interest in Thailand, both politically and economically, was juxtaposed to a small but significant cultural engagement in the country, made possible by the lack of an anti-colonial movement and the general eagerness of Thai communities to engage in American culture. Visitors from the USA complemented the dissemination of American media in Thailand to inform an already interested Thai audience in what ideological unity and inclusion into a US order might both look and feel like. Throughout the 1950s, these interactions betrayed Thai sensibilities,

202 *Conclusion*

which desired participation in a global culture, by consistently reinforcing the difference between 'us from the West' and 'you from Asia'.[3] Whether it was in the form of a fashion show or a cultural exchange programme, Americans came to learn about Thailand as being different from America, and in doing so enforced a reconceptualisation of what participation in global culture actually meant for Thais.

The project of elevating Thailand's value to the USA, and in turn of re-asserting its position within the new global order, would thus have to be undertaken by Thais themselves, and it was this that formed the basis of public relations under the Sarit regime. From 1958, the Thai state's projection of ideological ambiguity toward the Cold War was transformed into a message of unity, as the Thai state combined US anti-communist ideology with its own desire to capture the hearts and minds of urban Thai communities. In doing so, the state provided urban Thai society with the cultural narratives it needed to participate in American consumer culture, transforming Thailand into a playground for US visitors, and using the interest this generated to foster pride and a sense of global inclusion. Dramatised displays of Thai culture fed directly into the vision of Thailand with which Americans felt familiar, and were consumed with rigour by urban Thais who sought involvement with the global consumer culture such displays represented. Anxieties of a faltering development were repeatedly exploited in both US and Thai propaganda material to maintain commitment to the alliance, which, for as long as it survived, promised unfettered progress. In both *Seriphap*, the local publication of the United States Information Service (USIS), and the Tourist Organisation's Thai language magazine, images of Thainess were constructed out of assertions of traditional cultural heritage and shown in harmony with a modernity emanating exclusively from the United States. American rockets and space expeditions were presented as part of the Thai world as much as the American, while rural Thai communities were depicted living comfortably and happily as part of the American world order.

What was proven during the Sarit revolution, therefore, was that drawing Thailand to America was not in itself the problem for Thai society. Rather, it was the ideological integrity of the move, and the extent to which a narration of the integration fell within existing narratives of statehood and nation building in a changed political context. Certainly, a successful alliance could not last if it failed to ensure Thai subservience to American influence; but it would also fail if it could not live up to assertions of growth and prosperity under US tutelage. By aligning state-building exercises with the principles of modernisation theory, the new regime thus reconciled tensions that had developed since the end of the Second World War. Thai statecraft under the Sarit government was re-directed into the project of re-discovering what it meant to be Thai, not just through remembering once again who 'we' might be, but also by understanding what 'we' might be to American consumers.

The US framing of Thailand during the Cold War is therefore significant because American constructions provided much of the cultural framework within which urban Thai communities sought to reconcile their troubled post-war identity. United through their mutual homage to commodity as a vehicle for the expression of national citizenship, the purchase of Thai silk as an international brand was an example of how urban Thais integrated into a free world culture. By purchasing silk produced on the looms of the poor, urban Thais were able to participate in, and increasingly learn about, Thailand's status within an American imperial order. On one hand this included the betterment of rural or *klong*-side lives. Through development schemes and economic pro-grammes, many of which aimed to harness the purchasing power of the urban or international consumer, Thailand would emerge as a more comfortable society for all. Yet, through the beatification of a Thai under-class as both 'traditional' and 'authentic', Thailand would be held in suspended animation, caught within an externally imposed tension between the future and the past. It is a tension that has remained to this day.

Notes

1 Pinai Sirikiatkul, '*Na thi ni mai mi "Khwamsueam" thanon ratchadamnoen pho so 2484–2488*' [A place without "cultural slackness": Rajadamnern Boulevard, 1941–1945], *Warasan nachua, Wa duai prawattisat sathapattayakam lae sathapattayakam thai* (NAJUA), 6, Bangkok: 2010, pp. 9–50.
2 This was made evident when Phibun decided to travel to Washington in 1955. The ambassador had battled with Secretary of State John Foster Dulles to offer an invitation, only succeeding after admitting it was a *fait accompli*.
3 This is the terminology employed by Naoki Sakai in his article '"You Asians": on the historical role of the West and Asia binary', in Tomiko Yoda and Harry Harootunian (eds) *Japan after Japan, Social and Cultural Life from the Recessionary 1990s to the Present*, Durham, NC: Duke University Press, 2006, pp. 167–195.

Bibliography

Archival materials

National Archives of Thailand

Much of the archival material in this study comes from the National Archives of Thailand, and is identified as such by prefacing the reference with 'NA'. Materials in the Thai National Archives are organised first by department or ministry and collection. For example, (3) SR 0201 would refer to the third collection of materials from the Cabinet Secretary. The rest of the reference refers to the topic with which the files are concerned. If the reference is (3) SR 0201.72, this would be documents from the Cabinet Secretary that deal specifically with hotels. Further sub-groups are then designated with added decimal places and numbers. The final piece of information will be a slash followed by a final number, eg. (3) SR 0201.72/1. This reference refers to the specific file, which generally is concerned with one 'story'. In this example, the file would contain everything over a given period concerning the Rattanakosin Hotel.

National Archives at College Park, MD

State Department archives held at the US National Archives at College Park are organised by Decimal file, which refers to the period with which they are dealing. For example, Decimal file 50–54 means that it is part of the collection of documents concerned with the period 1950–1954. The rest of the reference refers to the location of the file, specified by the file number and box number.

Wheaton College Archives

The only collection from which this study draws is the Margaret and Kenneth F. Landon papers. They cover a period from 1824–2000 and are organised by series, subseries, box and folder. So, for example, 1/6/38/10 would indicate that the file was in Series 1 (Bibliographical)/Sub-series 6 (Diaries/Calendars 1928–1961)/Box 38/Folder 10 (Kenneth Landon's Diary, 27 Oct 1945–26 Feb 1946).

Newspapers and periodicals

Anusan Osotho
Bangkok Post
Bangkok World Sunday Magazine
Business Week
Collier's
'Daily Mail' Pictorial News
Democracy
Holiday Time in Thailand
House & Garden
House Beautiful
Glamour
Life
Life International
Khao
Khao Phanit
Khon Muang
The New York Times
Phap Khao Sayam Nikon
Phim Thai
Prachachat
Prachathippatai
San Seri
Sang Ton-eng
Saturday Review
Sayam Nikon
Sayam Samai
Sayam Rat
Suphap Satri
Thai Rat
Ta khlong thai mai
Thongtiao Sapda
Vogue
The Washington Daily News
The Washington Post and Times-Herald

Thai-language sources

Anuson ngan phutthaphayahayatra than chonlamak nai kan chalong 25 phutthasatawat [Brochure to accompany the Buddhist Barge Ceremony for the celebrations for the 25th Buddhist centenary], Bangkok: 14 May 1957.

Chanida Chitbundid, *Kronggkan an nueang ma chak phraratchadamri: kansathapana phraratcha-amnat nam nai Phrabat Somdet Phrachao Yu Hua* [The Royally Initiated Projects: The Making of King Bhumibol's Royal Hegemony], Bangkok: Foundation for the Promotion of Social Sciences and Humanities Textbooks Project, 2007.

Chatri Prakittanonthakan, *Khanarat chalong ratthathmmanun: prawattisat kan mueng lang 2475 phan sathapattayakam "amnat"* [Celebrating the People's Constitution: A

206   Bibliography

Thai Political History of Architecture following 1932 through "Power"], Bangkok: Arts and Culture, 2005.

Institute for Thai Studies, '*Krabuan phayuhayatra chonlamak*' [The Royal Barge Procession], *Chat phim nueng nai okat phraratchaphithi mahamongkon chaloem phrachonmaphansa 6 rop*, Bangkok: Institute for Thai Studies, Thammasat University, 5 December 1999.

Kukrit Pramoj, *Panha pracham wan* [Problems of Everyday Life], Bangkok: Rong phim sin akson, 1956.

Kukrit Pramoj, *Panha pracham wan chut thi 2* [Problems of Everyday Life, Set 2], Bangkok: Rong phim sin akson, 1956.

Kukrit Pramoj, *Panha pracham wan chut thi 3* [Problems of Everyday Life, Set 3], Bangkok: Rong phim sin akson, 1956.

Kukrit Pramoj, *Panha pracham wan chut thi 4* [Problems of Everyday Life, Set 4], Bangkok: Rong phim sin akson, 1958.

Kukrit Pramoj, *Panha pracham wan chut thi 5* [Problems of Everyday Life, Set 5], Bangkok: Rong phim sin akson, 1958.

Kukrit Pramoj, *Panha pracham wan chut thi 6* [Problems of Everyday Life, Set 6], Bangkok: Rong phim sin akson, 1958.

Kukrit Pramoj, *Panha pracham wan chut thi 7* [Problems of Everyday Life, Set 7] Bangkok: Rong phim sin akson, 1958.

Kukrit Pramoj, *Kukrit Pramoj kap panha khong thai samai lueak tang mai riaproi* [Kukrit Pramoh and Thai Problems of Everyday Life in the era of Messy Elections], Bangkok: Kasem bannakit, 1960.

Kukrit Pramoj, *Panha pracham wan chut mai mai* [Problems of Everyday Life: The newest set], Bangkok: Samnak phim kaona, 1964.

Public Relations Department of Thailand, *70 pi Krom pracha samphan* [70 years of the Public Relations Department], Bangkok: Public Relations Department of Thailand, 2004.

Kullada Kesboonchoo Mead, '*Kanmueang Thai yuk Sarit-Thanom phaitai krhongsang amnat lok*' [Thai Politics from Sarit to Thanom under the world power structure], unpublished study, Chulalongkorn University, Bangkok, 2007.

Nakarin Mektrairat, *Khwamkhit khwamru lae amnat kanmueang nai kanpatiwat sayam* [Knowledge and Political Power in the 1932 Siam Revolution], Bangkok: Fa diaokan, 2003.

Nattupoll Chaiching, '*Kanmueng thai samai rattaban Chomphon Po Phibun Songkram phai tai rabiap lok khong Saharat America phoso 2491–2500*' [Thai Politics in the era of Field Marshal Phibun Songkram under the American International System], PhD thesis, Department of Political Science, Chulalongkorn University, 2009.

Patarawdee Puchadapirom, *Watthanatham banthoeng nai chat Thai: kan plian plaeng khong watthanatham khwam banthoeng nai sangkhom Krung Thep Maha Nakhon pho.so. 2491–2500*, [Entertainment Culture in Thailand: Change in Entertainment Culture in Bangkok Society, 1948–1950], Bangkok: Samnak phim matichon, 2007.

Pinai Sirikiatkul, 'Na thi ni mai mi "Khwamsueam" thanon ratchadamnoen pho so 2484–2488' [A place without "cultural slackness": Rajadamnern Boulevard, 1941–1945], *Warasan nachua, Wa dui prawattisat sathapattayakam lae sathapattayakam thai (NAJUA)*, 6, Bangkok, 2010, pp. 9–50.

Bibliography 207

Phonrueatri Somphop Phirom, *Ruea phraratchaphithi phayuhayatra chonlamak* [The procession of the Royal Barges], Bangkok: Samnak phim Amarin Printing and Publishing, 1996.

Prakan Klinfong, '*Kansadet phraratchadamnoen thongthi tangchangwat khong Phrabat Somdet Phrachao Yu Hua Bhumibol Adulyadej phutthasakkarat 2483–2530*' [His Majesty King Bhumipol Adulyadej's Visits to Provincial Areas, 1950–1987], MA thesis, Chulalongkorn University, Bangkok, 2008.

Pacharalada Juliapechr, *Naeo khit rueang kueng phutthakan nai sangkhom thai phutthasakkarat: 2475–2500* [The concept of 'Buddhist Meridian' in Thai society, 1932–1957], MA thesis, Thammasat University, Bangkok, 2005.

Prayun Phitsanakha, *Apasra Hongsakul nang ngam chakkawan chak Prathet Thai* [Apasra Hongsakul, Miss Universe from Thailand], Bangkok: Rongphim Fueang Akson, 1965.

Saichon Satyanran, *Kukrit kap praditthakam "Khwam pen Thai" lem 1, yuk Chomphon Po Phibun Songkram* [Kukrit and the Construction of Thainess Book 1: The Era of Phibun Songkram], Bangkok: Samnak phim matichon, 2007.

Saichon Satyanran, *Kukrit kap praditthakam "Khwam pen Thai" lem 2, yuk Chomphon Sarit thueng thotsawat 2530* [Kukrit and the Construction of Thainess Book 2, From Sarit to 2530s], Bangkok: Samnak phim matichon, 2007.

Saichon Satyanran, *Phraya Anuman Rajadhon: Prat samanchon phu niramit "khwam pen Thai"*, Bangkok: Samnak phim matichon, 2013.

Saranmit Prachansit, '*Kitchakan hotel nai Prathet Thai phutthasakkarat 2406–2478*' [Hotel Business in Thailand 1853–1935], MA thesis, Chulalongkorn University, Bangkok, 2000.

Sopha Chanamool, *Chat Thai nai thatsana panyachon hua kao na* [The Thai Nation from the Perspective of Progressive Intellectuals], Bangkok: Samnak phim matichon, 2007.

Sorasan Phaengsapha, *Ratri pradap thi Hua Hin* [Hua Hin's Evening Star], Bangkok: Samnak phim sa san di, 2002.

Suphatra Kopitsukkhasakun, '*Kan prakuat nang sao Thai phutthasakkarat 2477–2530*' [The Miss Thailand Competition, 1935–1987], Master's thesis, Thammasat University, Bangkok, 1988.

Suthachai Yimprasert, *Phaen ching chat thai, wa duai rat lae kantotan ratthasamai Chompon Po Phibun Songkram khrang thi song (phutthasakkarat 2491–2500)* [Planning the Thai Nation: The State and the State's Opposition in the Era of Phibun Songkram during his Second Term], Bangkok: Samnak phim 6 tularamluek, 2007.

Thanomjit Michin, '*Chomphon Po Phibun Songkram kap ngan chalong 25 phuttasatawat 2495–2500*' [Phibun Songkram and the 25th centennial celebrations of the Buddhist calendar, 1952–1957], MA thesis, Thammasat University, Bangkok, 1988.

Wichai Napharatsami, *Lai chiwit Jit Pumisak* [The Many Lives of Jit Pumisak], Bangkok: Fa diaokan, 2003.

English-language sources

Agamben, Giorgio, *Homo Sacer: Sovereign Power and Bare Life*, Stanford, CA: Stanford University Press, 1998.

Agamben, Giorgio, *State of Exception*, Chicago, IL: University of Chicago Press, 2005.

208 Bibliography

Akira, Suehiro, *Capital Accumulation in Thailand 1855–1985*, Chiang Mai: Silkworm Books, 1996.

Aldrich, Richard J., *The Hidden Hand: Britain, America and Cold War Secret Intelligence*, New York: Overlook Press, 2002.

Allred, Jeff, *American Modernism and Depression Documentary*, Oxford: Oxford University Press, 2010.

Amenta, Edwin, *Bold Relief: Institutional Politics and the Origins of Modern American Social Policy*, Princeton, NJ: Princeton University Press, 1998.

Anderson, Benedict, 'Studies of the Thai State: the state of Thai studies', in Eliezer B. Ayal (ed.) *The Study of Thailand: Analyses of Knowledge, Approaches, and prospects in Anthropology, Art History, Economic, History and Political Science*, Athens, OH: Centre for International Studies, Ohio University, 1978, pp. 193–247.

Anderson, Benedict (ed.), *In the Mirror: Literature and Politics in Siam in the American Era*, Bangkok: Duang Kamol, 1985.

Anderson, Benedict, *Spectre of Comparisons: Nationalism, Southeast Asia and the World*, London and New York: Verso, 2002.

Appadurai, Arjun, *Modernity at Large: Cultural Dimensions in Globalization*, Minneapolis, MN: University of Minnesota Press, 1996.

Augustine, Andreas and Williamson, Andrew, *The Oriental, Bangkok*, Bangkok, 2000.

Baker, Chris and Pasuk Phongpaichit, *A History of Thailand*, New York: Cambridge University Press, 2005.

Bardsley, Jan, 'Girl royalty: the 1959 coronation of Japan's first Miss Universe', *Asian Studies Review*, 32(2008): 375–391.

Barme, Scott, *Luang Wichit and the Creation of a Thai Identity*, Singapore: Institute of Southeast Asian Studies, 1993.

Barme, Scott, *Man Woman Bangkok, Love, Sex and Popular Culture in Thailand*, Lanham, MD: Rowman & Littlefield, 2002.

Barme, Scott and Batson, Benjamin, *Siam's Political Future: Documents from the End of the Absolute Monarchy*, South East Asia Program, Department of Asian Studies, Ithaca, NY: Cornell University, 1976.

Benedict, Ruth, *Thai Culture and Behaviour, An Unpublished Wartime Study Dated 1943*, South East Asia Program, Department of Asian Studies, Ithaca, NY: Cornell University, 1953.

Benedict, Ruth, *The Chrysanthemum and the Sword, Patterns of Japanese Culture*, New York: Mariner Books, 2005.

Bernays, Edward, *Propaganda*, Brooklyn, NY: Ig Publishing, 1928.

Brown, Anthony Cave, *The Last Hero, Wild Bill Donovan: The Biography and Political Experience of Major General William J. Donnovan, Founder of the OSS and 'father' of the CIA, from his Personal and Secret Papers and the Diaries of Ruth Donovan*, New York: Vintage Books, 1984.

Brown, Ian, *The Elite and the Economy in Siam, c1890–1920*, Singapore: Oxford University Press, 1988.

Buxton, William J., 'From the Rockefeller Center to the Lincoln Center: musings on the "Rockefeller half century"', in William J. Buxton (ed.) *Patronising the Public: American Philanthropy's Transformation of Culture, Communication and the Humanities*, Lanham, MD: Lexington Books, 2009.

Callahan, William, *Cultural Governance and Resistance in Pacific Asia*, New York: Routledge, 2006.

Bibliography 209

Cohen, Lizbeth, *A Consumer's Republic: The Politics of Mass Consumption in Postwar America*, New York: First Vintage Books, 2004.

Copeland, Matthew, 'Contested nationalism and the 1932 overthrow of the absolute monarchy in Siam', PhD thesis, Australia National University, 1993.

Denes, Alexander, 'Recovering Khmer ethnic identity from the Thai national past: an ethnography of the localism movement in Surin Province', PhD thesis, Cornell University, 2006.

Department of Overseas Trade, *Economic Conditions in Siam, 1933–1934*, London: Department of Overseas Trade, 1935.

Dixon, Chris, *The Thai Economy: Uneven Development and Internationalisation*, London and New York: Routledge, 1999.

Donaldson, Gary, *Abundance and Anxiety, America 1945–1960*, Westport, CT: Greenwood, 1997.

Duara, Prasenjit, *Sovereignty and Authenticity: Manchuko and the East Asian Modern*, Lanham, MD: Rowman & Littlefield, 2004.

Eagleton, Terry, *Ideology: An Introduction*, London: Verso, 1991.

Ehrenreich, Barbara and Ehrenreich, John, 'The professional managerial class', in Pat Walker (ed.) *Between Labor and Capital*, Controversies Vol. 1, Boston, MA: Southend Press Political, 1979.

Elbaum, Max, *Revolution in the Air: Sixties Radicals Turn to Lenin, Mao and Che*, New York: Verso, 2002.

Endy, Christopher, *Cold War Holidays: American Tourism in France*, Chapel Hill, NC: University of North Carolina Press, 2004.

Esterick, Penny Van, *Materializing Thailand*, Oxford: Berg, 2000.

Feangfu, Janit, '(Ir)resitably modern: the construction of modern Thai identities in Thai literature during the Cold War era, 1958–1976', PhD thesis, University of London, 2011.

Fineman, Daniel, *A Special Relationship: The United States and Military Government in Thailand 1947–1958*, Honolulu, HI: University of Hawai'i Press, 1997.

Foerstel, Lenora and Gilliam, Angela, *Confronting the Margaret Mead Legacy, Scholarship, Empire and the South Pacific*, Philadelphia, PA: Temple University Press, 1992.

Foley, Matthew, *Cold War and National Assertion in Southeast Asia: Britain, The United States and Burma, 1948–62*, London and New York: Routledge, 2010.

Glassman, Jim, *Thailand at the Margins, Internationalization of the State and the Transformation of Labour*, Oxford: Oxford University Press, 2004.

Glassman, Jim, 'On the borders of Southeast Asia: Cold War geography and the construction of the other', *Political Geography* 24(2005): 784–807.

Gray, Christine, 'Thailand – the soteriological state in the 1970s', PhD thesis, University of Chicago, 1986.

Handley, Paul, *The King never Smiles, A Biography of King Bhumibol Adulyadej*, New Haven, CT: Yale University Press, 2006.

Harootunian, Harry, *History's Disquiet, Modernity, Cultural Practice, and the Practice of Everyday Life*, New York: Columbia University Press, 2000.

Harrison, Rachel, 'The man with the golden gauntlets: Mit Chaibancha's Insi Thorng and the hybridization of red and yellow perils in Thai Cold War action cinema', in Tony Day (ed.) *Cultures at War: The Cold War and Cultural Expression in Southeast Asia*, Ithaca, NY: Cornell University Press, 2010.

210 Bibliography

Harrison, Rachel and Jackson, Peter (eds), *The Ambiguous Allure of the West: Traces of the Colonial in Thailand*, Hong Kong: Hong Kong University Press, 2010.

Hell, Stefan, *Siam and the League of Nations, Modernization, Sovereignty and Multilateral Diplomacy 1920–1940*, Bangkok: Riverbooks, 2010.

Herzstein, Robert, *Henry R. Luce, A Political Portrait of the Man who Created the American Century*, New York: Charles Scribner's Sons, 1994.

Herzstein, Robert, *Henry R. Luce, Time and the American Crusade in Asia*, Cambridge: Cambridge University Press, 2005.

Huggan, Graham, *The Post Colonial Exotic: Marketing at the Margins*, London: Routledge, 2001.

Ingram, James C., *Economic Change in Thailand Since 1850*, Stanford, CA: Stanford University Press, 1955.

Iriye, Akira, *Cultural Internationalism and World Order*, Baltimore, MD: Johns Hopkins University Press, 1997.

Jackson, Peter A., 'An American death in Bangkok, the murder of Darrell Berrigan and the hybrid origins of gay identity in 1960s Thailand', *Journal of Lesbian and Gay Studies*, 5(3) (1999): 361–411.

Jackson, Peter A., 'The Thai regime of images', *SOJOUN: Journal of Social Issues in Southeast Asia*, 19(2) (2004): 181–218.

Kasian Tejapira, *Commodifying Marxism, The Foundation of Modern Thai Radical Culture, 1927–1958*, Melbourne and Kyoto: Kyoto University Press, 2001.

Klausner, William, 'Cool heart', *Journal of Social Sciences, Chulalongkorn University*, 4(2) (1966): 117–124.

Klein, Christina, *Cold War Orientalism, Asia in the Middlebrow Imagination, 1945–1961*, Berkeley, CA: University of California Press, 2003.

Kissinger, Henry, *Ending the Vietnam War: A History of America's Involvement in and Extrication from the Vietnam War*, New York: Simon & Schuster, 2003.

Kullada Kesboonchoo Mead, *The Rise and Decline of Thai Absolutism*, London: Routledge Curzon, 2004.

Kurlantzick, Joshua, *The Ideal Man, The Tragedy of Jim Thompson and the American Way of War*, Hoboken, NJ: Wiley, 2001.

Lederer, William J. and Burdick, Eugene, *The Ugly American*, New York: Fawcet, 1958.

Loos, Tamara, *Subject Siam: Family, Law and Colonial Modernity in Siam*, Ithaca, NY: Cornell University Press, 2006.

Lulitanond, Prasit, *A Postman's Life 1910–1997*, Bangkok: Post Publishing Company, 1999.

MacDonald, Alexander, *Bangkok Editor*, New York: Macmillan, 1949.

MacKenzie, John M., *Propaganda and Empire: The Manipulation of British Public Opinion, 1880–1960*, Manchester: Manchester University Press, 1984.

Manza, Jeff, 'Political sociological models of the U.S. New Deal', *Annual Review of Sociology*, 26(2000): 297–322.

Marchand, Roland, *Advertising the American Dream: Making Way for Modernity, 1920–1940*, Berkeley, CA: University of California Press, 1986.

Mollenkopf, John (ed.), *Power, Culture, and Place: Essays on New York City*, New York: Russell Sage Foundation, 1988.

McConachie, Bruce A., *American Theatre in the Culture of the Cold War: Producing and Contesting Containment 1947–1962*, Iowa City, IA: University of Iowa Press, 2003.

Michener, James A., *The Voice of Asia*, New York: Random House, 1951.

Bibliography 211

Neal, Arthur G., *National Trauma and Collective Memory: Major Events in the American Century*, New York: M.E. Sharpe, 1998.

Nehrer, Arlene, 'Prelude to the Alliance: the expansion of the American economic interest in Thailand during the 1940s', PhD thesis, Northern Illinois University, 1980.

Ninkovich, Frank, *Modernity and Power: A History of the Domino Theory in the Twentieth Century*, Chicago, IL: University of Chicago Press, 1994.

Nivat Kromamun Bidyalabh, H. H. Prince Dhani, 'Introduction', in William Skinner (ed.) *The Social Sciences and Thailand: A Compilation of Articles on Various Social-Science Fields and their Application to Thailand*, Bangkok: Cornell Research Center, 1956, p. 1.

Nobel, David W., *Death of a Nation: American Culture and the End of Exceptionalism*, Minneapolis, MN: University of Minnesota Press, 2002.

Osgood, Kenneth, *Total Cold War: Eisenhower's Secret Propaganda Battle at Home and Abroad*, Lawrence, KS: University Press of Kansas, 2006.

Outka, Elizabeth, *Consuming Traditions, Modernity, Modernism and the Commodified Authentic*, New York: Oxford University Press, 2009.

Pellegi, Maurizio, *Lord of Things: The Fashioning of the Siamese Monarchy's Modern Image*, Honolulu, HI: University of Haiwai'i Press, 2002.

Pellegi, Maurizio, 'Refashioning civilization: dress and body practice in Thai nation building', in Mina Roces and Louise Edwards (eds) *The Politics of Dress in Asia and the Americas*, Eastbourne: Sussex Academic Press, 2010.

Phya Anuman Rajadhon, *Life and Ritual in Old Siam: Three Studies of Thai Life and Customs*, translated by William Gedney, New Haven, CT: HRAF Press, 1961.

Prasit Lulitanond, *A Postman's Life 1910–1997*, Bangkok: Post Publishing Company, 1999.

Phillips, Herbert, *Thai Peasant Personality, The Patterning of Interpersonal Behaviour in the Village of Bang Chan*, Berkeley and Los Angeles, CA: University of California Press, 1966.

Phillips, Matthew, 'Crafting nationalist consumption: public relations and the Thai textile movement under the People's Party, 1932–1945', *South East Asia Research*, 21(4) (2013): 673–691.

Puey Ungphakorn, *Economic Development in Thailand 1950–1962*, Bangkok: Thammasat University, 1963.

Quaritch Wales, H. G., *Siamese State Ceremonies: Their History and Function*, London: Bernard Quaritch Ltd, 1931.

Reynolds, Bruce E., *Thailand's Secret War: OSS, SOE and the Free Thai Underground During World War II*, Cambridge: Cambridge University Press, 2005.

Reynolds, Craig J., *Thai Radical Discourse: The Real Face of Thai Feudalism Today*, Ithaca, NY: Cornell Southeast Asia Program, 1994.

Reynolds, Craig J., *Seditious Histories, Contesting Thai and Southeast Asian Pasts*, Seattle, WA and Singapore: University of Washington Press, 2006.

Riggs, Fred, *Thailand: The Modernisation of a Bureaucratic Polity*, Honolulu, HI: East-West Centre Press, 1966.

Robin, Ron, *The Making of the Cold War Enemy, Culture and Politics in the Military–Intellectual Complex*, Princeton, NJ: Princeton University Press, 2001.

Rostow, Walt W., *The Processes of Economic Growth*, New York: W. W. Norton, 1952.

Samuel, Lawrence R., *The End of Innocence: The 1964–1965 New York World's Fair*, New York: Syracuse University Press, 2010.

212 *Bibliography*

Sakai, Naoki, '"You Asians": on the historical role of the West and Asia binary', in Tomiko Yoda and Harry Harootunian (eds) *Japan after Japan, Social and Cultural Life from Recessionary 1990s to the Present*, Durham, NC: Duke University Press, 2006.

Schweitzer, Marlis, *When Broadway was the Runway: Theatre, Fashion, and American Culture*, Philadelphia, PA: University of Pennsylvania Press, 2009.

Scott, Peter Dale, 'Operation Paper, the United States and drugs in Thailand and Burma', *Asia Pacific Journal*, November (2010), www.japanfocus.org/-Peter_Dale-Scott/3436.

Seksan Prasoetkun, 'The transformation of the Thai state and economic change, 1855–1945', PhD thesis, Cornell University, 1989.

Sharp, Lauriston and Hanks, Lucien Mason, *Bang Chan: Social History of a Rural Community in Thailand*, Ithaca, NY: Cornell University Press, 1978.

Shefter, Martin (ed.), *Capital of the American Century: The National and International Influence of New York City*, New York: Russell Sage Foundation, 1993.

Sirikit, Her Majesty Queen, *In Memory of the State Visits of His Majesty the King*, 2nd edn, Bangkok, 12 August 2004 [1st edn 12 August 1968].

Skinner, William G., *Chinese Society in Thailand: An Analytical History*, Ithaca, NY: Cornell University Press, 1957.

Skwiot, Christine, *The Purposes of Paradise, U.S. Tourism and Empire in Cuba and Hawai'i*, Philadelphia, PA: University of Pennsylvania Press, 2010.

Springhall, John, '"Kicking out the Vietminh": how Britain allowed France to reoccupy South Indochina, 1945–46', *Journal of Contemporary History*, 40(1) (2005): 115–130.

Stowe, Judith A., *Siam becomes Thailand*, London: Hurst, 1991.

Streckfuss, David, *Truth on Trial in Thailand: Defamation, Treason, and Lese-majeste*, Abingdon: Routledge, 2011.

Subrahmanyan, Arjun, 'Reinventing Siam: ideas and culture in Thailand, 1920–1944', PhD thesis, University of California, 2013.

Suri, Jeremi, *Henry Kissinger and the American Century*, Cambridge, MA: Belknap Press of Harvard University, 2007.

Suwannathat-pian, Kobukua, *Thailand's Durable Premier, Phibun Through Three Decades, 1932–1957*, Singapore: Oxford University Press, 1995.

Suwannathat-pian, Kobukua, *Kings, Country and Constitutions: Thailand's Political Development 1932–2000*, Abingdon: Routledge, 2013.

Swan, William L., *Japan's Economic Relations with Thailand: The Rise to 'Top Trader' 1875–1942*, Bangkok: White Lotus, 2009.

Tarling, Nicholas, *Britain, Southeast Asia and the Onset of the Cold War, 1945–1950*, Cambridge: Cambridge University Press, 1998.

Thak Chaloemtiarana, *Thailand: The Politics of Despotic Paternalism*, Ithaca, NY: Cornell Southeast Asia Program, 2007.

Thamsook Numnonda, 'Phibunsongkram's Thai nation building programme during the Japanese military presence 1941–1945', *Journal of Southeast Asian Studies*, 9(2) (1978): 234–247.

Thompson, John B., *Ideology and Modern Culture: Critical Social Theory in the Era of Mass Communication*, Cambridge: Polity Press, 1990.

Thongchai Winichakul, *Siam Mapped: A History of the Geo-body of a Nation*, Chiangmai: Silkworm Books, 1994.

Thongchai Winichakul, 'The others within: travel and ethno-spatial differentiation of Siamese subjects 1885–1910', in Andrew Turton (ed.) *Civility and Savagery, Social identity in Tai states*, Richmond: Curzon, 2000.

Thongchai Winichakul, 'Nationalism and the radical intelligentsia in Thailand', *Third World Quarterly*, 29(3) (2008): 575–591.

Tourist Bureau, Bangkok, *Democratic Thailand*, Bangkok: Government Tourist Bureau, Department of Public Relations, 1957.

Trivedi, Lisa, *Clothing Ghandi's Nation: Homespun and Modern India*, Bloomington, IN: Indiana University Press, 2007.

Van Beek, Steve and Manivat, Vilas, *Kukrit Pramoj, His Wit and Wisdom, Writings Speeches and Interviews*, Bangkok: Duang Kamol, 1983.

Wallerstein, Immanuel, 'What Cold War in Asia: an interpretive essay', in Y. Zheng, H. Liu and M. Szonyi (eds) *The Cold War in Asia: The Battle for Hearts and Minds*, Leiden: Brill, 2010.

Warren, William, *Jim Thompson: The Unsolved Mystery*, Singapore: Archipelago Press, 1998.

Westad, Odd Arne, *The Global Cold War*, Cambridge: Cambridge University Press, 2007.

Whitfield, Stephen J., *The Culture of the Cold War*, Baltimore, MD: Johns Hopkins University Press, 1996.

Woods, Randall Bennet, *The Quest for Identity, America since 1945*, Cambridge: Cambridge University Press, 2005.

Wyatt, David K., *Thailand: A Short History*, 2nd edn, New Haven, CT: Yale University Press, 2003.

Yoshihara, Mari, 'Re-gendering the enemy, Orientalist discourse and national character studies during World War II', in Nancy Lusignan Schultz (ed.) *Fear Itself, Enemies, Real and Imagined in American Culture*, New York: Purdue University Press: 1999.

Zinn, Howard, *Postwar America, 1945–1971*, Cambridge, MA: South End Press, 2002.

Websites

http://history.state.gov/conferences/2010-southeast-asia/secretary-kissinger [accessed 12 October 2014].

www.youtube.com/watch?v=mtCAEb_nu6g&feature=player_embedded [accessed 5 December 2014].

www.youtube.com/watch?v=gLqzCga2AWA [accessed 5 December 2014].

TV documentaries and films

Golden Temple Paradise (Circle Film Enterprises, 1953).
March of Time, Oasis on a Troubled Continent (Time Inc., 1953).
Walt Disney's Siam (Walt Disney/Buena Vista Film Distributing Corp., 1954).

Oral history interviews from the Jim Thompson Oral History Project

Ann Donaldson, 26 October 2006.
Anne Tofield, 28 October 2006.
William Warren, Bangkok, 3 November 2006.
William Klausner, 6 November 2006.

Index

aid, US to Thailand: 6, 40, 122–124, 145, 172, 201; Thai public opinion about 98, 148

American Century 22, 200; as defined by Henry Luce 26–27; in *Vogue* 26–27; post-war references 2, 28, 29–33, 35

Ananda, King Rama VIII (1935–1946) 92

anxiety, American: about communism 121, 32–35; about decolonisation 27, 29, 44

anxiety, Thai: about cultural lag 57, 162, 157, 173; about decolonization, 4, 96–97, 107; about economic developments post war 54, 71–75, 83, 96–98, 157; about economy before 1945 58, 60–61, 85; about lost territory 4, 82–83; about international status of Thailand 60–62, 83, 173; about relationship to United States 97–98, 148, 180, 201; about sovereignty 4, 9, 58, 84, 124, 201; about Thai identity postwar 95, 89–90, 99; about third world war 97, 126

Apasra Hongsakula 16, 179–180, 191–193

art, Thai 21, 55 107, 159; in Bangkok 90, 93, 102, 129, 162–165; Fua Haripitak 163; Sawasdi Tantisuk 164; Silpa Bhirasi 131, 163; Taval Dajanee 163

Bang Chan Project 103, 110–111

Bandung Conference 44, 112, 125, 127; *see also* neutrality

Bangkok; political centre 56, 71, 87–88, 92, 123–124, 127; and cosmopolitanism 71–75, 88, 97, 111–112, 179–180, 186; cultural centre (1932–1944) 8, 58–60, 65–66, 72–73, 117–118, 120; cultural centre during Cold War 55–56, 73, 75–76, 103–107, 110, 172; economic centre 64, 146; exhibitions during Cold War 118, 121; expatriate life 21–22, 36–37, 45–49, 87–88, 90–92, 125; as regional hub in Cold War 102, 132, 160; tourist location 102, 152–153, 159–160, 162–165; in US media 35–37, 40–43, 45, 101–102

Bao Dai, Emperor of the State of Vietnam 5–6

beauty pageants: Miss Thailand 59, 76, 77, 191; Miss Universe 16, 179–180, 191–192; Miss World 160; *see also* Apasra Hongsakula

Benedict, Ruth 31, 84–88, 100, 102, 104

Bhumibol, King Rama IX (1946–) 1, 106, 130, 133, 138–140; and Thai national character 36; as tourist icon 152–153, 168; world tour 181–183, 185–188, 193

Bird, Willis 105, 121

Britain: foreign policy in Southeast Asia 2, 87, 88; and postwar occupation 83, 88, 91–92, 95, 157; Thai attitudes toward 3, 64, 88; in US media 27, 29, 34, 56

Buddhism 127; Buddhist centenary 16, 118, 127, 131–134; and Thai national character 35, 135–137

bureaucracy, Thai government 57, 117, 145, 162; and 1932 revolution 58–60, 62, 69, 119, 156; in postwar 112, 122, 157–158, 172

Burma 2, 96–98, 108, 118, 123

Central Intelligence Agency (CIA) 28, 123, 127, 148

Index 215

Chiang Mai 107–109
China, People's Republic of 2, 5, 92, 106, 127, 195; in US media 32–34
China, Republic of 64
Chinese in Thailand 8, 61, 64, 104–105, 130, 135; and communism 125, 149; and integration 130, 145, 172
Chulalongkorn, King Rama V (1868–1910) 128
Chulalongkorn University 73, 94, 133
citizenship; following 1932 revolution 59, 60–63, 66, 68–70, 75, 77; postwar debate over nature of 89, 93, 95, 99–101, 104, 112; Thai citizenship under Sarit 140, 146–147, 150, 154, 160, 172–173; in the United States 1, 13, 24–25, 27, 151
class 1, 6–7, 14, 23–24, 66, 95, 187, 192–193; and 1932 revolution 56–58, 60, 67; American consumers as global elite 36, 41–42, 48–49, 55; emergence of high society in Bangkok 56, 73–76, 110–111, 158; and the grandstand 16, 155, 168; professional-managerial 24, 49; Thai integration into global elite 146–147, 165, 167–168, 179–181, 184, 187–193; and the theatre 38, 48–49
communist insurgency 1–3, 5, 35–36, 123, 125
Condé Nast 26, 40, 55, 76; *Glamour* 30–31; *House and Garden* 40–41, 47, 159; *Vogue* 26–27, 29–31, 41, 47, 50, 54–56, 75–76, 100, 193–194; *Vogue, Americana edition* 26–27, 29–30
Constitution Day Fair 59, 65, 117–118, 120–121, 131–132 191; US 1953 stand at the fair 121–122, 130
consumerism: and Cold War internationalism in United States 28, 31, 39, 41–42, 47, 151; consumption of rural Thailand 8, 109, 146–147, 165, 193; Thai integration into US consumer practices 109, 118, 172–173, 188, 190–191, 195, 202; and Thai nationalism interwar 59–60, 65–66, 199–200; Thai postwar hunger for imports 57–58, 71–75, 83, 157; US interwar 23–25; *see also* rural Thailand *and* Thai Silk
Cornell Research Centre 85, 102, 106

decolonisation 4–5, 76, 84, 87, 112, 125; as obstacle to US hegemony 2, 34–35

democracy: 1957 election 118, 127, 131–132, 139, 147–148, 158; as western import 30, 34, 85, 99, 149, 187
design: America as design centre 26–27, 37, 39–40, 73; innovation of Thai design 42, 45–48, 109, 156–159, 179, 188–190
Dhani, Prince 106
dress 137–138; and cultural edicts 62–63, 66–69, 119; and economic sovereignty 8, 15, 63; as mark of global elite 41–43, 72–77, 102, 169–171, 188–189, 191; and self-improvement 56, 59–60, 71; and Thai exceptionalism 90, 107–108, 159, 162, 182; *see also* national costume
Dulles, John Foster, US Secretary of State 126

economy, Thai: control of imports 7, 61, 75; economic policy following 1932 revolution 7, 13, 57–61, 63, 67, 199; integration into global economy 13, 66, 107, 109, 145, 153
economy, United States 24–25, 29, 32, 39, 41
Eisenhower, Dwight D. US President 126, 132, 182–183

Fine Arts Department 67, 90, 120, 129, 180
First Indochina War 2–5, 8, 125,
floating market 14, 47, 164, 169–171, 173; *klongs* [canals] in US media 41–42; klongside life 21–22, 46–47, 49, 101–102; Thai interest in 146, 161–162, 164, 169–171, 190, 194
France, 2–3; as cultural centre 26, 37; war with Thailand 1941 8, 66, 83, 94, 158; *see also* First Indochina War
Free Thai Movement [*Seri Thai*] 28, 87–88, 92

Gedney, William 105–106
Great Depression 24, 28,

Hollywood 38, 72, 76, 180–181, 195
hotels 41, 102, 151, 156–160, 172, 190; Erawan 16, 157, 159–160, 180; Hua Hin 156; Oriental 22, 156, 169, 173; Rattanakosin 156–157

ideology 8, 10–11, 25, 49, 98–99; anti-communism and Phibun 3–5, 92,

216 *Index*

125–126; anti-communism and Thailand 44, 98, 130, 146, 149–152, 201–202; communism as ideology 2, 32–34, 98, 103, 123–125, 149–150; progress in postwar Thailand 90, 103–105, 122, 172, 202; progress and Thai nationalism 54–56, 58, 60–63, 67, 73, 119–120; progress in US imagination 32, 41, 45, 47, 88–89, 103; self-improvement as ideology 59–60, 62, 65, 73; *see also* nationalism, Thai
India 96, 108; and textiles 64, 68, 183; in US media 34, 55–56, 76

Japan: commercial relationship with Thailand 64, 109; and Cold War 32, 34, 118, 132; and national character 85–87, 183; and second world war 28, 68, 71, 82, 87, 91, 157
jazz 185–186
Jit Pumisak 106–107

Kennedy, Ted and Joan 48
Khuang Aphaiwong 92
King and I, The 13, 37, 44, 49, 192; reception in United States 38–41, 44, 75; Thai responses toward 186–187
Klausner, William 48
Kopkaeo, Mom 54, 72
Korean War 6, 33, 35, 44, 74, 98–99, 102
Kukrit Pramoj 11, 93–95, 97–101, 106, 135, 181, 184

League of Nations 7, 61, 63
Leftists 8, 11; activity in Bangkok 106–107, 124, 132, 145; crackdowns on; 125, 148–149
Luang Wichitwathakan 62, 104
Luce, Henry 25, 28, 32; *see also* American Century; as defined by Henry Luce

MacDonald, Alexander 37, 74, 88, 157
Mead, Margaret 27–31, 84–85, 100
media, Thai: Thai photo magazines postwar 15, 54–55, 57, 71–77, 107–113, 135; Thai newspapers postwar 89, 91, 123, 130, 133, 181–187; *see also* propaganda *and* Tourist Organisation of Thailand
Michener, James 3, 33–36, 44–45, 151
Military, Thai 6–8, 57, 123; involvement in Cold War 98, 123; status postwar 83, 87, 91, 123, 146, 148–149

modernisation theory 42, 103, 106, 153–155, 165, 195

Nation Day, Thailand 62, 65, 96–97, 119–120
national character 27; American national character 27–31; national character studies 31, 83–85; Thai national character 61, 86–90, 100, 111, 150, 154
national costume 69, 76–77, 89, 108, 180–185, 188–189
National Council of Culture 72, 129–130
National Security Council 32–33
Nationalism, Thai: propagation under People's Party 12, 57–60, 62–66, 82, 117, 193; postwar ideas about 12, 89–90, 100, 106, 109, 187
neutrality 5–6, 112, 132, 146–147
New York 14, 32, 121, 160, 193, 195; Broadway 23, 38–39, 40, 49; as cultural centre 22–27, 37–40, 42, 47–49, 54–55; King Bhumipol and Queen Sirikit visit to 181–182, 184, 190; World Fair (1939) 25–26; World Fair (1964) 48, 180
non-alignment (*see* neutrality)
nuclear armaments 29, 32, 82, 91

Office of Strategic Services (OSS) 87–88, 91–92; and Jim Thompson 14, 22, 28, 37, 46; *see also*, Central Intelligence Agency (CIA)

Pacific Area Travel Association (PATA) 151, 154–155
people-to-people diplomacy 154; *see also* propaganda
People's Party 57, 59, 94
Peurifoy, John E., US Ambassador to Thailand (1954–55) 122, 127
Phao Sriyanond, Police Chief 6, 123, 127, 148
Phibun Songkhram, Field Marshal: American attitude toward 82, 86, 88, 92; as anti-communist 5–6, 92, 125; Buddhist centenary 118, 127–133; national ideology postwar 118–121; as Prime Minister, first term 7–8, 62–63, 71, 82; as Prime Minister, second term 73, 87, 91–92, 123–124, 145–146, 194; and *ratthaniyom* 62–63, 66–68; rivalry with royalists 87, 93, 130–131; and Thai public opinion 96, 106, 112, 126,

132–136, 139–140, 147–148; visit to the United States 91, 118, 126, 181
Phya Anuman Rajadhon 11, 90, 104–107, 129
Prachathipat [Democract Party] 92, 123, 133
Prajadhipok, King Rama VII (1925–1935) 57
Pridi Banomyong 60, 87, 92, 122–123
propaganda: Japanese 120–122; under People's Party 7–8, 15, 56–59, 62, 65, 75; under Sarit Thanarat 147, 149–150, 152; and Second World War 68–71, 119–120, 157; spectacle as a form of 64–65, 117–118, 131; Soviet 2, 117, 121, 151; United States 3, 117–118, 121–122, 124–125, 147
Psychological Strategy Board 3, 125; *see also* propaganda

ratthaniyom [cultural edicts] 62–63, 66, 68, 72, 120
Roosevelt, Eleanor 41
Roosevelt, Franklin D. 24–25
Royal Barges 117–118, 128–130, 138; as tourist attraction 153, 167–168
Royalists 57, 60, 87, 89–92, 123, 130
rural Thailand: in American imagination 45, 85–89, 102–103, 105, 110, 195, 202–203; and handicrafts 109, 156, 172, 190; integration into national community 61, 66–67, 69–70; royal engagement with 130; as site of cultural nation 1, 8, 11, 104–106, 111–112; and Tourist Organisation of Thailand 146–147, 154–156, 162–163, 165; and unbalanced development 13–14

Sarit Thanarat, Field Marshal 6, 123, 127; and 1958 revolution 9, 13–14, 147–150, 160, 172; and cultural policy 10–11, 140, 145–146, 151, 158, 163
Seni Pramoj 87–88
Sirikit, Queen 130, 168, 181, 183, 186–188, 193–194; and Thai dress 182–185
Southeast Asia Treaty Organization (SEATO) 125, 127, 201
Stanton, Edward, US Ambassador to Thailand (1947–1953) 92

textiles 54, 61–66, 68; *pha tip* (untreated Thai cotton) 68; *see also* Thai Silk
Thai Airways International 163, 180, 191
Thai silk 14–15, 21, 48; invention of 22, 37, 45, 91; marketing to Americans 32, 37–38, 40–43, 49, 156, 171–172; Thai consumption of 75–76, 159, 180, 184, 188–191, 193–195
Thaibok fabrics 14, 37, 40, 42–43
Thammasat University 58, 132
Thompson, James (Jim) HW, American entrepreneur 23–24, 28, 92; as antidote to 'Ugly' American 22, 40, 45–47, 156, 195; disappearance of 21–22, 194; house on the *klong* 21, 23, 42, 44–50, 194; and Thai silk 21, 32, 37–40, 91, 156, 189; and tourism 23, 41–42, 49, 156
tourism: US tourism to Thailand 1, 12, 22–23, 41, 47–48, 49, 101–102; and Thai nationalism 59, 156–159; *see also* Tourist Organisation of Thailand
Tourist Organisation of Thailand: *Anusan Osotho* (magazine) 147, 158–161, 163, 165–166; and Cha-lermchai, General 154–155, 160–161, 168–170; publicity to Americans 152–156, 159–160, 162–163; setting up of 147, 151; Surin Elephant round-up 146, 154–155, 165

Ugly American, novel (1958) 45, 154
unequal treaties 7, 60–61
United Nations Educational, Scientific and Cultural Organization (UNESCO) 90, 93, 102, 106
United States Information Service (USIS) 121, 124, 131, 202

Vajiravudh Fair 192
Vietnam War 12, 37, 195; *see also* First Indochina War

Wan Waithayakorn, Prince 127
Warren, William 21, 28, 45–46
Wiri Phasnawid, Thai dress maker 188–189
World Bank 145, 150, 172

eBooks
from Taylor & Francis
Helping you to choose the right eBooks for your Library

Add to your library's digital collection today with Taylor & Francis eBooks. We have over 50,000 eBooks in the Humanities, Social Sciences, Behavioural Sciences, Built Environment and Law, from leading imprints, including Routledge, Focal Press and Psychology Press.

Choose from a range of subject packages or create your own!

Benefits for you
- Free MARC records
- COUNTER-compliant usage statistics
- Flexible purchase and pricing options
- 70% approx of our eBooks are now DRM-free.

Benefits for your user
- Off-site, anytime access via Athens or referring URL
- Print or copy pages or chapters
- Full content search
- Bookmark, highlight and annotate text
- Access to thousands of pages of quality research at the click of a button.

Free Trials Available

We offer free trials to qualifying academic, corporate and government customers.

eCollections
Choose from 20 different subject eCollections, including:

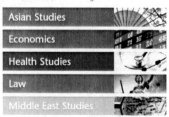

- Asian Studies
- Economics
- Health Studies
- Law
- Middle East Studies

eFocus
We have 16 cutting-edge interdisciplinary collections, including:

- Development Studies
- The Environment
- Islam
- Korea
- Urban Studies

For more information, pricing enquiries or to order a free trial, please contact your local sales team:

UK/Rest of World: **online.sales@tandf.co.uk**
USA/Canada/Latin America: **e-reference@taylorandfrancis.com**
East/Southeast Asia: **martin.jack@tandf.com.sg**
India: **journalsales@tandfindia.com**

www.tandfebooks.com